Sociology of Religion

Sociology of Religion

An Historical Introduction

ROBERTO CIPRIANI

Translated by
Laura Ferrarotti

ALDINE DE GRUYTER
NEW YORK

About the Author

Roberto Cipriani is professor of sociology at the University of Rome, Italy. He has served as a visiting professor at the University of Saõ Paolo in Brazil and at Laval University in Quebec and has conducted research in Greece and in Mexico. He has also served as editor in chief of *International Sociology*. This is the first of his many books to be translated into English, on subjects ranging from the work of Lévi-Strauss to symbolic legitimation. He has also made documentary films based on his varied research.

Originally published as *Manuale di sociologia della religione*
Copyright © 1997 Edizioni Borla s.r.l.

ALDINE DE GRUYTER
A division of Walter de Gruyter, Inc.
200 Saw Mill River Road
Hawthorne, New York 10532

This publication is printed on acid free paper ∞

Library of Congress Cataloging-in-Publication Data

Cipriani, Roberto.
    [Manuale di sociologia della religione. English]
    Sociology of religion : an historical introduction / Roberto Cipriani ; translated by Laura Ferrarotti ; edited and revised by Katrina McLeod and William D'Antonio.
      p. cm.
    Includes bibliographical references and index.
    ISBN 0-202-30591-0 (alk. paper) — ISBN 0-202-30592-9 (pbk. : alk. paper)
     1. Religion and sociology. I. Title.

BL60.C5613 2000
306.6—dc21
                                      00-027071
Manufactured in the United States of America

10 9 8 7 6 5 4 3 2 1

CONTENTS

PART III   THE CONTEMPORARIES

PART IV   RECENT DEVELOPMENTS

List of Tables

Preface to the English Edition

This book was conceived from the start as intended for an international reading public composed both of scholars and of students. As a result, it is at the same time broad in its treatment of the discipline as a whole—the sociology of religion—and of the individual authors presented, whether European or American.

Taking account of the difficulty of traversing so vast a body of material, we also devised some synthetic charts, outlines in graphic format, to say nothing of a list summarizing the salient points of every scientific contribution whose key concepts are brought into play, the influences undergone and exerted, also indicating which published work we think would be the most significant as a point of reference.

Rather than a "textbook," this volume represents a documented introduction to the history of sociological thought as applied to religious phenomena, without overemphasizing the critical debate that concerns each individual author, in order not to weigh down a text whose girth is already conspicuous.

Its point of departure is a bit remote, because a subject like the sociology of religion does not arise spontaneously; rather, it develops slowly, setting out from a philosophical approach (perhaps one of the most important innovations of this book). Such a philosophic point of departure is largely justified and legitimated subsequently, bit by bit, as we proceed along the course of years down to our own days. Besides, the sociology of religion, just like sociology in general, cannot be devoid of roots of a philosophic character.

The organization of the contents has posed some problems, because in completing a given chapter on a certain skein of thought one arrives at a conclusion with an author who lived after the one with whom the following chapter begins (for instance, the chapter on the social anthropologist Marcel Mauss concludes before the one on Emile Durkheim). But the chronological indications that accompany the authors' names help in immediately placing individual scholars in their proper time setting, so that the reader will not be deceived by the order followed in the presentation of the text.

The development is necessarily by authors rather than subjects, precisely to avoid the fragmentation, already a tangled affair, of the discipline under examination. Particular attention has been devoted to the connections among the diverse protagonists on the socioreligious scene, from which clearly emerges the strong impulse that North American sociology has provided the sociology of religion, particularly in the second half of the twentieth century.

It is not possible, however, to isolate American sociology of religion from European, nor can the latter remain in its splendid isolation. For some time now, in truth, a traffic in exchanged ideas between the two Atlantic coasts has increased notably. And this book is a confirmation of the exchange, inasmuch as it is intended as a bridge between the two shores, in such a way as to facilitate communication and to produce new fruits. These will surely not fail to grow, given the premises and the promises that are already in evidence here.

The Sociological Definition of Religion

The simplest way of defining the sociology of religion is to say that it is an application of sociological theories and methods to religious phenomena. Historically, there have been very close ties between sociology and the sociology of religion. The slow and uneven development of theory and methods in the general field of sociology affected the development of the sociology of religion, but the latter has also benefited from increasing precision and scientific validity in the general field of sociology. It is a significant fact that the great "classic" theorists of general sociology, such as Comte, Durkheim, Simmel, Weber, Sorokin, and Parsons, were also major exponents of the sociology of religion.

There is a particular point at which the different approaches of these and other sociological writers agree and disagree. Some sociologists maintain an approach to the sociology of religion that is militantly confessional or anticonfessional; others, instead, assume a position of neutrality, refusing any confessional involvement or application of their work. But few sociologists of religion take a position equidistant from these two alternatives. The personal beliefs of each sociologist emerge clearly from the definitions of religion to which each adheres. Yves Lambert has devoted a study to this (1991) in which he makes a distinction between substantive and functional definitions of religion. The former refers to substantive elements: religious practice, the supernatural, the invisible, ritual, etc. The latter, instead, emphasizes the functional connotation of religion, that is, the role of religion in society. When the sociology of religion first got started, substantive definitions were prevalent; later—particularly with the debate on secularization—functional approaches became more influential. But both approaches were shot through with and conditioned by problems of belief (or unbelief) and by the confessional belonging (or not belonging) of the individual scholar or sociologist.

The theories of Weber and Durkheim are examples of a tendency toward the substantive approach to religion; Luckmann and Luhmann are examples of sociologists who have adopted a more explicitly functional approach.

1

DEFINITIONS OF RELIGION THAT TEND TO THE SUBSTANTIVE

For Durkheim, "a religion is a unified system of beliefs and practices relative to sacred things, that is to say, things set apart and forbidden—beliefs and practices which unite into one single moral community, called a church, all those who adhere to them" (Durkheim [1912] 1995:44). The substantive elements of this definition are beliefs, practices, unapproachable sacred entities, and the church. In an earlier definition Durkheim had been more concerned with religious phenomena than with religion and made no mention either of "community" or of the "sacred" (Durkheim [1898] 1996:67).

By contrast, Max Weber never gave a specific definition of religion. We can, however, find a few indications from his writings. For example, in his study of the economic ethos of world religions, Weber described them as "systems for regulating human existence," which had been successful in "grouping around themselves a large number of faithful" (Weber [1921–22] 1976a:327).

Jean Séguy has correctly observed:

> In the first lines of paragraph 1 of Chapter V of *Economy and Society*—which deals expressly with the sociology of religion (*Religionssoziologie*)—Weber considers it impossible to provide a definition of religion at the beginning of his work. "At least one can attempt such a definition when the work is finished." But at the end he thinks no more about it. (Séguy 1988a:174)

Perhaps the reason for this is that a definition of what forms and content were to be considered "religious" would have put at risk Weber's sense of scientific neutrality, of his value-free position (*Wertfreiheit*). Or perhaps, as Séguy suggests, the reason was Weber's reluctance to enter into a rather outdated controversy, like that of Feuerbach on the essence of religion.

What remains evident, however, is Weber's intention: to study collective religious action, that is, action in community, and its reference to supernatural powers. In fact, Weber gave his attention to the regulation of the relations between the human and the supernatural; as a result, his implicit definition of religion was also functional since that regulation serves to manage the relation between the human and the supernatural. In addition, Weber's approach, although it lacked basic definitions, was to use the method of *verstehen* (that is, attempting to understand the event from the point of view of the social actors themselves), in particular through an effort to understand the religious life of other social subjects who, as protagonists, themselves have given definitions of their beliefs, of their religious views of the world, of their rituals. Therefore, by grasping the definition that individuals give of their religion, it is possible to assume a point of view that is empirically grounded, without having to be concerned about the possibility of the sociologist's own interpretation.

Another relevant element in Weber's analysis that should be taken into account, according to Séguy, is his recourse to religious analogies and metaphors, that is, religious modalities that are used analogically or metaphorically in a secular context, as is the case with what Weber calls the "polytheism" of values used to indicate plurality and the "sacrality" of valuative forms, the outcome of ethical individualism.

Weber did not personally support the idea of a plurality of values but as a sociologist he could not but take their existence into account. He writes that since life must be grounded in itself and must be understood on its own terms, it only knows of an unceasing struggle of those gods with one another. Or speaking directly, the ultimately possible attitudes toward life are irreconcilable, and hence their struggle can never be brought to a final conclusion (Weber 1962a:152). The following question, as posed by Weber, therefore becomes pertinent: "Which of the warring gods should we serve? Or should we serve perhaps an entirely different god, and who is he?" (ibid.:153).

Because they can be bearers of meaning, some cultural forms that are not specifically religious can take the place of religion. These tendencies, which had already been described by Weber in terms of the metaphorization of religion, find confirmation today. As Séguy further notes, some metaphoric religions have taken their cue from what

> Luckmann calls "invisible religions" (1967); others are nearer to the "implicit religion" of Arnaldo Nesti (1985) or to the "diffused religion" of Robert Towler (1974) and Roberto Cipriani (1988b) or to the "political religion" of Raymond Aron ([1955] 1977) and of Jean-Pierre Sironneau (1982). The concept of "metaphorical" religion has the merit of being globalizing but this brings with it difficulties: the sheer variety of the phenomena which come close to this concept. (Séguy 1988a:180)

This outlook for the future of religion is not only Weberian. Durkheim also seems to conceive of a possibly more functional sort of religion, alluding to

> present-day aspirations toward a religion that would consist entirely of interior and subjective states and be freely constructed by each one of us. But no matter how real those aspirations, they cannot affect our definition: this definition can be applied only to real, accomplished facts, not to uncertain possibilities. Religions can be defined as they are now or as they have been, not as they may be tending more or less vaguely to become. It is possible that this religious individualism is destined to become fact; but to be able to say in what measure, we must first know what religion is, of what elements it is

made, from what causes it results, and what functions it performs—all questions whose answers cannot be preordained, for we have not crossed the
threshold of research. Only at the end of this study will I try to look into the
future. (Durkheim [1912] 1995:44)

Thus, one already knows Durkheim's definition of religion. But at the
end of his text, Durkheim refrained from making predictions: "To be sure,
it cannot be said at this moment how far these explanations can be
extended and if they can lay every problem to rest" (ibid.:448). It is, however, the case that Durkheim's reference to religious subjectivism is a prel-
ude to later developments in the sociological analysis of religion, such as
the more marked functionalism in Luckmann's definition of religion, in
his theories of "invisible religion," and in particular his idea of an "individual religiosity."

THE FUNCTIONAL DEFINITIONS OF RELIGION

In terms of definitions of religion, Luckmann specifies:

Once a substantive definition of religion has been accepted one can, of
course, hopefully or fearfully raise the question whether religion is, or has
become, an exceptional phenomenon. If we take up the suggestion submit-
ted by Durkheim—or, at least, implied in his work—and define religion by
its universal social function that question ceases to make sense. In order to
be useful for the sociological theory of religion the suggestion must be spec-
ified. This will involve some difficulties which we shall try to overcome. One
thing, however, can be asserted confidently here. A functional definition of
religion avoids both the customary ideological bias and the "ethnocentric"
narrowness of the substantive definition of the phenomenon. (Luckmann
1967:42)

For Luckmann it is not religious practices that have primary sociological significance but rather "symbolic universes," which "are objectivated
meaning-systems that relate the experiences of everyday life to a 'transcendent' layer of reality. Other systems of meaning do not point beyond
the world of everyday life; that is, they do not contain a 'transcendent' reference" (ibid.:44). For this description of religion as "symbolic universe,"
Luckmann has taken his inspiration from the phenomenological sociology
of his teacher Alfred Schutz, who had studied the different forms of
everyday life and of symbolic relations, which he understood as the "transcendence of nature and of society." But the more remote origin of this
approach lies in pragmatism, which defines a concept with reference to its
practical consequences (James 1904), and in the functionalism of William

James ([1890] 1912), who considered religion to be a subuniverse with the same claims to validity as scientific theory, politics, and art. Schutz, however, preferred to call these subuniverses "finite regions of meaning," each of which is characterized by a specific "cognitive style" of reality.

Luckmann's definition of religion, however, goes well beyond the usual types of description. He argues that "it is in keeping with an elementary sense of the concept of religion to call the transcendence of biological nature by the human organism a religious phenomenon. . . . This phenomenon rests upon the functional relation of Self and society" (Luckmann 1967:49). His objective is to move on to "modern religious themes" such as the autonomy of the individual, self-expression, self-realization, the ethos of mobility, sexuality, and familism, which stand for "invisible religion," in distinction to the visibility of religious practices. But with this description of religion, Luckmann opens himself to criticism: in particular, of overextending the concept of religion and of thus going much beyond experiences that are usually considered to be religious. Luckmann, however, anticipates this criticism:

> We may, therefore, regard the social processes that lead to the formation of Self as fundamentally religious. This view, incidentally, does no violence to the etymology of the term. It may be objected from a theological and 'substantivist' position on religion that in this view religion becomes an all-encompassing phenomenon. We suggest that this is not a valid objection. The transcendence of biological nature is a universal phenomenon of mankind. (ibid.)

In other words, in Luckmann's view, religion remains a "bond" or tie, and in this sense true to its etymology. The "bond" does not necessarily refer to a linkage between human beings and the divinities of organized, historical religions, but rather to being bound to a worldview. Luckmann thus considers a definition of religion that refers to the "supernatural" a "shortcut"; instead, using the classic theory of the "social construction of reality" (Berger and Luckmann 1966), he raises the problem of the "universal anthropological condition of religion" and therefore of religion as a "distinct part of social reality." In particular, Luckmann insists:

> The transcendence of biological nature by human organisms is a fundamentally religious process. We may now continue by saying that socialization, as the concrete process in which such transcendence is achieved, is fundamentally religious. It rests on the universal anthropological condition of religion, individuation of consciousness and conscience in social processes, and is actualized in the internalization of the configuration of meaning underlying a historical social order. We shall call this configuration of meaning a world view. (Luckmann 1967:51)

For Luckmann, therefore, religion can be defined as a worldview. In fact "the world view, as an 'objective' and historical social reality, performs an essentially religious function and defines it as an *elementary social form of religion*. This social form is universal in human society" (ibid.:53).

The definition of religion put forward by Niklas Luhmann also belongs to the functionalist perspective:

> [Religion] carries out the function of transforming the indeterminate world for the social system, since it could not be circumscribed towards the external (environment) and towards the internal (system), in a determinable world in which system and environment can have a relationship which excludes from both an arbitrary change. In other words, religion must justify and make tolerable all typologies, self-identifications, categorizations and any form of expectation should proceed in a reductive form and remain open to criticism. Even religion itself must remain at the level of an accessible common sense and must represent appresentation. But in its long history it makes a special effort to include representative forms which might imply the risk of pure representation. As a consequence, there is the problem of a specialization that makes evident both the function and its limitations. (Luhmann 1991:36)

The function of religion for Luhmann is to reduce uncertainty and complexity, to determine that which seems to be indeterminate, and to make accessible what seems to be inaccessible. The supernatural dimension, therefore, comes in handy because it serves to reduce complexity. But, above all, religion, for Luhmann, is a system that lacks a divine referent: the giver of meaning is absent. The only referent of the religious system is to itself. The system is self-made, self-generated, self-constitutive.

As Sergio Belardinelli has correctly noted in his introduction to the Italian edition of Luhmann's *Funktion der Religion*, "The proper function of religion in systems theory is stated from the very beginning of the text: 'to represent appresentation'" (ibid.:1). Schutz had also discussed appresentation (1962), referring to Husserl's fifth *Cartesian meditation* ([1950] 1977), in which Husserl spoke of "appresentation" or "analogical perception," a modality that joined together, whether knowingly or unknowingly, two different but connectible elements (for example, smoke and fire). The perception of what is seen sends one back to what is not seen: "the frontside, which is apperceived in immediacy or given to us in presentation, appresents the unseen backside in an analogical way"; as a consequence "the appresenting term, that which is present in immediate apperception, is coupled or paired with the appresented term" (Schutz 1962:295). Appresentation presupposes another presence of which only a part is visible. It is at this point that we find the real limit of appresentation: it is not able to represent that to which it refers. Religion tries to do so, that is, it tries to represent what cannot be represented. While remaining within its system, religion seems, more than other systems, to allude to the external environment and therefore succeeds to some extent in grasping both "system" (internal) and "environment" (external) at the same time; that is, religion succeeds in grasping the world as a whole. Nonetheless, religion is connected to the contingency of reality, so that God himself becomes a contingent element thought out to respond to the requirements of reducing complexity.

Another aspect deserves attention: a religion is a "system" made up of those who belong to it as believers; outside religion, there is the "environment" of unbelievers; both are part of the world. So Luhmann is not interested in the problem of God as a transcendent being to whom the believer relates; but he is instead concerned with the functional adequacy of religion in reference to the complex, contemporary differentiation of society. According to Luhmann's systems theory, the function of religion can be defined only in reference to the relation between system, environment, and world. Thus the principle at work in the metadifferentiation (*Ausdifferenzierung*) of religion, which remains an autonomous, partial system, is the capacity for self-transformation and self-specialization, which comes into effect not through the use of one of its internal functions as partial system but with recourse to the global social system of which it expresses a specific function (Luhmann 1991).

In other words, Luhmann rejects the idea of an "integrating systemic function" for religion (ibid.:24–26), which is typical of Durkheim's approach, and instead suggests giving attention to the difference between system and environment, and to processes of generating meaning. Luhmann argues:

> Functional analysis, in contrast with the definitive approach, allows and actually forces a radical reference to the underlying issues as regards entire categories of functional equivalents. The lack of precision, being inevitable, is therefore explicitly admitted even if from a purely verbal point of view it can be denied—just as when reference is made in the name of religion to the sacred, to the numinous or to the superior being. By such definition the analytic process is prematurely finished. These analyses play fast and loose with the religious experience, to its own object, in such a way as to provoke a short circuit. Functional analysis rather prefers a distanced approach that gives value to connections toward the external, in the sense of a multiple use of concepts, and to the use of theoretical approaches from different conceptual settings. As regards its own object, it increases the ability for decomposition and recomposition. (ibid.:24–26)

Despite Luhmann's assertions, however, the suspicion lingers that systems theory might represent a sort of straightjacket for the understanding of religion, trapped in an iron logic that allows little space for alternatives in the field of sociological possibility. As Luhmann is, of course, well aware:

> A conception of religion that is connected exclusively to a functional deter-
> mination is often criticized due to its indetermination. On the one hand it is
> too comprehensive because it includes lived experiences and also items that
> are not considered religious. On the other hand, it says too little because a
> single abstract functional denotation is not sufficient to understand the inter-
> nal variety and the limited variability of religion. These shortcomings in the
> formulation of the concept cannot be resolved by limiting the functional
> determination through the indication of "how" to satisfy its function,
> and therefore by describing religion as a belief in a superhuman entity.
> (ibid.:88–89)

Therefore the functions to be analyzed are plural, because

> the intent is that in religion theory each social system, and therefore society
> as a whole, must resolve more than one problem, as it is bound to satisfy a
> multiplicity of functions. The capacity of development of a system theory
> and of a functional theory of religion, will be successful to the extent that it
> will be able to push the analysis beyond a mere catalogue of functions and
> dysfunction. (ibid.)

The capacity of religion to confront insecurity and to reformulate its significance is not a secondary matter. In fact, "It interprets events and possibilities, giving them a meaningful order and making therefore possible the
increment of tolerable insecurity" (ibid.:88).

TOWARD A LESS REDUCTIVE DESCRIPTION OF RELIGION

Our examination of both the substantive and the functional definitions
of religion has made evident the necessity to appeal to definitions of religion that are more open, more pluralistic, and not inscribed in a single
explanatory horizon or within a single confessional perspective. In other
words, an appropriate sociological approach to religion would lead us to
set aside concepts derived from purely subjective experience and to base
any theory or explanation on a much larger spectrum of plural, pluralist,
and universal approaches. To this end, it would be useful to find a common denominator that could ground the largest possible number of routes
related to quite different religious matrices. The difficult part is finding the
constituent elements of this common denominator that could apply to different historical periods and cultures.

A first element of this common denominator could be the notion of meta-empirical reference in the attribution of meaning to human existence, in its various modes of articulation, and to events, whether everyday and repetitive or singular and exceptional. This recourse to phenomena that cannot be directly experienced and are not objectively verifiable should, however, be taken as a possible avenue of approach because some social-religious actors (those who may well in fact have had religious experiences) can do without an unverifiable, metaphysical "transfer," and can even consider their religious experiences to be objective, almost material. In this context, one may think of immanentism, which considers every question within the experiential dimension, or of pantheisms, which attribute creative force to nature.

The meta-empirical approach is therefore just a hypothesis for orienting oneself in a complex field; it is what Blumer (1954) has called a "sensitizing concept," that is, a minimal theoretical definition, which can be refashioned and adapted to different concrete situations. In this way, no contrast arises between the transcendent world and reality. In essence, it is as if one were to look at nonhuman presence in reality, and on the other hand from the viewpoint of an explicative meaning taking root within this same reality. The first of these two visions does not exclude the second; they are not mutually opposed. They can, indeed, sometimes converge at the same point: the understanding and explanation of life in a religious key.

But a fundamental contribution to the definition of what one might mean by religion also comes from field research, which orients and verifies, suggests and focuses, demarcates and puts both the premises and the provisional definitions that are correlated with them into discussion.

PART I

The Origins

1

The Historical-Philosophical Background

THE HISTORICAL-CRITICAL METHOD

The beginning of a scientific approach to the study of religious phenomena originated a long time ago and developed at a rather slow pace. It dates back to the seventh century and is linked to the new Galilean science, to Cartesian rationalism, and to Spinozism, that is, to the need to free religious studies from fideistic and ideological claims. In this regard Piergiorgio Grassi wrote, "Today we can see more clearly how Spinoza's thought spread within late seventeenth century English culture by influencing the political and religious debate. . . . Spinoza wished to bring biblical hermeneutics back to the *ratio*" (1984:54–55).

Baruch (Benedict) Spinoza lived in Holland from 1632 to 1677; his parents were of Spanish and Portuguese origin. Spinoza's Jewish origins are a trait in common with other scholars who have been crucial for the development of the study of religion. Spinoza has been criticized in various ways (Grassi 1984), e.g., for being "Jewish" or for being "excluded from his own community." "He died without the assistance of the clergy and without belief in a recognized God." He was declared a "symbol of atheism," a "godless philosopher, a threat to religion and society." But he has been also seen as a "discreet and simple man," a "virtuous atheist," a "sober and frugal person, obedient to his country's laws, indifferent to wealth, a man of faultless morality" (ibid.). Spinoza's *Tractatus theologico-politicus* ([1670] 1991) did not find an easy road to success, because it was a text that is critical of the belief in prophecy, miracles, and theocracy.

Spinoza strenuously defended being a free thinker. For the sake of his autonomy, he went so far as to reject economic support from Louis XIV and an appointment offered to teach at the University of Heidelberg. Spinoza fought against prejudices that keep us from knowing the truth. Following Descartes, he adopted a deductive methodology. His motivation was mostly a moral one (which brings him close to Durkheim among others). He supported the superiority of the state over the church. His main objective was the possibility of expressing his thoughts in complete freedom. This freedom should be coupled together with a rationalistic attitude, the

13

basis of scientific knowledge leading to laws that would be valid at any place and time. Truth could be achieved through the deductive method—that is, reality should be understood by first considering important and reliable ideas, which could be then applied to specific cases, going from the general to the particular.

Spinoza's historical-critical method was directly linked to political questions designed to achieve a freer society, which would be open to new solutions, including a secular approach to religion.

Aside from the considerations described above, there are obviously other, more strictly philosophical implications in Spinoza's thought. However, what is of interest here is Spinoza's avant-garde position with respect to later social scientifically oriented developments.

VICO (1668–1744):
CIVIL THEOLOGY IN THE LIGHT OF PROVIDENCE

Notwithstanding an aversion toward Cartesianism and toward the rationalistic and empirical presuppositions that are at the origin of sociology, Giambattista Vico contributed to a change in the study of religious phenomena. Through his historical approach to philosophical questions, he saw the origin of religion and the idea of God in the history of humanity. In fact, in the *New Science* he said: "The civil world for all peoples begins with religion" (1999:(8) 8), a statement he repeated later.

According to Vico, through history (the *new science*)—with its own laws and paths—it is possible to explain society, nature, and reality in general. From the age of the gods, or the age of "mere feeling," there followed the age of the heroes, or the age of "imagination." Finally there was the age of man, ruled by "reason." Differently said: "People first feel things without noticing them, then notice them with inner distress and disturbance, and finally reflect on them with a clear mind" (ibid.:94).

Every society reflects the main traits of its particular age. So society will be in turn theocratic, aristocratic, and then democratic. But at the end of each cycle (of the three phases) there is a crisis and everything starts again, with cyclical returns, or *ricorsi*, to the age of the gods. Myth remains dominant until the advent of the third phase, that of human reason.

According to Vico, divine providence (a leitmotiv throughout the *New Science*) is at the origin of all these developments. History, in fact, is a sort of "civil theology reasoned in the light of providence." To this logic should be attributed Vico's idea of the "strength of religion":

Divine providence initiated the process by which fierce and violent men were led from their lawless condition to enter civilization and create nations. Providence did this by awakening in them a confused idea of divinity, which in their ignorance they ascribed to objects incompatible with the divine. Still, in their fear of this imaginary divinity, they began to create some order in their lives. (ibid.:87)

This principle of the *New Science* implies that religion carries out an educational activity even under difficult conditions. Even violent peoples accustomed to the use of weapons can become meek and promote social order. Vico discusses in advance this postulate in the seventh axiom (or metaphysical principle), which "proves that divine providence exists and that it acts as a divine legislative mind. For out of the passion of people intent on their personal advantage, which might cause them to live as wild and solitary beasts, it makes civil institutions which keep them within human society" (ibid.:78). It is clear from this last statement that there is a connection between religion and society, between religious beliefs and civil order.

Pasquale Soccio has observed in his introduction to Vico's *New Science* that this is

a civil theology reasoned by providence—let us stress the adjective *civil*—that is, a divine providence that acts through natural means in the formation of simple human knowledge which chronologically precedes educated knowledge. The word *reasoned* here is used to demonstrate the natural and historical order of human things and facts. The work of providence is especially evident at the origin of humanity, when it acts through "merely natural routes" and reveals itself as acting from reason and good sense, thus guiding human occurrences toward justice, society and common well-being. Thus, those selfish individuals who think to act according to "different and opposite paths" are instead positively influenced by the work of providence toward man's tendency for living in society. (1983:214)

The conclusion of Vico's work was in praise of religion:

Providence caused the world's first governments to base themselves on religion, which alone made the state of families possible. Next, as they developed into heroic civil governments, or aristocracies, religion clearly provided the principal stable foundation. Then, as they advanced to popular governments, religion likewise served as the people's means of attaining democracies. Finally, as they come to rest in monarchical governments, this same religion must be the shield of rulers. If peoples lose their religion, nothing remains to keep them living in society. They have no shield for their defense, no basis for their decisions, no foundation for their stability, and no form by which they exist in the world. (1999:490)

The centrality of religion is constant. It is like an everlasting "shield" for civil life and thus a necessary ingredient in the social history of peoples.

In the end Vico openly shows his religious bias by stating:

> Only religion can make people perform virtuous works by appealing to their
> senses, which effectively move people to action. . . . There is an essential dif-
> ference between our true Christian religion and all the other religions, which
> are false. In Christianity, divine grace inspires virtuous works for the sake of
> an infinite and eternal good. And since this good lies beyond the senses, the
> mind must move the senses to virtuous actions. (ibid.:490–91)

It necessarily follows that this "New Science is indissolubly linked to the
study of piety; and unless one is pious, one cannot be truly wise"
(ibid.:491).

Later analysis of religious fact omitted piety as a crucial ingredient for
wisdom and scientific knowledge. Vico's discussion of religion remains
useful in particular for its diachronic analysis, which uncovers the close
ties between religion and different societies.

HUME'S NATURAL RELIGION (1711–1776)

The birth of a scientific subject like the sociology of religion is not a sud-
den event. Prior to the appearance of the sociology of religion as an independent field of study, there were highly contrasting attitudes toward
religion. On the one hand, religion was heavily attacked, especially in its
organized forms; on the other hand, individual confessional creeds
were strenuously defended. More rarely, a neutral position emerged that
aimed at a mere social analysis—not yet a sociological one—of religious
phenomena.

The beginning of the sociology of religion can be traced back through
various paths. However, the development of a philosophy of religion has
contributed more than other disciplines to the social sciences' initial interest in religious phenomena. In fact, the alliance between philosophy and
sociology is an undeniable fact.

It should be stressed, however, that the scholars discussed in the following section of this book cannot be considered protosociologists of religion. In fact, the term *sociology* came into existence during their lifetime.
However, the contributions by Hume, Feuerbach, Tocqueville, Marx, and
Bergson are discussed in this volume because of their historical importance and theoretical weight, which was crucial for later scientific
developments.

These authors' observations on religion became both vantage points
and dividing lines, since they followed different ideologies and philosophical orientations. The study of religion later became more objective, as

it adapted the rules of experimental science to social phenomena. Between the end of the nineteenth century and the beginning of the twentieth century, the contribution of positivism became crucial. It is from this philosophical current that sociology emerged.

However, the path of the development of the sociology of religion is not clear-cut; in fact, it does not lead directly to Durkheim and Weber if one considers the work of the philosophers who were active in the eighteenth and nineteenth centuries. The quest for his path should be undertaken with great care in order to detect speculative currents and cultural attitudes that underscore the role of religion within society.

The Scottish philosopher David Hume (1711–76) is the first author who should be considered for his essentially empirical approach to the analysis of religion. He spoke of a *natural religion* whose roots are found at the instinctual level, since human beings are instinctively motivated by three elements: happiness, poverty, and death. The desire for pleasure, together with the fear of poverty and death, have led people to seek satisfactory answers and explanations in religion through the creation and divination of anthropomorphic figures—a device to conquer all sorts of fears.

It is possible to infer from this the importance of Hume's thought for the development of the empirical interpretation of religion. His thought also influenced the growth of a more modern theory of knowledge applied to religion. This theory relies on a concrete perception of reality and avoids theological hypotheses and assumptions that cannot be empirically demonstrated.

Among the leading members of the so-called Scottish moralists (as they are sometimes called) or the Scottish realistic school were Adam Ferguson ([1767] 1980) and John Millar ([1771] 1996). They dealt with inquiries concerning civil society (Montesquieu's influence is clear) together with important conceptual hypotheses applied to sociologically relevant realities, such as groups, conflict, property, "association" (which is a form of cooperation aimed at the creation of associative institutions, such as religious ones), division of labor, anomie, power. However, most of these terms were not defined according to today's sociological usage. David Hume—the philosopher, economist, and historian (1754–63) who also authored a history of England—worked in an environment that favored the empirical approach. However, if on the one hand he rejected the hypothesis of God because it is empirically unverifiable, on the other hand he attributed an important role to emotions in directing the individual's life. Even though they lack an empirical basis, people's beliefs appear to be consistent in their support of ethics, religion, and other social experiences that give sense to life.

Hume's *Treatise of Human Nature* (1739–40) was published anonymously in two installments. The first volume, divided into two books, appeared in 1739 and the second volume was published in 1740 in three different books. The three books of the second volume deal with knowledge (book I), passions (book II), and ethics (book III). Religious questions are discussed in an unusual and daring way for the time. Religion is examined and subjected to experience. Hume's better known observations on religion appeared partly in *A Treatise*. These notions are resumed in *Four Dissertations: The Natural History of Religion, of the Passions, of Tragedy, of the Standard of Taste* ([1757] 1996) and especially in *Dialogues concerning Natural Religion* ([1779] 1998).

For Hume, feeling is the foundation of religion, since experience bases itself on perceptions. However, from experience derive ideas to which emotions, memories, and anticipations are linked. The existence of God cannot be proven. For this reason both the person of faith and the nonbeliever share the same hopelessness when it comes to explaining the idea of God, which is a barely probable and unnecessary anthropomorphic character. This also explains a certain skepticism on the part of the believer. Since they cannot be rationally explained, miracles are seen through a skeptical lens (Hume 1748), also because scientific progress is more and more able to discover new horizons and to provide new explanations for various phenomena. Miracles as such then seem to be linked to a superstitious attitude and to the desire to see a supernatural event. In fact, there are usually very few witnesses to a miracle and their versions of what happened generally tend to conflict. According to Hume:

> It is experience only which gives authority to human testimony; and it is the same experience which assures us of the laws of nature. When, therefore, these two kinds of experience are contrary, we have nothing to do but to subtract the one from the other, and embrace an opinion either on one side or the other, with that assurance which arises from the remainder. (Hume [1757] 1996:146).

From a more sociological perspective, Hume underlines the difference between monotheistic and polytheistic peoples. The first have a more rationalistic view of the world, whereas the second are tied to a less critical approach. However, polytheist peoples are more accepting of different views and are in general more socially open (Hume 1996:47). Moreover, polytheism is more familiar with the metaphysical dimension since the gods appear to be closer to human subjects.

Hume maintains that all knowledge falls under the control of experience. Hume's method resembles that of Newton in physics. Hume sees social reality almost as pertaining to the field of physics. This analytical attitude holds true both for the *Treatise* (Hume [1739–40] 1986)—a juvenile work later rejected, written during his first stay in France (in La Flèche, where Descartes was educated)—and his later works (which were published under his name).

Briefly, one can say that Hume does not deny the possibility of religion. In fact, he would not be able to since experience shows the existence of a religious phenomenology. His skeptical attitude is then mainly with regard to the *evidence* of religious facts, which it is not possible to prove empirically and rationally. Religious beliefs turn out to be feelings and not knowledge. In fact, human beings are more mindful of feelings than of reason.

Notwithstanding his basic skepticism, Hume is mainly concerned with moral questions. The ties between ethics and religion are not fortuitous. In fact, he disagrees with certain ways of debating morals or with fanatical attitudes toward religion, but he does not completely deny them. On the contrary, through his moderate attitude he disdains religion's miraculism on the one hand, and its rational and empirical claims on the other. Hume's attitude toward morals seems to anticipate the same concerns of Durkheim a century later. It is not by chance that Hume, like Durkheim, was interested in the topic of suicide (Hume [1777] 1996). In 1757 Hume wrote an essay on this topic, which was published posthumously twenty years later.

In his time Hume was a controversial scholar. His reputation for being an atheist prevented him from obtaining a professorship. He became a friend of the economist Adam Smith and had a well-known quarrel with Rousseau (Hume helped the Swiss philosopher escape to Staffordshire to avoid his French prosecutors, who considered him a revolutionary for his egalitarian and libertarian ideas). Despite his being an antimetaphysical thinker, the Scottish philosopher had among his acquaintances a number of clergymen. He remained a nonbeliever till the end of his life and, as he wrote in a work published posthumously (Hume [1777] 1996), he did not believe in the immortality of the soul. Notwithstanding this, his fellow countrymen called him "Saint David."

David Hume's empirical inductivism is linked to the positivist thought of August Comte, the father of sociology. It also anticipates the *methodological atheism* developed by Peter Berger [(1967) 1973], a scientific option based on the necessity of discarding anything that is not empirically based. Hume's thought has not been sufficiently considered by sociology and social science historians, especially not by philosophers of religion. The latter all seem to agree—apart from scholars Bucaro (1988:50–57) and Olivetti (1992:226–28)—upon a *damnatio memoriae*, condemning the Edinburgh philosopher to oblivion. Olivetti writes: "When the philosophy of religion emerged as a separate philosophical field of study, it essentially developed as a theory of religious society—or community—and as a theory of society *überhaupt*," that is, in general. This double characteristic—the socioreligious in particular and the social in general, is further confirmed in reference to Hume: "Philosophy of religion (and the name itself) developed historically as a consequence of the crisis of ontological metaphysics. This holds true for both the Kantian and post-Kantian traditions, and also for the empirical tradition (cf. Hume's *Dialogues on Natural Religion*)" (ibid.:225–26).

The Protestant pastor Friedrich Schleiermacher (1768–1834) is also worth mentioning for his interest in the philosophy of religion. A professor of dogmatic theology at the University of Berlin, Schleiermacher viewed religion as a "feeling of utter dependence" of the finite being on the infinite being, which is the reality of the world or God. This "feeling" or "utter self-consciousness" is the religious consciousness that belongs to a divine being. Such a God is everything. This perspective is essentially Spinozian and pantheist, since it considers religion as completely autonomous with respect to other human activities, including the historical churches.

According to Schleiermacher, society and religion itself appear as an aggregate of relationships among individuals who due to their own peculiarities acquired a special place within the infinite. Religion then should not be interpreted by means of morality and scientific reasoning. What prevails in the end is religious feeling, which is different from religion as an institution. From primitive fetishism, to polytheism, to the classical age, and to Christianity, religion became more and more a subjective experience within the individual. From the religious experience, from religious feeling (*Gefühl*), a "pious self-consciousness" develops, which generates "pious communities," among which one can find the Christian church.

> Thus it was religion when the ancients, annihilating the limitations of time and space, regarded every unique type of life throughout the whole world as the work and reign of an omnipresent being. They had intuited a unique mode of acting of the universe in its unity, and designated this intuition accordingly. . . . It was religion when they rose above the brittle iron age of the world, full of fissures and unevenness, and again sought the golden age on Olympus among the happy life of the gods. . . . To present all events in the world as the actions of a god is religion; it expresses its connection to an infinite totality. (Schleiermacher [1799] 1988:105)

As it is possible to tell from Schleiermacher's most famous work, *On Religion: Speeches on Its Cultured Despisers* (published anonymously in 1799), dogmas and doctrines have a secondary importance. In his last work, *The Christian Faith*, published in 1821, Schleiermacher fully applied the inductive method to the religious experience. He emphasized that "pious self-consciousness" precedes institutionalized religion. Indeed, the foundation of religion comes after religious feeling, that is, after experience. In this regard, sociologist Peter Berger prefers the term *experience*. Berger writes:

One of the basic criticisms that has been made of Schleiermacher has been to the effect that his method was the predecessor of Feuerbach's. It would be more accurate to say that Schleiermacher's method is the opposite of Feuerbach's. The latter . . . sought to reduce infinity to finitude, to translate theology into anthropology. Schleiermacher, by contrast, only uses an anthropological starting point in his theologizing, and he views the finite as being shot through with manifestations of the infinite. In his discussion of miracles (a tender topic in an intellectual milieu saturated with Enlightenment rationalism) he argues that the world is full of them, in the sense of *signs and intimations of the infinite* even in the most natural and common events. (Berger 1979:118–19)

Schleiermacher's notion of the "feeling of utter dependence" influenced Rudolf Otto's ([1917] 1958) idea of the sacred. Moreover, Schleiermacher's inductive method is notably close to William James's analytic scheme.

THE ANTHROPOLOGICAL ESSENCE OF RELIGION IN FEUERBACH (1804–1872)

Ludwig Feuerbach was born in Bavaria and studied theology at the University of Heidelberg. He then studied philosophy in Berlin, where Hegel was one of his teachers. Feuerbach is usually considered as having atheist views (which he, however, denied). He considered faith a device to project human qualities. Thus, the Holy Trinity would be linked to three traits typical of mankind: reason, will, and love. Through his humanistic theology he claimed that with atheism humankind became an object of cult. Thus, it is possible to practice a "religion of humanity" (this was also thought by Auguste Comte).

Like Hume, Feuerbach published an essay anonymously—*Thoughts on Death and Immortality* ([1830] 1980)—in which he declared that he did not believe in immortality (because of this assertion he lost his university position). He then published two essays: *On Philosophy and Christianity* (1839) and *The Essence of Christianity* ([1841] 1989). In the first essay he looked at the disappearance of Christianity, which would be, he thought, reduced to a mere idea. In the second essay, religion is seen exclusively as a person's awareness of the infinite. Similar to Hume's ideas, according to Feuerbach, God is man's projection. This is the so-called anthropological essence of religion as opposed to the theological one, in which God is seen as situated outside earthly reality. God then becomes the object of a religious materialism through sacraments, prayers, and beliefs in revelation. It thus becomes clear that God's goodness, love, and ethical laws are nothing but illusions that simply match the needs of human nature.

Feuerbach's religious and human-centered projectionism leads to a human interpretation of the religious fact, to a materialistic anthropology, and to a rejection of all forms of myth. God then goes through a process of humanization. Therefore, man should not be considered the image of God, but, rather God is a projected shadow deriving from man, who in turn alienates himself in divinity. Religion in general (and the Christian religion in particular) represents the relationship of man to his essence. God is the result of this human essence, which is raised to a metaphysical level and becomes an object of devotion. The divine is *essentially* human. Natural man (an expression that echoes Hume's natural religion) fulfills himself through being in contact with another man or with God through an egalitarian and rewarding form of dialogue. This idea has been developed by the religious philosopher Martin Buber, who published *Ich und Du* (*I and Thou*). From a Protestant perspective, there is also the contribution of Karl Barth—a supporter of the anti-Nazi movement—who influenced Dietrich Bonhoeffer and was a theorist of ecumenism.

At this point, an evaluation expressed by Buber on the central role of this kind of dialectic is worth mentioning:

> Feuerbach initiated that discovery of the "Thou," which has been called the "Copernican deed" of modern thought, and an "elemental event." It has been just as momentous as the discovery of the "I" by Idealism, and must lead to a second new beginning of European thinking, which refers us beyond the first Cartesian entry of the newer Philosophy. He gave me, in the days of my youth, the decisive stimulus. (Gollwitzer 1970:58, footnote 34)

Just as the origins of the scientific approach in sociology could be traced back to Descartes's experimental method, one could also assume that the development of a nonmetaphysical approach to religious phenomena originated to some extent from Feuerbach's anthropology.

It should also be mentioned that Feuerbach tried to solve the conflict between reason and feeling. While he clearly favored the latter, at the same time he encouraged people to shift from prayer to work, from the relationship with God to one with other human beings, from the tension with the other world to tension with the present one. According to Feuerbach, the essence of man resided in man himself, not in God or in religion. God and religion separated man from himself. There was a need, then, to recover man's essence by anthropologizing both God and religion, bearing in mind that they were man's mental projections. Through the denial of God and religion, man affirmed himself; thus it was he himself who became God, and not God who became man. Hence, humanism became a kind of atheism.

Feuerbach, who was a leading figure of the Hegelian left, rejected the quasi-religion represented by Hegel's idealistic philosophy (Hegel claimed that the essence of things resided in the concept of ideas, thanks to which all matter existed), preferring a more realistic and sensationalist kind of materialism, which paved the way for Marx and Engels. However, Marx wrote in 1845 (published posthumously in 1888) a concise criticism of Feuerbach, the *Theses on Feuerbach*. In this volume, Marx accused Feuerbach of lacking "revolutionary" sensitivity (thesis I) since he did not draw a distinction between theory and practice, between thought and human sensitive nature, ignoring the passage that goes from the interpretation of the world to changing it (thesis XI). In thesis IV Marx stated:

> Feuerbach starts out from the fact of religious self-alienation, the duplication of the world into a religious, imaginary world and a real one. His work consists in the dissolution of the religious world into its secular basis. He overlooks the fact that after completing this work, the chief thing still remains to be done. For the fact that the secular foundation lifts itself above itself and establishes itself in the clouds as an independent realm is only to be explained by the self-cleavage and self-contradictoriness of this secular basis. The latter must itself, therefore, first be understood in its contradiction and then, by the removal of the contradiction, revolutionised in practice. (Marx [1888] 1935:74)

Even more explicit for the sociological perspective are theses VI and VII: "Feuerbach resolves the religious essence into the human. But the human essence is no abstraction inherent in each single individual. In its reality it is the *ensemble* of the social relations" (ibid.:74–75). Thus, for Marx, Feuerbach would not perceive the individual as a social being but as isolated in his subjective religious feeling, which he shares, just as a natural fact, with other individuals: "Feuerbach, consequently, does not see that the 'religious sentiment' is itself a *social product*, and that the abstract individual whom he analyses belongs in reality to a particular form of society" (ibid.:75). Marx was not a sociologist but the sociological weight of his reflections in the *Theses on Feuerbach* cannot be ignored.

"THE OPIUM OF THE PEOPLE" AND "THE SIGH OF THE OPPRESSED CREATURE" ACCORDING TO MARX (1818–1883)

Karl Marx was born into a German family of Jewish origin that later converted to Lutheranism. Contrary to what is normally thought, Marx's vision of religion is not unilateral. He wrote that "*religious* distress is at the same time the expression of real distress and the *protest* against the real distress" (Marx 1844, in Marx and Engels 1959). The choice of religion as a "poor" solution is a result of material poverty, but it also shows the non-acceptance of the actual condition and this paves the way for revolt against any form of enslavement. In fact: "Religion is the sigh of the oppressed creature, the heart of the heartless world, just as it is the spirit of an unspiritual situation. It is the *opium* of the people" (Marx [1844] 1959). Thus, the longing for religion is also a social ambition to free oneself from oppression, to overcome spiritless and hard conditions. However, religion itself would keep human beings from going a step beyond simple protest, that is, it prevents a real revolutionary action against the *status quo*. Hence, for Marx religion is not effective enough—it is always on the verge of revolution but never accomplishes it.

We should emphasize that for Marx social relations (including the relations of production) were crucial in explaining many different dynamics, as well as those which pertain to the change and preservation of existence. The various processes described by Marx are the alienation of the object, that is, the product of the work, which grows foreign to the worker) and the alienation of the process (workers, that is, are not fulfilled in their job and at the same time they lose their ties with humanity). Another process is that of social alienation brought on by the growing separateness among social beings, and by the fact that the product of work belongs to another subject, who then profits from it. All these processes are also present in religion. Indeed, Marx wrote that the more man puts in God, the less he keeps for himself (Marx [1844] 1959)

In this regard, Bucaro rightly states:

> As far as the expressions employed are concerned, Marx has used Feuerbach's concepts of religious alienation. At the content level, however, Marx reverses Feuerbach's ideas and limits the whole to the alienation of the worker's relationship with the product of his work, retaining this kind of alienation as the basic one, from which all other forms of alienation originate. Religious alienation has been used by Marx to describe the main form of alienation, that is, that of the worker's object with respect to the producer. Thus for Marx religious alienation is neither the first nor the most important one. Here lies the difference between Marx's thought and earlier philosophy, including that of Feuerbach. According to Marx, religion originates as the product of the total inversion of society and not as the result of man's unfulfilled desires and dreams. Religion becomes the theoretical consciousness of this reversal. (Bucaro 1988:67)

Above all, however, religion has an ideological character, especially considering its part in maintaining capitalist society. As a system of ideas, religion sustains the interests of the determinate social classes (the ruling ones). Religion turns out to be an illusion that prevents anyone from acting according to an antibourgeois and anticapitalist perspective.

But religion was not solely "the opium of the people" and "class exploitation." Marx acknowledged religion as also "wisdom of the other world" and a special form of knowledge even though lacking freedom and rationality.

The references to divinity were the result of a social construction of reality. "This state, this society produce religion, *a perverted world consciousness, because they are a perverted world*" (Marx [1844] 1959:262). This quotation presents an old problem: the confusion between theoretical analysis of religion and its use from an ideological point of view. Sociologist Marcello Fedele in his introduction to an anthology of writings on religion by Marx and Engels rightly points out that often when discussing Marxism and Christianity, "The logico-sociological question regarding the nature of religious ideology has been substituted with the partial and limited historical-political analysis of the social contents of Christianity and its doctrine" (1973:42).

Indeed, Marx's analytical standpoint appears to be reductive when compared to Feuerbach's position. Feuerbach supported the idea of a global perspective with regard to people, going beyond the restricted realm of the socioeconomic dimension. In this sense, it is possible to explain Marx's transition from understanding religious reality to overcoming religion itself. Marx argued that the disappearance of religion would be a basic condition for the advent of a society without classes in which not even atheism (or theism) would have reason to exist. In the end, the negation of God turns out to be unnecessary in a situation governed by a kind of socialism based on man's "positive consciousness." Marx's objective was the creation of a "truth of this world," unconcerned about "heaven" except for its being part of nature.

Happiness itself originates from the suppression of religion since the illusions that keep human essence from grasping "true reality" are in this way eliminated.

According to Marx, fighting against religion means fighting against a given reality. More explicitly: "The criticism of religion disillusions man, to make him think and act and shape his reality like a man who has been disillusioned and has come to reason, so that he will revolve round himself and therefore round his true sun. Religion is only the illusory sun, which revolves round man as long as he does not revolve round himself" (Marx [1844] 1959:263)

Criticism against religion is an important feature in Marx's thinking from his early years right up to his years of maturity. Scholar Luciano Parinetto writes:

> Understanding the *mystery* of *religious* alienation is *propaedeutic* to understanding the mystery of the *form of commodities*. The person who is well aware of religion's subtle mystifications could also grasp those pertaining to capital and be wary of it. Whoever is not critical of *capital* is not a good critic

of *religion*. The analogy between the *fetishism of commodities* and *religion* becomes even more apt considering that the religious object is also apparently independent with respect to its human producer, just as occurs in the case of commodities with respect to the workers. (Parinetto 1976:73)

Aside from the contributions of Otto Maduro (1979), the trend of the Marxist sociology of religion never really fully developed consistently. This is, however, not the case with other disciplines, from economics to politics.

2

The Universal Religion of Auguste Comte
(1798–1857)

The French philosopher Auguste Comte has been the most important figure in positivist social science. He was also the secretary of Saint-Simon, who was a socialist and a supporter of a new kind of Christianity based on the ethics of brotherhood. Comte, who coined the term "sociology," strongly believed in the possibility of science solving all the problems of humanity, which he defined as the "Great Being," and he proclaimed himself the "high priest" of science. He viewed science as the last of three phases of human evolution: The first phase is the "theological" one, in which reality is explained through the existence of the gods. Comte defined the second phase as the "metaphysical" one, since it is based on pure abstractions. The third phase is the "positive" one, founded on the observation and correlation of facts. Finally, "positive philosophy" would coordinate all the various sciences of which sociology emerges as the most complex, because its function is to control the evolution of society.

As Comte noted in his writings, disciplines like metaphysics and theological philosophy were unable to show the social perspective. In fact, metaphysical philosophy is devoted to a subjective perspective, while theological philosophy subordinates real life to a chimerical destiny. But Comte's new philosophy adopted the social point of view as the universal basis for the final systematization. The two previous disciplines could not possibly have allowed for the development of purely disinterested feelings, and went so far as to deny their existence dogmatically, either through useless scholastic quibbling or a constant preoccupation with personal salvation (Comte 1830–42).

Comte was enthusiastic about the idea of a "religion of humanity" and went so far as to found a trinitarian cult based on the "Great Being" (humankind), the "Great Fetish" (the world), and the "Great Mean or Middle" (space). Altruism—another term he coined—is at the center of Comte's intellectual activity and is worshipped and put into practice by the religion of humanity. In the volume *Catéchisme positiviste* (Comte 1852)

27

Comte introduced the reader to the essential contents of the "universal religion." However, to have a good grasp of Comte's thought it is important to refer to the well-known volume *Cours de philosophie positive* (Comte [1830–42] 1967) and to the *Système de politique positive, ou Traité de sociologie instituant la religion de l'humanité* (Comte 1851–54).

For Comte only those past, present, and also future generations that have or will have contributed to the universal order by generously "living for others" can be called truly human. Positivism itself becomes a religion, the "true, complete, and real" religion, differing greatly both from the theological phase and from the metaphysical one.

Notwithstanding his critical stance with regard to Comte's thought, Raymond Aron admits that

> Comte's religion—which, as you know, has not had a great worldly success—is not as absurd as is generally believed. In any case, it seems to me superior to many other religious or semireligious notions which other sociologists contributed to spread, either voluntarily or not. . . . [Therefore,] if one insists in wanting to create a religion from sociology (which I do not agree with), the only possible religion would be that of Auguste Comte. . . . [Besides,] what Comte wanted us to love is neither the French society of today, nor the Russian society of tomorrow, nor the American society of the day after tomorrow, but the essential humanity which certain men have been able to achieve and toward which all men should raise themselves. (Aron 1998:123)

These excellent people are the saints of Comte's universal religion. They are worshipped by positivistic philosophy in the Chapel of Humanity at 5 rue Payenne in Paris (the chapel has recently been reopened to the public). Again, Aron writes in this regard that "if Comte's 'humanity' consists more of dead than living members, it is not because there are statistically more dead than living men; it is because only the dead survive as the humanity we must love, the humanity worthy of what Comte called subjective immortality" (ibid.:122).

It is highly probable that the inspiration for Comte's idea of humanity derives from Saint-Simon. In fact, in Saint-Simon's *Lettres d'un habitant de Genève à ses contemporaines* (1802–3) one can read about a "religion of science," and in particular about religion as a human invention, as the only political institution that by its very nature tends to give humanity a general organization (Saint-Simon 1975:139). Just like Saint-Simon, Comte pursued the ideal of an organized humanity, regulated by religion as a major unifying factor, which also bears sociopolitical connotations when it comes to improving communal life. Comte's social solidarity is the underlying objective in reaction to the crisis of his time. His beliefs anticipated Durkheim's ideas; it would seem that Comte and Durkheim shared the same idea about social order. One must also bear in mind, however, the important influence that Saint-Simon had on both of them.

It is possible to sustain that in Comte's positivist sociology there is a sort of "religiosity" that does not clash with his conviction based on the observation of facts. His "social physics," later called sociology, postulates a scientific precision when it comes to the analysis of social phenomena. As far as religion is concerned, Comte first of all considered its historical origins (theological phase), while rejecting its abstract formulations (metaphysical phase), and ended his work by rejecting Christian and Catholic traditional solutions. Comte considered these solutions unsuitable for improving humanity, but considered positivist philosophy and the "religion of humanity," in particular, as more appropriate to this aim.

Through the historical-comparative approach, Comte also wanted to verify some laws by means of the hypothetical deductive method employed in physics. The final outcome is a diachronic view in which science has had a major role by freeing humanity in the past from theological and then from metaphysical claims, thus helping humanity in its progress from an infantile stage to an adult and more self-conscious one. Science itself turns out to be a useful tool for reconstructing a social theory that represents the "permanent spiritual basis of social order."

The overlapping of the scientific and the spiritual levels is typical of Comte. It is possible to grasp the simultaneous presence of the two levels both in the relationship between Comte and Clotilde de Vaux (his inspiring muse, "saint friend," "priestess of Humanity"), and with the realization of the "Chapel of Humanity" in Clotilde's house. On the front of the building one can read the following inscription: "L'Amour pour principe; L'Ordre pour base, Et le Progrès pour but" ("Love as principle; order as basis, and progress as aim"). This same inscription appears on the frontispiece of some books of essays published by Comte [cf. the volume quoted above, *Catéchisme positiviste* (Comte 1852)].

The chapel was founded in 1900 by a group of positivists. At present it is on the premises of a cultural association called *Apostolat Positiviste*. Almost everything in the chapel is described in ecclesiastic language. There is a "calendar of religious positivism" (it is divided into thirteen months of twenty-eight days each). Months and days are named after famous characters like Aristotle or Gutenberg. In the chapel there are various inscriptions more or less taken from Comte's writings: "Man becomes more and more religious," "Family, Homeland, Humanity," "Man works hard and Humanity leads him," "To live for others." Another inscription reads: "Auguste Comte, Founder of the Universal Religion and First High Priest of Humanity."

The chapel's walls are divided into regular spaces, each space representing the arts (architecture, sculpture, painting, music, and poetry) and forms of modernity (modern epic, modern industry, modern drama, modern philosophy, modern politics, modern science, the modern equality of women). Then a series of famous characters follows [Dante, Gutenberg, Shakespeare, Descartes, Frédéric (a well-known Belgian painter), Bichat (a famous anatomist-pathologist), Eloisa]. There are also important female characters who gave a great deal to humanity [Beatrice, Isabel of Castille, Elisa Mercoeur, Elizabeth of Bohemia (the daughter of James I of England), Sainte Geneviève, Sophie German (a mathematician), and the personification of childhood]. Some of these women come from the official religion of the church. However, most of them belong to many different fields, thereby confirming the multidisciplinary and "ecumenical" nature of Comte's philosophy and of his "universal religion." Finally, on the altar of the chapel there is an inscription in Italian: *Vergine Madre Figlia del tuo Figlio* ("Virgin Mother, Daughter of Your Son"). A little below there is the following inscription in Latin: *Amem te plus quam me nec me nisi propter te* ("If only I could love you more than I love myself and love myself only for you").

The relationship between Clotilde de Vaux and Auguste Comte is even more illuminating. They were both deeply disappointed by their previous marriages and began to see each other twice a week, in addition to exchanging letters every two days. Comte idealized Clotilde, believing her to be the great mediator between humanity and himself, the "high priest." The romantic-religious atmosphere completed the picture that renders the couple a perfect example of a fruitful sentimental and intellectual symbiosis. Wolf Lepenies has written a well-documented story of the couple that helps the reader to understand a lot more about the intertwining of reason and passion, science and religion, utopia and reality.

In this transformation of Positivism from a scientific thesis into a religion, a novel played an important role. On 30 April 1845 Comte lent Clotilde de Vaux a copy of Henry Fielding's *Tom Jones*. . . . Clotilde thanked him the following day; she hoped that she and Comte would soon be able to talk over Fielding's book together. These two letters are the first of the "correspondance sacrée". . . . Not without intellectual ambition she hoped to gain instruction and inspiration from a philosopher who, though he belonged to no university, had nonetheless acquired a reputation that extended far beyond Paris and France. . . . The transformation accomplished in Comte's way of thinking was profound. . . . On 2 June Catholics celebrate the feast of St. Clotilde. Comte, the critic of the age of theology, employed the opportunity to compose for Clotilde de Vaux an essay on the *commémoration sociale*. . . . He again warmed toward Catholicism—evidence for which is not least his reading of Augustine—and the systematic positivists seemed to him more and more to be the sole legitimate successors of the great men of the Middle Ages. . . . The Clotilde cult which Comte evolved even while she was still alive was a systematic compensation for an unfulfilled passion. . . . Comte was engaged in founding a religion. . . . Comte's affair with Clotilde de Vaux represents a bizarre episode in the history of the social sciences. . . . In the end every commonplace event that occurred in his incomparable year with Clotilde took on a religious significance. The religion of humanity and the rites with which Clotilde was and is venerated now have but few adherents. . . . Moreover, as we know today from documents in the local land-registry office, the positivists of Brazil and Liverpool purchased and renovated the wrong house: 5, rue Payenne; Clotilde lived in the building next to the present temple, 7, rue Payenne: it has long since been demolished. . . . The completed *Système de politique positive, ou traité de sociologie instituant la religion de l'humanité* is, as its title alone reveals, a kind of memorial to Clotilde. . . . Comte explained the fact that . . . his initial objective had been to prove the intellectual superiority of positivism over all systems of theology, while what he had subsequently to do was to demonstrate the moral excellence of the only true religion. (Lepenies 1988:27–38)

This long quotation consists of passages that convey an essential idea of the relationship between Comte and Clotilde. Nonetheless, it barely touches on the deep emotional and scientific exchange between the two. Every detail confirms the hypothesis of a "religion of humanity" of which Clotilde de Vaux is a crucial representative. It is not by chance that the image that appears on the altar of the Chapel of Humanity is probably Clotilde's.

The implications of this religion were specially analyzed in the essay *Catéchisme positiviste*—particularly in the first and ninth interview. The "religion of humanity" includes the individual and the social dimensions of human existence so as to form a "unity," since both the moral and the physical part point in the same direction. Comte talked about a real "synthesis" but this concept considers only the spiritual dimension. On the contrary, the idea of "unity" gathers together all aspects of human nature.

Thus, religion is needed in order to balance and adjust each individual nature and to create a connection among the various subjective realities. The political character of such a religion consists in perfecting humanity at the physical, intellectual, and moral levels.

3

Tocqueville (1805–1859)

Religion and Democracy

The French historian Alexis de Tocqueville is the well-known author of *Democracy in America*, published between 1835 and 1840 in Paris, almost at the same time as Comte's *Cours*. In his famous text, Tocqueville described the habits, customs, and beliefs of the liberal democratic tradition in the United States. According to Tocqueville, religion in particular sets the conditions for the creation and preservation of a stable society based on freedom. This could be the reason why in the United States the successful match between religious beliefs and liberal spirit helped democracy to endure. On the contrary, in France the centuries-old conflict between the church and the lay world kept the two spirits separate.

As a consequence, Americans were probably influenced by religion to make good use of democracy. Also their habits and customs formed the basis of democracy. As Giorgio Candeloro points out in his introduction to the Italian edition of *Democracy in America*: "For Tocqueville religion is one of the customs of Americans. He thinks religion has a great influence on politics." Tocqueville, who spent nine months in the United States, from May 1831 to February 1832,

> attributed to religion the instrumental function of maintaining morals and the established political order. He thus considered the respect that Americans had for religious beliefs in a positive light, notwithstanding the proliferation of religious sects in those years and that underneath this phenomenon there was probably a great deal of hypocrisy. (Candeloro 1996:11)

In his book *L'Ancien Régime et la Révolution* ([1856] 1988), Tocqueville argued that the French revolution resembled a religious revolution since it considered "man in general," going beyond the specific context and adopting a global perspective. The French revolution was concerned with "this world," while religious revolution aims at the "other world." Raymond Aron agrees that this correspondence between a political crisis and a religious revolution seems to be a typical trait of great revolutions in modern societies. He thinks that is possible to generalize this proposition: every political revolution retains certain peculiarities of the religious revolution when it wants to be effective at a universal level and pretends to be the only route to humanity's salvation (Aron [1955] 1977).

Returning to *Democracy in America*, at least two points deserve special attention: The first point is where Tocqueville dealt with "religion considered as a political institution which powerfully contributes to the maintenance of a democratic republic among the Americans" (Tocqueville 1966:300), the "indirect influence of religious opinions upon political society in the United States" (ibid.:303), and the "principal causes which render religion powerful in America" (ibid.:308).

In a detailed and well-documented way, the author presented his thesis regarding the religious basis of American democracy. He was mainly concerned with social stratification and wrote:

> Among the various Christian sects, Catholicism seems to me, on the contrary, to be one of the most favorable to equality of condition among men. In the Catholic Church the religious community is composed of only two elements: the priest and the people. The priest alone rises above the rank of his flock, and all below him are equal. (ibid.:300)

Almost anticipating an objection regarding the oligarchic structure of the Catholic church, Tocqueville added that "if Catholicism predisposes the faithful to obedience, it certainly does not prepare them for inequality." Indeed, "Catholicism is like an absolute monarchy; if the sovereign be removed, all the other classes of society are more equal than in republics." On the other hand, "no sooner is the priesthood entirely separated from the government, as is the case in the United States, that it is found that no class of men is more naturally disposed than the Catholics to transfer the doctrine of the equality of condition into the political world." As it turns out, Catholics are faithful and observant as far as their religion is concerned, but show a great deal of independence when dealing with politics. In fact,

> Religion in America takes no direct part in the government of society, but it must be regarded as the first of their political institutions; for if it does not impart a taste for freedom, it facilitates the use of it. . . . I do not know whether all Americans have a sincere faith in their religion—for who can search the human heart?—but I am certain that they hold it to be indispensable to the maintenance of republican institutions. (ibid.:300–6)

Tocqueville became more thorough as he wrote about his interviews: "Everybody attributed the peaceful dominion of religion in their country mainly to the separation of church and state" (ibid.:308). In fact, the clergy distanced itself from the political power, which Tocqueville saw as especially good, considering that "in forming an alliance with a political power, religion augments its authority over a few and forfeits the hope of reigning over all" (ibid.:310). The result of this seems a paradox—in order to be more influential, one must move away from politics. Thus, "in America religion is perhaps less powerful than it has been at certain periods and among certain nations; but its influence is more lasting" (ibid.:312). Tocqueville did not hide his being a Catholic and his concern about practical questions in order to "restore the Christian church of Europe to the energy of its earlier days" (ibid.:314). While it is difficult to agree with him on this point, other aspects of his masterwork appear more interesting. In particular, Chapters V, VI, and VII in Volume II, Book 1, which deal with "how religion in the United States avails itself of democratic tendencies" (ibid.:20), "the progress of Roman Catholicism in the United States" (ibid.:29), and "what causes democratic nations to incline towards pantheism" (ibid.:31). Moreover, Chapters IX, XII, and XV of Volume II, Book 2, deal with the following topics: "that the Americans apply the principle of self-interest rightly understood to religious matters" (ibid.:121), "why some Americans manifest a sort of fanatical spiritualism" (ibid.:134), and "how religious belief sometimes turns the thoughts of Americans to immaterial pleasures" (ibid.:143). "I do not believe," Tocqueville declares, "that self-interest is the sole motive of religious men, but I believe that self-interest is the principal means that religions themselves employ to govern men, and I do not question that in this way they strike the multitude and become popular" (ibid.:126).

The spread of religious sects in America is explained through a "fanatical and almost wild spiritualism" caused by the fact that "the soul has wants which must be satisfied" (ibid.:134). Tocqueville then wrote: "The greatest advantage of religion is to inspire diametrically contrary principles. There is no religion that does not place the object of man's desires above and beyond the treasures of earth and that does not naturally raise his soul to regions far above those of the senses" (ibid.:22). Hence, "Respecting all democratic tendencies not absolutely contrary to herself and by making use of several of them for her own purposes, religion sustains a successful struggle with that spirit of individual independence which is her most dangerous opponent" (ibid.:28). It is not by chance then, Tocqueville observed, that Catholicism makes a great deal of progress in the United States. It fails, however, to foresee "that our posterity will tend more and more to a division into only two parts, some relinquishing Christianity entirely and others returning to the Church of Rome" (ibid.:30). The French historian saw other improvements in pantheism, since "the human mind seeks to embrace a multitude of different objects at once, and it constantly strives to connect a variety of consequences with a single cause" (ibid.:31). Finally, it should be considered that "most religions are only general, simple, and practical means of teaching men the doctrine of the immortality of the soul. That is the greatest benefit which a democratic people derives from its belief, and hence belief is more necessary to such a people than to all others" (ibid.:145).

4

Bergson (1859–1941)
Religion and "Élan Vital"

Religion as social feeling is a distinctive feature of Bergson's stimulating and illuminating thought. The French thinker preferred a philosophical perspective that later underwent various developments, given its metadisciplinary character.

Henri Bergson was well aware of the developments of French philosophy during the nineteenth century. In his introduction to a book by Alexandre Gunn, Bergson wrote that the author had the merit to "have identified such developments with a few essential questions—science, freedom, progress, morals, religion" (Gunn 1922:8–9). These "preoccupations" are the thread that runs through Comte and Tocqueville up to Bergson's philosophy. Bergson, however, was also influenced by American philosophers like William James ([1902] 1961), the pragmatist philosopher whose ideas Bergson helped to spread in France.

In the essay *La pensée et le mouvant*, Bergson ([1934] 1946) stated that a new science is always dogmatic. Since this new science has a limited experience, it works less with facts than with a few simple ideas, whether these originated from the facts or not, which are treated almost deductively. Bergson was convinced that metaphysics, more than any other science, is exposed to this danger. He also thought that one had to clear one's mind to open the way to inner experience. Everyone has the capacity for intuition, which is, however, normally used for functions that are useful for practical life. The metaphysician works with a priori concepts that have been previously stored in language. These concepts, as if descending from heaven, reveal to the mind a supersensible reality. The Platonic theory of ideas originated in this way. This theory, through Aristotelism and Neoplatonism, came to inspire modern philosophers without their being conscious of it (ibid.).

These same observations seemed to apply to newly born sociology and to positivist scientism, which involved a very dogmatic current of thinking that relied on few a basic concepts. From a declared deductive reasoning one shifted to inductive practice, so that social facts lost their weight and importance. All sociological work revolved around these ideas rather than facts. On the contrary, according to Bergson, all inquiries should at first erase all presuppositions that prevent a close investigation of inner experience. Thus, Bergson was not in line with Comte's position regarding Positivism, since the latter seemed to be mainly based on mere theoretical reflections. Abstract elements should never predominate over empirical data. Bergson was also critical of Comte's universal religion since it was much more based on intellectual thought rather than on concrete facts.

To understand better man's inner dimension and to perceive his real motivations—the personal and social modes of religious experience—Bergson called for a more rigorous scientific method. Apart from being a philosopher, Bergson was also a mathematician and a first-rate writer—he obtained the Nobel Prize for literature in 1927. Thus, Bergson was accustomed to the precision of calculus, to the centrality of factual experience, to the difference between social statics and dynamics, and to an awareness of the difference between institutional and ecstatic religion.

Les deux sources de la morale et de la religion (Bergson [1974] 1986) was Bergson's most mature and well-known spiritual book (it ran to over one hundred editions in French). In this book Bergson distinguished between two main traits of human behavior: a static one and a dynamic one. The former leads to science but has a dogmatic, binding, and conservative character that usually connotes popular religion; on the other hand, the dynamic basis generates the ethics of the origins and the creativity of the mystic experience, which is typical of the founders of religion.

Bergson aimed at giving space to the spiritual dimension and strongly opposed rationalistic solutions that would heavily limit religious knowledge. It is not by chance that American pragmatist William James admired him greatly. They were friends and maintained a correspondence.

According to Bergson, the intuitive potentialities of the mind are superior to the logical order typical of reason. They deserve to be studied to capture reality's essential data, which often escapes a superficial and external analysis. Hence, after the positivistic and quantitative approach, it was not possible to escape the qualitative approach, especially when dealing with religious issues. This was the conclusion reached by Bergson after following a long path that also included Spencerian evolutionism (Spencer 1967).

In Bergson's opinion, analysis is the main scientific method. This holds true especially for inquiries concerning religion since it is crucial to go beyond exterior appearance. Thus, as Prontera writes,

> Within self-enclosed morality and static religion, which is characterized by prohibitions, habits and routine, the group's conservative calculus dominates. To be sure, this routine does produce mechanical cohesion but, at the

same time, it kills life and freedom. On the other hand, within open moral-ity and dynamic religion, the rejections of order, the breaking off of passivity and of habits give rise to a surge of love, which alone promotes new life forms and ways of being. The saints and the mystics are not only the wit-nesses but also the concrete agents of this deep renewal and rebirth, which means going back to the sources, to the creative energies. (Prontera 1991:771)

Briefly, reality must be seen differently from what it appears to be.

Bergson's vitalistic philosophy is essentially based on the concept of *élan vital*. It is a propulsive element of innovative forms both for the spirit and for matter. The universe itself is "a machine for the making of gods" (Berg-son [1974] 1986:317). It is a *"machine à faire des dieux"* in that it inspires, through cosmology, various representations of divine figures. *Élan vital*, however, eventually gets exhausted and self-enclosed societies develop that create and protect their own religion. As Bergson himself observed, this phenomenon could be *"a defensive reaction of nature against what might be depressing for the individual, and dissolvent for society"* (ibid.:205). However, the extraordinary strength of *élan vital* went beyond empty rituals and con-tributed to the growth of dynamic religion, that is, mysticism. Hence, as Bergson wrote, a few saints and prophets showed an incredible energy, boldness, and power of conception and realization (ibid.). In other words, the binding dogmas were replaced with an exceptional appeal of a special character that revealed the divine's *élan vital*. Society then became sponta-neous, dynamic, and free to express all of its original potential, which up to that moment had been obscured by a constraining society. On the other hand,

> What binds together the members of a given society is tradition, the need and the determination to defend the group against other groups and to set it above everything. To preserve, to tighten this bond is incontestably the aim of the religion we have found to be natural; it is common to the members of a group, it associates them intimately with each other in rites and cere-monies, it distinguishes the group from other groups, it guarantees the suc-cess of the common enterprise and is an assurance against the common danger. The fact that religion, such as it issued from the hands of nature, has simultaneously fulfilled, to use the language of the day, the two functions, moral and national, appears to us unquestionable: these two functions were in fact inevitably confounded in rudimentary societies where only custom existed. But that societies, as they developed, should have carried religion with them in the second direction, will be easily understood by reference to what we have just explained. (ibid.:206)

These words may remind us of Durkheim's ([1912] 1995) *Formes élémen-taires de la vie religieuse*, published in 1912, or even of Hume's natural religion.

At the philosophical level we cannot forget another important contribution to the study of religious phenomena. In fact, before discussing the contributions of cultural anthropology to religious studies, it would be worthwhile mentioning the important role played by Friedrich Nietzsche (1844–1900). Nietzsche had a noteworthy influence on Weber (Fleischmann 1964), especially on the issue regarding the relationship between the individual and political control. Moreover, the idea of a tie between religion and social stratification originated from Nietzsche. Weber elaborated on this idea and set the religious visions of one social class against the other. To support this notion, Weber resorted to "theodicy," the divine justice that distinguishes between good and bad conditions, between the chosen and the damned, and that justifies social stratification. The exaltation of suffering is sustained by the possibility of rebirth, of reincarnation, of salvation, in line with Hindu and Buddhist teachings. In Weber's opinion, class conflicts also have a religious component.

Nietzsche, who had been a professor in Basel, made an important contribution to the development of the sociology of knowledge (and religion). His philosophical approach is mainly characterized by suspicion and mistrust as preeminent tools when analyzing human reality. Moreover, Nietzsche ([1886] 1989) elaborated a concept of ideology—which has a strong link with religion—based on the "will to power" (*Will zur Macht*). According to his notion, what is true must be replaced by what one considers to be true. Above all things, man aims at self-dominion. When he does not succeed in this, he finds compensation in the idea of a future, in another life. This illusion, Nietzsche warned us, should not be cultivated. On the contrary, man must get stronger to become a "superman" (*Übermensch*).

Nietzsche's radical criticism of Jewish and Christian values, such as humility, purity, generosity, nobility, self-restraint, and the supernatural, led to the idea of the death of God. In fact, Christian moral theology made God too similar to human beings. In other words, God is a simple projection of the restless human consciousness. Thus, the "will to power" is the exaltation of the freedom of wanting obtained by the superman who conquers man. The superman is a completely new kind of being—a mixture of rationality and passion.

Nietzsche called for a "transvaluation of values and a revaluation of all values" to start a new era subsequent to the present one. Our era would be a transition stage that prepared the advent of the superman—a creator, upright, without prejudices, bold and intellectually strong, a solitary being, in order to be free in his creative action.

This perspective has been discussed and criticized a great deal. However, one cannot deny the important influence of Nietzsche's ideas on the theories of religious phenomenology (and also on Freudian psychoanalysis). In conclusion, as B. S. Turner wrote (1991:39), Nietzsche's godless theology has peculiar and lasting meaning for the sociology of religion. This is going to be true especially when considering Weber's criticism of modern society and Berger's analysis of the "crisis of credibility."

5

The Contribution of Anthropology

PRIMITIVE RELIGION AND ANIMISM:
EDWARD BURNETT TYLOR (1832–1917)

Edward Burnett Tylor (1832–1917) is considered the "founding father" of cultural anthropology. He was a Quaker and the first scholar who attempted an anthropological analysis of religion. He maintained that religion originated with animism, by which all elements of nature are considered to possess an independent life and should be thus considered "spiritual beings." The contents of primitive rites and the way they were put into practice justify this idea. Tylor's animism could be described as follows:

1st Various biological phenomena like sleep, dream, trance, diseases and death are attributed to spirits, who can abandon the body in which it resides. . . . 2nd The spirit of the deceased could appear in a dream, in a hallucination, in a vision. . . . Thus the veneration of the ancestors contributed to the genesis of the concept of the pure spirit. . . . 3rd At first the spirit was exclusively attributed to man's soul, but later it was connected to animals, plants and to all beings. . . . 4th The spirits could take possession of the bodies that do not belong to them. . . . The idea of good and evil spirits is already present; hence, there is the need to propitiate the evil ones. . . . 5th The notion of a good spirit spreads more and more. . . . 6th A particular god becomes progressively more important over the other gods. . . . 7th Tylor then recognizes the existence of peoples who by themselves reached the idea of a Supreme Being. . . . 8th Through animism it is possible to explain the origins and the carrying out of various worship practices like the prayer, sacrifice, ascetic practices, funeral and purification rites, etc. (Boccassino 1974:43–58)

This explanation of animism offers an instance of a typical evolutionist and mythologizing stance, especially if one considers the match between dream and reality. Thus, animism could not be considered to have a scientific basis. In fact, it does not entertain the possibility that people who belonged to very ancient cultures developed the idea of a "Supreme

Being" that is different from other spirits (Pettazzoni 1965). Moreover, Boccassino writes: "Tylor's system is based on the historical mistake that animism is a primordial condition common to all people" (1974:49).

In his book *Primitive Culture* ([1871] 1958) Tylor dealt extensively with animism, especially in the conclusion of volume I and in most of volume II, where he also wrote about rituals. Ugo Bonanate thinks that for Tylor

> the central importance of animism for the developments of religion lies in its being structured so as to determine consecutive developments. From the beliefs in the existence of single souls there is the subsequent passage to a completely animated world through which it is possible to explain all kinds of phenomena. . . . Animism is a general philosophy of nature in that it properly explains all aspects of man's life and of the world. (1975:10–11)

As Tylor himself wrote:

> Animism characterizes tribes very low in the scale of humanity, and thence ascends, deeply modified in its transmission, but from first to last preserving an unbroken continuity, into the midst of high modern culture. . . . Animism is, in fact, the groundwork of the Philosophy of Religion, from that of savages up to that of civilized men. (Tylor [1871] 1958:II, 10)

As far as magic is concerned, Tylor expressed a rather negative opinion: "Magic . . . belongs in its main principle to the lowest known stages of civilization, and the lower races, who have not partaken largely of the education of the world, still maintain it in vigour" (ibid.:I, 112).

During the years that followed the publication of *Primitive Culture*, animism gradually lost its scientific credibility, mainly due to Durkheim's criticism ([1912] 1995). Nevertheless, the debate around magic rituals was carried out and offered further occasion for original and illuminating investigations. Also the invective on primitive atheism or on primitive monotheism (with the idea of a "celestial being") has been progressively overcome.

MYTH AND RITE IN THE WORK OF ROBERTSON SMITH (1846–1894)

William Robertson Smith was a minister of the Free Church of Scotland. He is well-known especially for his studies on ancient Semitic religions and for being editor-in-chief of the ninth edition of the *Encyclopaedia Britannica*, published in 1889. Noteworthy is the entry *Sacrifice*, which Smith defined as the expression of the desire the members of a group have to feel united with the divine. These people share the same cult, especially through the practice of totemic rites.

Smith thought that there existed a blood relationship, a sort of alliance between an animal or a plant and a specific tribe. Usually the totem was a taboo for the members of a group; but sometimes the totem could be eaten for the well-being of the group or clan. The complete union between the group and the totem became thus realized. The sacrifice of the "thean-thropic animal" established a tie between the human and the divine. It represented the accomplishment of a communion that occurred through the totemic victim's flesh and blood. This allowed the confluence of the sacred with the profane.

The author of *Lectures on the Religion of the Semites* (Robertson Smith [1889] 1956) is also an expert on the Bible. He had a great influence on Frazer, Durkheim, and Freud. According to Smith:

> It is of the first importance to realize clearly from the outset that ritual and practical usage were, strictly speaking, the sum-total of ancient religions. Religion in primitive times was not a system of belief with practical applications; it was a body of fixed traditional practices, to which every member of society conformed as a matter of course. Men would not be men if they agreed to do certain things without having a reason for their action; but in ancient religion the reason was not first formulated as a doctrine and then expressed in practice, but conversely, practice preceded doctrinal theory. Men form general rules of conduct before they begin to express general principles in words; political institutions are older than political theories, and in like manner religious institutions are older that religious theories. (ibid.:20)

In other words, religious practice for Robertson Smith precedes doctrine and this holds true both in politics and in religion. Structure comes before theory. It is possible to infer, then, that at the start there could exist a structure without a theory, but never a theory without a concrete structure. At the same time, religion is not the product of an intellectual effort but rather the outcome of a specific culture, of a series of customs, of a communitarian social organization that conceives the rites. Rites are then followed by myths. Myths, in turn, are the theories, the ideological legitimization of the rites. However, writing about the chronological sequence involving rites and myths, Alfonso Maria di Nola warned:

> In those years research into religious forms of primitive populations contributed to sustaining an antimythological reaction that finds its most noteworthy expression in the work of W. Robertson Smith. Robertson Smith had been a pupil of J. F. MacLennan, who defined the structure of exogamy in primitive cultures and discovered totems. Robertson Smith had been highly influenced both by the studies by MacLennan that underlined the ritualistic aspects of the examined cultures, and by the totemic studies of J. G. Frazer, as they appeared in *Totemism* (1887). Hence, Robertson Smith marked the beginning of an erroneous methodological and historical perspective. Religious

studies got rid of this wrong perspective very late in time and with great difficulty. Robertson Smith assumed that totemism was a "basic form" of religious life. Through totemism he tried to explain sacrifice in the Semitic religions. He was the first, or at least one of the first, to point out the dynamic and interfunctional nature of the relationship between myth and rite. He then reached the incorrect—or, let us say, not always correct—conclusion of the historical priority of rite over myth. (di Nola 1974:94–95)

In describing Semitic religions, Robertson Smith ([1889] 1956) dwelt on the ambivalence of the sacred. He underlined the fact that the foundation of a sanctuary was usually connected with an appearance of the divine, that is, to a theophany (ibid.). He was, however, absolutely convinced that practices came before beliefs:

But the antique (ancient) religions had for the most part no creed; they consisted entirely of institutions and practices. No doubt men will not habitually follow certain practices without attaching a meaning to them; but as a rule we find that while the practice was rigorously fixed, the meaning attached to it was extremely vague, and the same rite was explained by different people in different ways, without any question of orthodoxy or heterodoxy arising in consequence. . . . The rite, in short, was connected not with a dogma but with a myth. (ibid.:16–17)

The following passage is even more to the point:

What was obligatory or meritorious was the exact performance of certain sacred acts prescribed by religious tradition. This being so, it follows that mythology ought not to take the prominent place that is too often assigned to it in the scientific study of ancient faiths. So far as myths consist in explanations of ritual, their value is altogether secondary, and it may be affirmed with confidence that in almost every case the myth was derived from the ritual, and not the ritual from the myth; for the ritual was fixed and the myth was variable, the ritual was obligatory and faith in the myth was at the discretion of the worshipper. Now by far the largest part of the myths of antique (ancient) religions are connected with the ritual of particular shrines, or with the religious observances of particular tribes and districts. (ibid.:17–18)

Among all the observations formulated by Robertson Smith on religious studies, one in particular turns out to be useful for the development of an analysis of religious phenomena that goes beyond the Christian-centered perspective: "Almost the only forms of religion seriously studied in Europe have been those of the various Christian Churches" (ibid.:16). This means that all the attempts to research outside a European context and in another period are biased with a misleading European perspective. In fact, this perspective assumes that in other peoples and historical ages are found the same elements, chronological order, and practices experienced by contemporary Europeans. However, if one is aware of this biased stance, then it is possible to perceive the different characteristics of religion in various cultures. In fact:

> To us moderns religion is above all a matter of individual conviction and rea-
> soned belief, but to the ancients it was a part of the citizen's public life,
> reduced to fixed forms, which he was not bound to understand and was not
> at liberty to criticize or to neglect. Religious nonconformity was an offence
> against the State; for if sacred tradition was tampered with the bases of soci-
> ety were undermined, and the favour of the gods was forfeited. (ibid.:21)

Robertson Smith's *Religion of the Semites* in many instances anticipated the same line of thought that would be developed by Durkheim: "A man did not choose his religion or frame it for himself; it came to him as part of the general scheme of social obligations and ordinances laid upon him, as a matter of course. . . . Religion did not exist for the saving of souls but for the preservation and welfare of society" (ibid.:28–29). In short, religion and everyday life were originally deeply interwoven. An individual who was born into a given family had to adhere to the religion of the family and the state. Religion is only one of the aspects of social life and is regulated by definite rules. It has the same traits found in a totem, since "religion is not an arbitrary relation of the individual man to a supernatural power, it is a relation of all the members of a community to a power that has the good of the community at heart, and protects its law and moral order" (ibid.:55). Durkheim's classic reflection eventually developed, in a more articulated way, along these same lines and with similar concerns about social stability.

MAGIC AND RELIGION IN FRAZER (1854–1941)

About Sir James George Frazer, born in Glasgow, and author of *The Golden Bough,* scholar Alfonso Maria di Nola writes that "he could be con-
sidered one of the alarming cultural myths that influenced negatively the developments of the historical-religious disciplines and that contributed to a misleading image of religious life outside these disciplines" (1974:99). Di Nola criticizes Frazer for being "ahistorical" and methodologically "naive." Moreover, Frazer had been rather superficial when he studied the phenomenon of the "mythical-ritual repetition," that is, the myths that recur in other cultures as well. He did not take into account the reasons for the repetition, for "what is repeated," by referring to specific shared models. He did not grasp the link between myth and rite. There are, in fact, "rit-
ual practices that are seldom individually based but that more often pertain to the group's religious experience. These rites are characterized by a particular relationship with the repeated form or, rather, by the uniqueness of the form itself" (ibid.:93).

In his studies Frazer employed a diachronic perspective; that is, he examined the practices and customs of different ages. Frazer placed magic at the beginning of the universe, while religion would develop later. Little by little, religion took the place of magic, but without disappearing completely, even in technologically advanced societies. Renaissance thinkers like Pomponazzi (1462–1525) and Campanella (1568–1639) made use of magic practices.

> Giovanni Pico della Mirandola (1463–1494) was convinced that magic and religion were deeply connected. *"Nulla est scientia,"* he said, *"quae nos magis certificet de divinitate Christi quam magia et Cabala."* From these examples it is possible to understand the real meaning of religious evolution. That is, the first and fundamental traits of the mythical thought are not completely destroyed. (Cassirer 1962:97)

Thus for Pico there was no science other than magic to prove Christ's divinity, and the continuity between magic and religion appears to be evident.

Frazer found theoretical support from Mannhardt's (1875–77) work on the spirits of the plants. He distinguished between two forms of magic—the homeopathic or imitative, and the contagious. Imitative magic is based on the idea of similarity, by which the similar produces the similar. On the other hand, contagious magic is based on the idea of contact: thus if an object is touched then its strength, its magic power, continues to influence the element that touched it. Indeed, "despite the fact that Frazer considers magic as a series of errors, he still conceives it as history and, even more, the beginning of history" (Cocchiara 1965:xxv).

In his monumental study *The Golden Bough*, Frazer ([1890, 1900, 1907] 1994) identified three moments in human evolution: magic, religion, and then science. This development is connected to the same outlook: in fact, the author provided such an impressive amount of data and information that he is considered more a renowned collector of records than a theoretician. However, his contribution to the knowledge of human society is important. Frazer was aware of the difficulty in defining the concept of religion. He then tended to define it along the line of his notion of magic, by writing that religion was:

> a propitiation or conciliation of powers superior to man which are believed to direct and control the course of nature and of human life. Thus, defined, religion consists of two elements, a theoretical and a practical, namely, a belief in powers higher than man and an attempt to propitiate or please them. Of the two, belief clearly comes first, since we must believe in the existence of a divine being before we can attempt to please him. (ibid.:I, 46)

While magic employed propitiatory techniques based on groundless reasons, religion sought a direct contact with divinity through belief, practice, faith, and deeds.

Thus in so far as religion assumes the world to be directed by conscious agents who may be turned from their purpose by persuasion, it stands in fundamental antagonism to magic as well as to science, both of which take for granted that the course of nature is determined, not by the passions or caprice of personal beings, but by the operation of immutable laws acting mechanically. In magic, indeed, the assumption is only implicit, but in science it is explicit. (ibid.:48)

It would be useful at this point to provide a concise example found by Frazer on the magic use of the "golden bough"—the title of his work:

Virgil definitely described the Golden Bough as growing on a holm-oak, and compares it with the mistletoe. The inference is almost inevitable that the Golden Bough was nothing but the mistletoe seen through the haze of poetry or of popular superstition. Now grounds have been shown for believing that the priest of the Arician grove—the King of the Wood—personified the tree on which grew the Golden Bough. Hence if that tree was the oak, the King of the Wood must have been a personification of the oak- spirit. It is, therefore, easy to understand why, before he could be slain, it was necessary to break the Golden Bough. . . . And to complete the parallel, it is only necessary to suppose that the King of the Wood was formerly burned, dead or alive, at the midsummer fire festival which, as we have seen, was annually celebrated in the Arician grove. . . . Thus it seems that at a remote age in the heart of Italy, beside the sweet Lake of Nemi, the same fiery tragedy was annually enacted. (ibid.:II, 796–97)

The name "golden bough" itself probably derives "from the rich golden yellow which a bough of mistletoe assumes when it has been cut and kept for some months; the bright tint is not confined to the leaves, but spreads to the stalks as well, so that the whole branch appears to be indeed a Golden Bough." Moreover, "the yellow colour of the withered bough may partly explain why the mistletoe has been sometimes supposed to possess the property of disclosing treasures in the earth; for on the principles of homeopathic magic there is a natural affinity between a yellow bough and yellow gold" (ibid.:II, 797). Furthermore, there is also the reference

to the priest of Diana, the King of the Wood, at Aricia in the oak forests of Italy. He may have personated in flesh and blood the great Italian god of the sky, Jupiter, who had kindly come down from heaven in the lightning flash to dwell among men in the mistletoe—the thunder-besom—the Golden Bough—growing on the sacred oak beside the still waters of the lake of Nemi. If that was so, we need not wonder that the priest guarded with drawn sword the mystic bough which contained the god's life and his own. The goddess whom he served and married was herself, if I am right, no other than the Queen of Heaven, the true wife of the sky-god. For she, too, loved the solitude of the woods and the lonely hills, and sailing overhead on clear nights in the likeness of the silver moon she looked down with pleasure on her own fair image reflected on the calm, the burnished surface of the lake, Diana's Mirror. (ibid.:II, 803–4)

This short example testifies to the way Frazer conducted the anthropological analysis—halfway between a romantic literary style, with its use of irony, and weak, strained interpretative constructions. Still, many scholars largely have used the materials gathered by Frazer, among them Freud and Eliade. The latter praises Frazer's erudition and literary talent and wrote that it is thanks to him that the "demons of vegetation" dominated ethnographic and history of religion studies until the beginning of the First World War (Eliade [1948] 1976:516). Freud also acknowledged Frazer's contributions and referred to him in his studies on magic, animism, and the similarity and contiguity principles. Freud even went so far as taking Frazer's side against some critics (Freud 1953b).

It is worth mentioning that Frazer wrote abundantly about totemism well before Durkheim and Freud did. According to Frazer:

Totemism is thus both a religious and a social system. In its religious aspect it consists of the relations of mutual respect and protection between a man and his totem; in its social aspect it consists of the relations of the clansmen to each other and to men of other clans. . . . The connection between a man and his totem is mutually beneficent; the totem protects the man, and the man shows his respect for the totem in various ways, by not killing it if it be an animal, and not cutting or gathering it if it be a plant. . . . Persons of the same totem may not marry or have sexual intercourse with each other. (Frazer 1887:3, 2, 58)

Freud would later quote these passages (Freud 1953b).

Finally, Frazer formulated three hypotheses on the origins of totemism, which are all based on a particular belief: "external soul," "magic induction of fertility," and "animal incarnation."

NEEDS, CULTURE, AND RELIGION: MALINOWSKI (1884–1942)

W. Robertson Smith was perhaps the first clearly to insist on the sociological context in all discussions which refer not merely to organization of groups but also to belief, to ritual, and to myth. He was followed by the leading French sociologist and anthropologist, Emile Durkheim, who developed one of the fullest and most inspiring systems of sociology. It, however, was marred by certain metaphysical preconceptions and, above all, by the complete rejection not merely of introspective psychological speculations, but also of any reference to the biological basis of human behavior. In many ways, however, Durkheim can be regarded as representing one of the soundest of those tendencies in modern anthropology which aim, above all, at the full scientific understanding of culture as a specific phenomenon. (Malinowski 1944:19)

From the reading of this passage by Bronislaw Malinowski (born in Cracow in 1884, and the first professor of social anthropology at the London School of Economics), it is possible to infer the kind of approach he adopted in studying culture and religion. He recognized Robertson Smith's crucial contribution to the history of the sociology of religion and at the same time clarified his own point of view. He criticized Durkheim for giving too much importance to the sociological data and undervaluing the psychological dimension, which was linked to the biological dimension. On the other hand, Malinowski attributed a great importance to both psychology and biology for the analysis of culture.

The theory of needs was a fundamental aspect of Malinowski's thought. He maintained that men had various organic needs that were generally adequately met only through group cooperation, the improvement of knowledge, and the development of ethnic values. In fact, he said:

> The essential fact of culture as we live it and experience it, as we can observe it scientifically, is the organization of human beings into permanent groups. Such groups are related by some agreement, some traditional law or custom. . . . It is always possible also to define and determine sociologically what effect the activities of such an organized human group produce, what needs they satisfy, what services they render to themselves and the community as a whole. (ibid.:43)

One of the general principles that encourages human cooperation is linked to reproduction. This principle justifies a series of social behaviors and institutions like marriage, the intergenerational relationships between parents and children, and the relationships in an extended family group. These different relationships are organized on a legal, economic, and religious basis. Another "integration principle" is directly linked to the professional and working world. Specific activities are then organized in order to reach a common aim. Thus, at the religious level there are "parishes, sects, and churches."

According to Malinowski, some forms of organization for the satisfaction of needs are present in all cultures. One example is provided by religion. Since it meets fundamental needs, religion has been present in every culture. Biological reasons, in fact, are not the only elements influencing human behavior. Cultural needs, or rather the cultural response to fundamental needs, should also be taken into account. This is the sense in which religion has had a relevant place in society.

Malinowski was critical of Frazer's theory on magic and religion and attacked in particular the two principles of similarity and continuity. He wrote: "In the light of our modern anthropological knowledge, this theory of magic, which also is a theory of the primitive outlook on the world, is untenable. We know now that primitive humanity was aware of the scientific laws of natural process" (ibid.:196). This was a sound objection. Malinowski, however, used it to overturn Frazer's point of view, since: "Frazer confirms not his untenable theory of magic as a misapplied principle of association, nor yet his evolutionary theory of three stages, but the sound and correct view that science, magic, and religion have always controlled different phases of human behavior" (ibid.:197). In this way Malinowski wanted to attest the substantial difference between magic and religion on the one hand and scientific knowledge on the other. "[That is why] we can here reformulate Frazer's theory: it is not the association of ideas, that like produces like or that contact persists, but the affirmation and enactment of desired ends and results, which form the psychological basis of magic" (ibid.:199). Moreover, "To Frazer magic is the direct coercion of natural forces by man; religion is the propitiation of divinities by the believer. The difference between the two, however, is to be found first in the subject matter: religion refers to the fundamental issues of human existence, while magic always turns round specific, concrete, and detailed problems" (ibid.:200). Thus, magic was mainly concerned with immediate and small problems, the particular present case, the individual questions, while religion covered a wider time span and a more general range of problems since it dealt with universal questions:

> Religion is concerned with death and immortality, with the worship of natural forces in an integral general manner, with the running up of man to the rulings of Providence. . . . In its dogmatic structure, religion always presents itself as a system of belief defining the place of man in the universe, the provenience of man, and his goal. Pragmatically, religion is necessary to the average individual to overcome the shattering disruptive anticipation of death, of disaster, and of destiny. It solves these problems through the belief in immortality or in a peaceful dissolution of man in the universe or his reunion with divinity. Socially, since religion is always the core of civilization and the mainspring of moral values, it becomes closely associated with every form or organization at lower and at higher levels. . . . Magic appears as a combination of ritual, act, and spoken spell. . . . Religion takes the form of public or private ceremonial, prayer, sacrifice and sacrament. (ibid.:200–1)

Magic thus seems a science in embryo that satisfies needs through culture. Once magic has vanished, man himself looks into the ultimate issues, into "the origins of humanity, into its destinies, and into the problems of life, death and the universe. Hence, as a direct result of man's need to build systems and to organize knowledge, there emerges also the need for religion" (ibid.:202).

Malinowski, a functionalist, was not merely an informed and accurate theoretician, as he appeared to be in *A Scientific Theory of Culture and Other Essays* (1944). In fact, many of the ideas that he developed were the results of fieldwork research in New Guinea, between 1914 and 1918 (Malinowski 1915), and especially in the Trobriand Islands, after which he published *Argonauts of the Western Pacific* (Malinowski 1922). Moreover, during the 1930s Malinowski carried out research in Africa. His anthology *Magic, Science and Religion and Other Essays* (Malinowski 1948), published posthumously, provides the reader with a comprehensive insight into socioreligious matters. This book also includes studies on the spirit of the dead in the Trobriand Islands and on myth. The leitmotiv is the conviction that every custom, every tradition, and each cultural element has a specific function and an important role in social life. It is the scholar's aim to understand and explain the relevance of such functions.

According to Malinowski's functionalist perspective, religion in the Trobriand Islands did not appear as a widespread phenomenon. On the other hand, magic had an important mythological background, which justified the celebration of rites, whenever there was the need. The spells, rites, and the conditions of practice of the officiant were the basis of magic. Magic had instrumental functions, namely productive, protective and destructive powers, and expressive, symbolic functions. Moreover, magic opposed religion and was linked to the subject's psychological needs. An individual resorted to magic when he or she underwent a period of crisis, when important choices had to be made. From here originated a kind of "ritualization of optimism," a positive outlook that aimed at overcoming difficulties. Besides, magic acted as a substitute procedure when there were no alternative means to solve various kinds of problems, especially existential ones. However, once new and decisive solutions were found and further knowledge was achieved, magic was expected to disappear. Malinowski seemed sure of this, especially after his periods in Africa.

SOCIAL STRUCTURE AND RELIGION:
RADCLIFFE-BROWN (1881–1955)

Alfred Reginald Radcliffe-Brown had a functionalist outlook. According to this perspective, social facts have their own laws, just like natural phenomena. He carried on fieldwork, especially in the Andaman Islands in 1906–8 (Radcliffe-Brown 1922) and in Australia in 1910–12.

According to Radcliffe-Brown, the magic rites performed, for instance, on the occasion of a birth or a death had a support function for the event itself and produced important social consequences. Every time in a society that an event occurred requiring an imposed social behavior, there was the establishment of a ritual relationship that connoted respect and assumed a traditional and ongoing character. "Thus the relationship between a Christian and the first day of the week is a typical example of ritual action"

(Radcliffe-Brown 1952). Skorupski (1983:72) objected, however, that there were various expressions and ritual forms that did not necessarily imply a respectful attitude. At most, they might have become a formal custom. In the end, in fact, there were also ritual performances toward nonsacred objects, or even toward unpleasant, dirty, and impure matters. In this case, the prohibitions themselves were part of the ritual. Hence

> A ritual prohibition is a rule of behaviour which is associated with a belief that an infraction will result in an undesirable change in the ritual status of the person who fails to keep to the rule. This change of ritual status is conceived in many different ways in different societies, but everywhere there is the idea that is involves the likelihood of some minor or major misfortune which will befall the person concerned. (Radcliffe-Brown 1952:134–35)

It was also necessary to distinguish between technical-instrumental ritual practices and symbolic-expressive ones. Religion usually made use of symbolic rituals. In fact,

> While in animal societies social coaptation depends on instinct, in human societies it depends upon the efficacy of symbols of many different kinds. . . . The primary basis of ritual, so the formulation would run, is the attribution of ritual value to objects and occasions which are either themselves objects of important common interests linking together the persons of a community or are symbolically representative of such objects. (ibid.: 150–51)

Radcliffe-Brown's functionalism was particularly concerned with structural aspects. In this sense it would be legitimate to call it "structural-functionalism," since it attributed a crucial role to the important aspects of social life and thus contributed to maintaining a structural continuity. Greatly inspired by Durkheim, Radcliffe-Brown's studies in the Andaman Islands—located in the Indian Ocean—seemed in fact to confirm Durkheim's hypothesis of religion's functions of maintaining collective identity and social solidarity. Social integration was maintained through the organization of festivals, dances, and ceremonies, which reinforced the social structure. This explained Radcliffe-Brown's concern for the concept of society rather than for that of culture. He employed concepts like social morphology to refer to the structure and social physiology when referring to functional laws. Even though he did not directly speak about needs as Malinowski did, Radcliffe-Brown talked about fundamental existential conditions.

Raymond Firth (1975:135–36) wrote that Radcliffe-Brown explained the symbolic meaning of Andaman myths in terms of their relationship with society. His interpretation of specific symbolic concepts and behaviors appeared clever and convincing, even though a little didactic. The comparative approach elaborated by Radcliffe-Brown was an appealing method of analysis also due to its stimulating reference to the various social levels. It has been used also by other scholars (Pinard de la Boullaye 1922; Schmidt 1934; Demarchi 1988).

Radcliffe-Brown himself—who taught social science at King Farouk University in Alexandria—clearly stated that "while I have defined social anthropology as the study of human society, there are some who define it as the study of culture" (1952:189). Also because of this choice Radcliffe-Brown was very close to Durkheim. However, as distinct from Durkheim, Radcliffe-Brown placed more relevance on social structure, claiming that it should be studied just like the patterns of natural sciences. He argued that human subjects adapted themselves to nature rather than undergoing a change at the cultural level. He went so far as stating that the research on social structure pertains to the realm of nature sciences in which the individuals are the basic structure. In any event, social matters are a special category of natural phenomena.

Just like Durkheim, Radcliffe-Brown attributed an undisputed place in social functions to religion. As he clearly maintained:

> We may entertain as at least a possibility the theory that any religion is an important or even essential part of the social machinery, as are morality and law, part of the complex system by which human beings are enabled to live together in an orderly arrangement of social relations. From this point of view we deal not with the origins but with the social functions of religions, i.e. the contribution that they make to the formation and maintenance of a social order. There are many persons who would say that it is only *true* religion (i.e. one's own) that can provide the foundation of an orderly social life. The hypothesis we are considering is that the social function of a religion is independent of its truth or falsity, that religions which we think to be erroneous or even absurd and repulsive, such as those of some savage tribes, may be important and effective parts of the social machinery, and that without these "false" religions social evolution and the development of modern civilisation would have been impossible. (ibid.:154)

Radcliffe-Brown here assumed a nonjudgmental and scientifically productive position. His aim was to document and verify the solidity of (structural) functionalism as it is applied to religious phenomenology. His conclusion testified to the wide social function of religion, or, rather, of religions, independently of their intrinsic value. What was crucial were religion's social relevance, communal life, and the existence itself of society.

In order to demonstrate the tight bond between religion and social structure, Radcliffe-Brown employed the material gathered on the cult of ancestors and Australian totemism. He emphasized how much religious practices reinforce social ties, strengthen social rules, and nourish morals and laws.

Radcliffe-Brown's conclusions were also a practical orientation for socioreligious studies. In synthesis his proposal was:

> (1) To understand a particular religion we must study its effects. The religion must therefore be studied *in action*. (2) Since human conduct is in large part controlled or directed by what have been called sentiments, conceived as mental dispositions, it is necessary to discover as far as possible what are the sentiments that are developed in the individual as the result of his participation in a particular religious cult. (3) In the study of any religion we must first of all examine the specifically religious action, the ceremonies and the collective or individual rites. (4) The emphasis on belief in specific doctrines which characterises some modern religions seems to be the result of certain social developments in societies of complex structure. (5) In some societies there is a direct and immediate relation between the religion and the social structure. This has been illustrated by ancestor-worship and Australian totemism. . . . But where there comes into existence a separate independent religious structure by the formation of different churches or sects or cult-groups within a people, the relation of religion to the total social structure is in many respects indirect and not always easy to trace. (6) As a general formula (for whatever such a formula may be worth) it is suggested that what is expressed in all religions is what I have called the sense of dependence in its double aspect, and that it is by constantly maintaining this sense of dependence that religions perform their social function. (ibid.:177)

The dependence Radcliffe-Brown was writing about concerns the fact that "religion is everywhere an expression in one form or another of a sense of dependence on a power outside ourselves, a power which we may speak of as a spiritual or moral power" (ibid.:157).

TOTAL SOCIAL FACT AND THE GIFT AS EXCHANGE IN MARCEL MAUSS (1872–1950)

Marcel Mauss was one of the authors who most influenced Radcliffe-Brown. Mauss is situated at the crossroads of various disciplines and themes. In fact, he first worked with his uncle and initial advisor Emile Durkheim, whom he later influenced greatly. Then he influenced his structuralist pupil Claude Lévi-Strauss, Lévy-Bruhl, and especially Henri Hubert, with whom he coauthored *Mélanges d'histoire des religions* (Hubert and Mauss 1909). We can thus define him as one of the most important scholars of the anthropology of religion of the first half of our century. It is difficult to decide whether he is a sociologist or an anthropologist. His works are all highly original and revolve around the themes of the gift as an exchange linked to social structures.

He first collaborated with and then directed the renowned annual journal *L'Année Sociologique* (the first issue came out in 1898). Mauss is well-known for being immensely knowledgeable in the social sciences. He was almost as learned a man as Frazer. A hard-working editor and untiring data cataloguer, he was also active in the cultural field, and founded the Institute of Semitic Ethnology in Paris. Unlike Radcliffe-Brown, Mauss never personally conducted fieldwork. However, he greatly stimulated the structural-functionalist current, and offered many important hints to other scholars, first of all to Lévi-Strauss. He was politically active with the socialists and with their daily newspaper *L'Humanité*. Together with Zola and Jaurès, Mauss was also a Dreyfusard.

Mauss exploited his extended linguistic knowledge in order to study nonliterate societies, and he was also aware of psychological issues. Hence, Mauss was a scholar in the round, someone who shifts easily from one discipline to another and gets the best from each.

After his essay on sacrifice (Mauss 1899), he published the essay *The Gift* (Mauss [1925] 1990), which became a classic. In this essay he presented data on Melanesian, Polynesian, and North American cultures. He analyzed in particular exchange and contractual behavior. Mauss's investigations usually had a limited scope, even though he adopted a comprehensive approach. As Martelli observed:

> Total social facts imply a higher level of methodological generalization, with a greater awareness of the complexity of social dynamism and multi-dimensional facts. Through this route it is possible to avoid excessive fragmentation and abstraction. . . . Mauss thought that total social facts could have various dimensions, from the macro (e.g., Athens, Rome: city-state or even capitals of an Empire), to the micro (middle French, or the inhabitant of a Melanesian island). These heterogeneous concepts, belonging to the category of total social fact, had in common their explicative power, that is, they allowed the researcher to discover essential traits of the society. All facts are social facts, but only a few of them could be considered total social facts. Because of their particular position or nature, they allowed the reconstruction of the complex relations and institutions of a specific society and, at the same time, threw light on human nature and the basis of sociability. (Martelli 1987:129–30)

Ruth Benedict (1887–1948) later worked on these ideas (1934) while elaborating her notion of "cultural pattern."

According to Mauss, some myths and religious symbols are typical total social facts that do not have any functions other than religious ones. Indeed, they are the main routes to understanding the culture to which they belong. Sacrifice itself may be seen as a total social fact. Its essential content is the consumption-destruction of the sacrificial victim, whatever it may be—an object, a plant, an animal, or human beings. The sacrificial also bears other meanings, like the idea of offering or of consecration. However, the fundamental notion behind sacrifice remained the victim as food to be eaten, something that should be burned or separated piece by piece, or a body that must be torn apart. The lethal separation of blood and body was an example of this. The participants in the sacrifice or the recipient of it—a god or an object, a place or a group of people, an activity or a building—might benefit from the sacrifice. This distinction was crucial in order to classify the various sacrificial rites.

Mauss thought that sacrifice was a religious act that modified the condition of the performers as much as the objects involved in it. The victim acted as a mediator between two different, opposite elements that never came in contact with each other, and thus the profane became sacred. These two realities participated in the sacrifice of the victim. Literally sacrifice meant to make sacred (*sacrum facere*) something that by nature was not sacred.

A further step in Mauss's elaborations is the notion of sacrifice as a gift, an exchange offering. Whoever enacted a sacrifice desired something in return, especially from the god to whom the sacrifice had been addressed, according to the usual give-and-take behavioral logic. In the Vedic religion of India sacrifice was not the simple offering of an object, but the *mana* of the giver that was offered with the gift and that was shared with the receiver. In this way, the receiver was subjected to the giver's power. Through the gift the two interlocutors became increasingly united and the receiver could in turn become the donor. *Mana*, which is mainly a Malaysian word, favored a whole series of possibilities, namely a tight relationship with the divinity, the totem, the dead, and nature. *Mana* then became an exploitable element that, on the other hand, could also dominate its believers. In this way magic appeared to differ from religion. In fact, it created asociality. Single people full of anxiety, fears, uncertainty about their future, but also full of hope, were especially attracted by the powers of *mana*.

The relationship between magic and religion was a crucial issue in Mauss. It is a controversial and difficult subject to deal with. Jean Cazeneuve tries to clarify some points:

> According to Mauss religious organization is composed of various groups that practice rites and believe in myths. While the rites are traditional practices aiming at a specific purpose, myths are traditional beliefs that society imposes upon the individual. In his ethnography course, Mauss in a broader sense considered magic as a part of religion but, in a stricter sense, he separated it from religion. Magic for Mauss is a body of rites and beliefs, namely a "systematization effort, a whole made of recipes and secrets and generally more individualized than religion." (Cazeneuve 1968:66)

As we can see, Mauss's definition of magic was close to Durkheim's idea of religion. The close resemblance of the two terms was thus confirmed. Besides, according to Mauss, it was not necessary to exclude magic completely from religious phenomena, but while considering the relationship between them, their difference should not be ignored (Mauss 1968:409). Mauss's purpose was clear and somehow anticipated Durkheim: in the sense that Mauss considered magic the primordial form of collective representations that later became the foundation of the human intellect (Mauss 1902–3, 1975:142).

Indeed,

> Magic practices are always considered to go against the rules and are anomalous. They are usually carried out secretly. Hence magic rites are viewed as being aloof from organized cult and tend, on the contrary, toward forbidden practices. The magicians find themselves in a particular and unusual situation in the society that recognizes their role. Hence people's opinions help the establishment of the magicians as such and the influence they have. The same holds true for rites and magic representations which are defined by the collectivity. People's belief in magic sets its basis, even though magic is for many aspects on the fringes of society. (Cazeneuve 1968:69)

Mauss's hypotheses on magicians constituted the novelty of his approach as opposed to other explanations, like Tylor's animism or Frazer's notion of magic as a pseudoscience. Through various examples Mauss ([1925] 1990) demonstrated that magic rites followed social norms and collective expectations. According to Mauss (ibid.) an individual could become a magician in three ways: revelation, consecration, and tradition. Mauss also tended to reject the criticisms that accused magicians of being deceivers for personal interests. Mauss used the example of the Australian magicians who filled their mouths with small stones and then claimed that their initiator spirit did this. Mauss explained that this was done to satisfy social expectations for being a magician. These acts should not be interpreted as a deception for personal interest but rather as simulations the magician performed as a sort of functionary. Society invested him with an authority in which he himself had to believe. He was naturally endowed with the spirit of his function. Thus he had to assume a serious stance so that people would take him seriously, as he took himself seriously (Mauss [1925] 1990, 1975).

The belief in magic issued from the *mana*, which was an exceptional and recognized force. The *mana* assigned to things, events, and people a magic or religious attribute. To Cazeneuve the *mana* possessed a personal and impersonal strength at the same time, a material and spiritual character. The *mana* was placed in an "other" hidden dimension of space, beyond categories like height, length, and width. The *mana* was the shared basis for religious or magic beliefs and practices. The common origin of religion and magic lay in the common emotional conditions. In line with Durkheim's position, Cazeneuve emphasized that the real difference between magic and religion was the existence, in the latter, of a church. In any case, the *mana* could not be eliminated.

Mauss always emphasized that some rites were certainly religious: for instance, the regular, public, and compulsive ones, such as holidays and sacraments. However, according to Frazer, some of these rites were not religious. There were also other rites that were usually magic. These were the rites connected with producing evil against someone. They were explicitly prohibited and punished, and this made evident the antagonism between magical rites and religious rites. It was precisely the prohibition that characterized in magical terms the evil eye. Thus magic and religion were two polar extremes. In all religions there were ideals in whose name hymns and sacrifices were celebrated and that were protected by prohibitions. Magic avoided these special fields. It always tended toward the evil eye and provided those aspects of the image of magical rites that mankind had learned to expect (Mauss 1902–3, 1975:21–22).

Essentially, Mauss maintained that magic was an "interplay of value judgment" just as religion was. Emotional meanings were attributed to the various objects that belonged to its system. These value judgments, however, were not the work of individual spirits; they expressed social feelings that have taken shape, at times fatally or causally, with respect to some arbitrary choices of animals and plants, professions and sexes, stars and physical phenomena, soil conformation, matter, and so forth. For Mauss the notion of *mana*, like that of sacred, in the last analysis was nothing but a category of the collective thinking that created its judgment, imposed a classification, and established its lines of influence as well as the limits of its isolation (Mauss 1902–3, 1975:120–21). In conclusion, for Mauss a magical rite was any rite that was not part of an organized cult, that is, private, secret, with a tendency toward the prohibited. Mauss maintained that he did not define magic on the basis of the form of its rites, but on the basis of the conditions in which these rites were produced and the place they had in the complex of social habits (Mauss 1902–3, 1975:120–21, [1925] 1990).

Mauss also stated that magic was connected with science as well as with technique. It was not only a practical art, but also a treasure of ideas. Magic recognized the importance of knowledge, and this was one of its most important factors. In fact, for magic knowledge was power. While religion through its intellectual elements tended toward metaphysics, magic tried to understand in a pragmatic way how nature worked (Mauss 1902–3, 1975:140–41).

Indeed the central core of Mauss's contribution lies in the exchange relationship started by the gift (Mauss [1925] 1990). The gift symbolized the establishment of a relationship and bore a social value beyond its exchange value. First of all, a relationship of reciprocity was established. Each present contributed to strengthening the community's cohesion. Just as with sacrifice, the gift was a collective concern. The individual who gave up possession of an object adopted a position of abnegation, a complete dedication to the well-being of the community. As a result, the whole of society benefited and a new balance was reached.

We should also briefly note Mauss's work on prayer (Mauss 1968). As Martelli observed,

> Prayer has all the traits of the religious rite. First of all, it is an act and must not be confused with the mythical dream nor with theological speculations. It is a *traditional* act that is included in a ritual and linked to tradition. Prayer is effective in the same *sui generis* effectiveness of religion. Even when prayer is pure adoration, as is the case in monotheistic religions, it is still an exhortation addressed to the divinity to take action. Sometimes there are oral rites, like the spell, that are very close to prayer. Nevertheless, Mauss places prayer among the oral religious rites that include various forms like taking an oath, a verbal contract of religious alliance, to express good wishes, blessings and curses, etc. Even here, the boundaries between oral rites are not clearly defined. In fact, a prayer could have the value of an oath, the same way as a wish could have the form of a prayer, etc. (Martelli 1987:48)

In short, as Mauss (1968:414) emphasized, prayer was nothing more than an oral religious rite concerning sacred matters.

Marcel Mauss disagreed with Durkheim on the idea of the sacred as the basis of religious phenomena. Mauss viewed in the notion of *mana* a much more ancient and comprehensive concept that allowed a more flexible classification of various religious, magic, divinatory, and folkloric phenomena pertaining to different historical moments and parts of the world. Robert Henry Codrington (1891) also formulated this idea in his studies on Malayan societies. According to Mauss, the notion of *mana* clarified the social origins of the magic powers. It also subsumed and unified the variegated body of religious phenomena respecting, however, cultural differences thanks to its flexible polysemy. The *mana*, then, included "magic and divinization, the folk and popular superstitions which are to be considered religious phenomena in a broader sense" (Mauss 1947). Conversely, the idea of the sacred pertained to religion in a stricter sense.

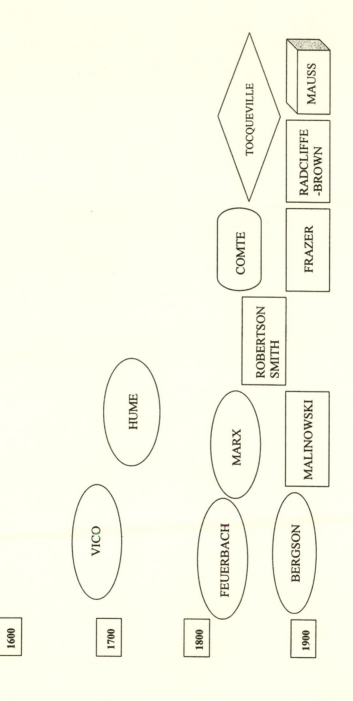

Synoptic Table 1: From Vico to Mauss

PART II

The Classics

1

Durkheim's (1858–1917) Religious Forms

RELIGIOUS LIFE AND SOCIETY

Emile Durkheim contributed to the growth of a whole current of socioreligious studies that had started long before him and that aimed at the establishment of the sociology of religion as an autonomous discipline. The development of this discipline has been favored by the contribution of many scholars with a wide range of interests.

Durkheim was at the center of a large group of followers. Aside from Mauss, there were also Henri Hubert, Robert Hertz, Lucien Lévy-Bruhl, and Arnold van Gennep. Durkheim's work was influenced by Robertson Smith, and Fustel de Coulanges ([1864] 1980) influenced him to consider religion as an essential part of social life. Coulanges studied Greek and Roman classic religions and identified the solidaristic character of the cult of the nature gods and of the dead (at a domestic level). He claimed that marriage and the *patria potestas* originated from religion, just like family relationships, private property, and inheritance. The family, a religious association more than a natural kind of group, increased with time until it achieved the dimension of a city. Here the common cult functioned as a tie among the people who shared the same ritual, the same altar or temple, the same sacred flame, which was carefully fed.

Religion and family ties were two important elements in Durkheim's childhood. His father Moses was a rabbi and his mother Melanie was very devoted to the family. The home was the *point de repère,* a community and sacred place at the same time. Moreover, Judaism strengthened the ties within and outside the family by the sharing of the same rituals, both at home and with others.

The forms of religious life were the specific topics of Durkheim's most mature work (Durkheim [1912] 1995) and also the most criticized ones. Durkheim's complete writings add up to forty-three works, including book reviews. They all deal with religion as the main topic or at least as a relevant sociological subject.

In order to offer a clearer and comprehensive outline of Durkheim's thought, it would be better to leave aside as much as possible the debates around the sociologist's work, which still continue, by a large number of scholars. The critical bibliography is immense and includes thousands of titles. More than Weber, Durkheim is probably the most quoted author as far as the sociology of religion is concerned.

It would be best at this point to directly describe Durkheim's text through the beginning of *The Elementary Forms of Religious Life: The Totemic System in Australia* (ibid.). The title of the introduction, "Religious Sociology and Theory of Knowledge," already sounds like a kind of proclamation. The linking of religion and knowledge, which would be developed, especially by Berger and Luckmann, places Durkheim's work within the parameters of two branches of sociology: the sociology of religion and the sociology of knowledge. However, at the macrosociological level, the subject also has a wider perspective. In the introduction, Durkheim wrote that the purpose of the book was to study primitive religion, because it was the simplest religion ever known. In order to be defined as primitive, a religious system should have two prerequisites: First, it should be placed in the simplest social context at the organizational level, and second, it should be explained without reference to previous religious systems. This is the reason why the religious system to be studied should be the most primitive and simplest possible. As far as the term "primitive" is concerned, Durkheim was aware of the possible ambiguous meaning of the word. He explained:

> It will be seen that I give the word "origins," like the word "primitive," an entirely relative sense. I do not mean by it an absolute beginning but the simplest social state known at present—the state beyond which it is at present impossible for us to go. When I speak about origins and the beginnings of history or religious thought, this is the sense in which those phrases must be understood. (ibid.:7, footnote 3)

For Durkheim, archaic religion, more than other religions, enabled us to better understand people's religious disposition, which is a permanent and essential aspect of humanity. One must then trace back the oldest religions to grasp religiosity's invariant elements. More than an archaeological study, this research must be carried out as a sociological investigation to understand people in their present state by isolating their original conditions.

Durkheim was convinced that the most primitive religions, with respect to the Australian tribes, must not be studied with a Western outlook, but by keeping in mind concrete human needs. Notwithstanding the eccentricity of some myths or rites, the sociologist must look under the exterior layer to find the essence of religiosity itself. In fact, there is no such thing as a false religion. Each religion has its founding reasons, primary needs, basic reasons, and motivations that nourish it. From this it is possible to begin to research the common roots of every religious expression.

Why is one supposed to study "inferior" societies?

> The lesser development of individuality, the smaller scale of the group, and the homogeneity of external circumstances all contribute to reducing the differences and variations to a minimum. The group regularly produces an intellectual and moral uniformity of which we find only rare examples in the more advanced societies. Everything is common to everyone. . . . At the same time that all is uniform, all is simple. . . . Inessential, secondary and luxurious developments have not yet come to hide what is primary. Everything is boiled down to what is absolutely indispensable, to that without which there would be no religion. But the indispensable is also the fundamental, in other words, that which it is above all important for us to know. (ibid.:5)

This primitive nucleus is later going to be defined by the concept of structure. A successful as well as a controversial concept, structure is a fundamental notion in the vast production of Claude Lévi–Strauss (Cipriani 1988a), a *sui generis* follower of Durkheim.

There are at least two stable points that must be underlined. On the one hand, "It has long been known that the first systems of representations that man made of the world and himself were of religious origin. There is no religion that is not both a cosmology and a speculation about the divine" (Durkheim [1912] 1995:8). The initial knowledge of the world, the original *Weltanschauung*, is chiefly a religious one. Cosmos and divinity are one thing just like knowledge and religion. On the other hand, in his conclusion to the book, Durkheim wrote that:

> Religion is an eminently social thing. Religious representations are collective representations that express collective realities; rites are ways of acting that are born only in the midst of assembled groups and whose purpose is to evoke, maintain, or recreate certain mental states of those groups. But if the categories are of religious origin, then they must participate in what is common to all religion: They, too, must be social things, products of collective thought. At the very least—since with our present understanding of these matters, radical and exclusive theses are to be guarded against—it is legitimate to say that they are rich in social elements. (ibid.:9)

Religion and society seem to overlap, to be interwoven in an inextricable way. The social reality is religious, the religious condition is social—their legitimation is reciprocal. Either the community is a religious one or otherwise it does not exist at all. However, Durkheim felt he was pushing the identity between society and religion too far. He thus became cautious on

the issue, stating that his ideas were based on the present state of knowledge, which was a typical scientific assertion. Nevertheless, he underlined
the religious origins of the time sequence. Furthermore, "Spatial organization was modeled on social organization and replicates it. Far from being
built into human nature, no idea exists, up to and including the distinction
between right and left, that is not, in all probability, the product of religious, hence collective, representations" (ibid.:11–12).

The relationship between society and religion recalls the analogous one
between the individual and society: "Man is double. In him are two
beings: an individual being that has its basis in the body and whose sphere
of action is strictly limited by this fact, and a social being that represents
within us the highest reality in the intellectual and moral realm that is
knowable through observation: I mean society" (ibid.:15–16).

SACRED AND PROFANE

Durkheim was also an excellent critic of other scholars' theories of religion. He tore these theories apart, but his reflections were also keen and
convincing. He discussed the concept of the supernatural through a
dialectical examination that took into account the theories of Herbert
Spencer ([1882–85] 1967) and those of Max Müller (1889), and the concept
of the divine, referring to the works of Edward B. Tylor ([1871] 1958) and
James Frazer. Then Durkheim briefly concluded that "there are rites without gods, and rites from which gods derive" (Durkheim [1912] 1995:33).
He later stated:

> Religious phenomena fall into two basic categories: beliefs and rites. The
> first are states of opinion and consist of representations; the second are par-
> ticular modes of action. Between these two categories of phenomena lies all
> that separates thinking from doing. . . . It is the object of the rite that must be
> characterized, in order to characterize the rite itself. The special nature of
> that object is expressed in the belief. Therefore, only after having defined the
> belief can we define the rite. Whether simple or complex, all known religious
> beliefs display a common feature: they presuppose a classification of the real
> or ideal things that men conceive of into two classes—two opposite *genera*—
> that are widely designated by two distinct terms, which the words *profane*
> and *sacred* translate fairly well. . . . The sacred and the profane are always
> and everywhere conceived by the human intellect as separate *genera*, as two
> worlds with nothing in common. The energies at play in one are not merely
> those encountered in the other, but raised to a higher degree; they are differ-
> ent in kind. This opposition has been conceived differently in different reli-
> gions. . . . But while the forms of the contrast are variable, the fact of it is
> universal. (ibid.:36)

This clear-cut separation between sacred and profane, which probably derives from Durkheim's personal education, is one of the sociologist's least convincing statements. It seems as if Durkheim himself was aware of this and tried to clarify the question:

This is not to say that a being can never pass from one of these worlds to the other. But when this passage occurs, the manner in which it occurs demonstrates the fundamental duality of the two realms, for it implies a true metamorphosis. Rites of initiation, which are practiced by a great many peoples, demonstrate this especially well. Initiation is a long series of rites to introduce the young man into religious life. For the first time, he comes out of the purely profane world, where he has passed his childhood, and enters into the circle of sacred things. This change of status is conceived not as a mere development of preexisting seeds but as a transformation *totius substantiae*. At that moment, the young man is said to die, and the existence of the particular person he was, to cease—instantaneously to be replaced by another. He is born again in a new form. (ibid.:36–37)

Durkheim clearly expresses the idea that sacred and profane are two distinct matters. Moreover:

The sacred thing is, *par excellence,* that which the profane must not and cannot touch with impunity. To be sure, this prohibition cannot go so far as to make all communication between the two worlds impossible, for if the profane could in no way enter into relations with the sacred, the sacred would be of no use. This placing in relationship in itself is always a delicate operation that requires precautions and a more or less complex initiation. Yet such an operation is impossible if the profane does not lose its specific traits, and if it does not become sacred itself in some measure and to some degree. The two *genera* cannot, at the same time, both come close to one another and remain what they were. (ibid.:38)

The French sociologist sometimes underscored the separation between sacred and profane, whereas at other times he denied it, at least in part. Indeed, reality does not allow drastic positions and absolute statements.

As is well-known, Durkheim did not directly carry out fieldwork research, but he used the research and writings of other scholars for his analysis of Australian tribal cultures. Although the data appeared to be uniform at a superficial level, they were complex and sometimes ambiguous and contradictory. Durkheim's work on the empirical data was careful and true to the content. Durkheim's Jewish background remained influential also in his maturity, notwithstanding the agnosticism he professed. The seriousness and rigorous approach, the scientific attitude that he took on, seemed to be his new religion. He wanted to discover the origins of religious sentiment and he was not interested in attacking the irrationality behind religious belief. His aim lay in understanding the role of religious feelings within society, the solidarity and communitarian outcome, and, finally, why society appeared as a new divine entity.

Compared with Comte's ideas, Durkheim's perspective appears to be more plausible.

> In many respects Durkheim's doctrine of bracketing society and religion comes perilously near Comte's ludicrous idea of a religion of humanity; but whereas Comte's idea was to be realized at some future time when science would reign supreme in society, Durkheim's view was that society is—always has been in fact—the religion of man. This was an extreme example of realism and reification of an idea almost medieval in its implications. (Abraham 1973:100)

Talcott Parsons (1968) assumed a different position regarding Durkheim. He emphasized the correspondence of the distinction between sacred and profane and that between moral obligation and personal advantage. Even more stimulating was a further reflection by Parsons concerning the sacred character, which was not given by the object but by its being considered a symbol, a cultural element bearing meanings connected to beliefs and feelings, in a word to "representations." Thus, Parsons preferred to talk about symbolic systems and in particular of "religious systems of representations" that were integrated within the social structure thanks mainly to the moral dimension. He considered the symbolic system elaborated by Durkheim to have a collective connotation because it was mainly a cultural system. The small degree of differentiation that one found among the so-called primitive cultures allowed one to identify the "elementary forms," that is, the origins of religious life. According to Durkheim the social sphere was also cultural. Parsons recognized Durkheim's contribution in distinguishing between social and cultural systems. However, since Durkheim limited his research to less differentiated societies, this prevented him from establishing whether the nexus between his "representations" and social structure also held true for more complex societies. However, the problem lay more in the starting conditions of Durkheim's research, because culture was considered at the same time a social and a religious phenomenon. However, this cannot be verified in the case of more complex societies.

Moreover, as Parsons recognized, Durkheim's reflections were a turning point in the studies on religion. Unlike Edward Tylor ([1871] 1958), Herbert Spencer ([1882–85] 1967), and Karl Marx ([1888] 1935), Durkheim did not envisage the disappearance of religion. On the contrary, he believed that religion in contemporary society held the same crucial role as it did in primitive times. Possibly in the future there would be a "functional equivalent" of religion, as was the case with Luckmann's so-called invisible religion (Luckmann 1967). On the other hand, it is clear from the start that Durkheim's *The Elementary Forms of Religious Life* was not an attack on religion.

This is confirmed by the reading of the text.

> But characteristically, the religious phenomenon is such that it always assumes a bipartite division of the universe, known and knowable, into two *genera* that include all that exists but radically exclude one another. Sacred things are things protected and isolated by prohibitions; profane things are those things to which the prohibitions are applied and that must keep at a distance from what is sacred. Religious beliefs are those representations that express the nature of sacred things and the relations they have with other sacred things or with profane things. Finally, rites are rules of conduct that prescribe how man must conduct himself with sacred things. When a certain number of sacred things have relations of coordination and subordination with one another, so as to form a system that has a certain coherence and does not belong to any other system of the same sort, then the beliefs and rites, taken together, constitute a religion. (Durkheim [1912] 1995:38)

In this concise presentation of Durkheim's ideas on religion, the sacred and the profane, it is possible to see the main features of Parsons's interpretation of Durkheim. Also, one can easily perceive once more the apodictic tone of Durkheim's position—the world is "always" divided into sacred and profane. Thus, half-measure solutions must be discarded. Of course, one should take this opinion with some caution; Durkheim was himself occasionally aware of this.

MAGIC, RELIGION, AND THE CHURCH

Before defining religion, Durkheim attempted a definition of magic in order to prevent any possible confusion between these two terms. Durkheim's predecessors and contemporaries had already extensively studied magic. They considered it a basic *tópos*, but they failed to provide it with sufficient empirical support. Thus,

> Magic, too, is made up of beliefs and rites. Like religion, it has its own myths and dogmas, but these are less well developed, probably because, given its pursuit of technical and utilitarian ends, magic does not waste time in pure speculation. Magic also has its ceremonies, sacrifices, purifications, prayers, songs and dances. Those beings that the magician invokes and the forces he puts to work are not only of the same nature as the forces addressed by religion but very often are the same forces. In the most primitive societies, the souls of the dead are in essence sacred things and objects of religious rites,

but at the same time, they have played a major role in magic. In Australia as well as in Melanesia, in ancient Greece as well as among Christian peoples, the souls, bones, and hair of the dead figure among the tools most often used by the magician. (ibid.:39–40)

Having defined magic, Durkheim could then define the church: "A society whose members are united because they imagine the sacred world and its relations with the profane world in the same way, and because they translate this common representation into identical practices" (ibid.:41).

A few timely remarks are necessary at this point. First of all, the use of the term "society" sounds in this case too broad and generic. Durkheim should have used the word "organization" or "community," as he did in other instances when talking about the church. Second, the unifying character provided by the shared idea of the world and of cultic practices was strongly emphasized. Third, the relations between sacred and profane were stated again to be an essential factor for the establishment of a church. Hence, religion and church overlapped to the point that the two terms became inseparable. If religious life existed, then there was also a church. Smaller groups were nothing but "chapels pertaining to a bigger church."

Also within the realm of magic there were groups of followers. However, their cohesion and sense of community were almost nonexistent, hence *"there is no Church of magic"* (ibid.:42, emphasis in original). The ties between the magician and his clients were just as short-lived as those between a magic creed and its followers. The same magic experience did not last for a particularly long time. Moreover, "the magician has a clientele, not a Church." Each client turned to him independently of other clients. Thus an individualistic attitude was typical of magic and it contrasted with the solidarity attitude of the church. In this regard, Durkheim quoted Robertson Smith ([1889] 1956), but then he could not make too drastic a separation between magic and religion, between magic and church. Experience continued to demonstrate that the gap between the two was not absolute. However, Durkheim gave a memorable definition of church: "a moral community made up of all the faithful, both laity and priests" (Durkheim [1912] 1995:42).

Durkheim anticipated some aspects of a future sociology of religion that would tend to stress individual religious expression. He hinted at "individual religions" and formulated an intriguing and clever question: "Not only are these individual religions very common throughout history, but some people today pose the question whether such religions are not destined to become the dominant form of religious life— whether a day will not come when the only cult will be the one that each person freely practices in his innermost self" (ibid.:43). Thus we have the original explanation of contemporary religious subjectivism, of Luckmann's "invisible religion" (1967), of the "modern religious actor" (Corradi 1993).

Durkheim, however, was so intrigued by his idea of sociocentrism that he hastily added a note: "These individual cults are not distinct and autonomous religious systems but simply aspects of the religion common to the whole Church of which the individuals are part" (Durkheim [1912] 1995:43). In any case, each cult fell within a church.

Later on in his text, Durkheim dealt again with religious subjectivism: "a religion that would consist entirely of interior and subjective states and be freely constructed by each one of us" (ibid.:44). However, Durkheim immediately decided to abandon or to postpone this feasible dimension of religion. In the meantime he provided the reader with the following concise and articulated definition of religion: "*a religion is a unified system of beliefs and practices relative to sacred things, that is to say, things set apart and forbidden—beliefs and practices which unite into one single moral community called a Church, all those who adhere to them*" (ibid.:44, emphasis in original). Durkheim then talked about a cohesive "unified system" based on the abstraction of beliefs as well as on the concreteness of the practices. Individuals were united among them thanks to the beliefs and practices through the sense of community manifested by the church. Briefly, "The idea of religion is inseparable from the idea of a Church. . . . Religion must be an eminently collective thing" (ibid.:44).

The author then restated the same concept: religion was characterized by being a social fact. Beliefs and practices were symbols of society. Being together was at the origins of the religious forms. Hence, Durkheim rejected both Edward B. Tylor's ([1871] 1958) animistic thesis by which every element of nature was believed to have a soul and Max Müller's (1889) naturistic theory.

Then, in the last part of *The Elementary Forms of Religious Life*, Durkheim turned to studying the simplest primitive society, the Arunta, in order to discover the most original religious forms. He spoke extensively about the totem and wanted to show that the clan was named after the totem to which all the rituals were devoted. This primitive society believed that a mysterious force animated the totem, which was considered capable of punishing violations. Since the plant or the animal chosen to be the totem did not possess special characteristics, one could take the totem to be essentially a symbol representing the god and the clan at the same time. The totem and the clan identified with each other in the same way as religion and society.

The Arunta studied by Durkheim first underwent a period of individualism, followed by a more religious phase, characterized by group solidarity. Society itself assumed moral authority and urged the individuals to observe their rules. A strong social community commitment that overcame individual aims was then established.

In his analysis Durkheim ([1912] 1995) dealt with a whole range of questions concerning the various Australian totemic forms, which are difficult to present here in detail. In any case, some of the most significant discussions concerned the differences between spirits and gods; between negative cults with prohibitions and ascetic rites, and positive cults with sacrifices and offerings, mimetic rites, which are representative, commemorative, and piacular; and between the beneficent and the evil sacred.

In his conclusion, Durkheim stressed that "there is something eternal in religion that is destined to outlive the succession of particular symbols in which religious thought has clothed itself. There can be no society that does not experience the need at regular intervals to maintain and strengthen the collective feelings and ideas that provide its coherence and its distinct individuality" (ibid.:429). Moreover, Durkheim makes a clear-cut prediction: "Religion obviously cannot play the same role in the future as it did in the past. However, religion seems destined to transform itself rather than disappear" (ibid.:432).

2

Weber's (1864–1920) Universal Religions

CALVINISM AND CAPITALISM

Max Weber was influenced by a large group of noteworthy theologians and historians, among them the theologian Otto Baumgarten and his father Hermann, a well-known historian, and American theologian William Emery Channing (1780–1842). Weber was also influenced by discussions on religious matters with his brother Alfred. He became a pupil of the historian Theodor Mommsen and then joined the Evangelical social movement, in the process meeting the "proletarian pastor" Friedrich Naumann; he carried out a research project among workers through questionnaires that he distributed to pastors. Weber became friends with the theologian Ernst Troeltsch, and was later associated with Georg Simmel. In 1904 he visited the United States and was struck by the organizational and religious spirit that he observed there. After this long training, Max Weber started working on his fundamental essay *The Protestant Ethic and the Spirit of Capitalism* (Weber [1904–5] 1976b).

His name has often been associated with Marx's; in fact, he has been called the "Marx of the bourgeoisie"; the shadow of Marx, his designated opponent, is thus always present. However, his research into religious phenomena demonstrates that Weber's interests were very different. Through religious phenomena he first uncovered the Protestant ethic by following the same path that led, in his last years, to the publication of a series of monographs on the economic ethics of many of the world's religions.

In Weber's opinion, the Marxist analysis of capitalism was too deterministic. Weber, on the other hand, was convinced that ideas developed within religious tradition could influence behavior. Calvinism offered an ideological basis for capitalist development. In fact, by means of the concept of predestination, an individual felt the necessity to demonstrate his membership among the elect. This could be indicated by prosperity, which demonstrated the positive outcome of the individual's economic activity. The concept of predestination was also linked to the concept of vocation

75

(*Beruf*), together with forms of asceticism and hardship. All of this, in Weber's view, encouraged productivity and thus the accumulation of capital, because people usually chose to reinvest wealth in new enterprises instead of living off their earnings.

Weber did not completely ignore the more strictly economic dimension of the development of capitalism, but his aim was to refute a materialist understanding of history. He recognized the strength of capitalism in modern social reality, but he was convinced that social dynamics were not monocausal. That is why he added the religious aspect to the merely economic one.

Weber's analyses were not faultless; his excessive erudition was sometimes not verifiable and difficult to master. Often his arguments led away from his immediate objectives so that they became almost an intellectual gratification. Nevertheless, he is a cornerstone for studies in religious phenomenology, especially for his objective outlook, an unusual attitude in socioreligious studies.

In his essay *The Protestant Ethic and the Spirit of Capitalism*, Max Weber examined in particular the ethics of Calvinism, Pietism, Methodism, and the Baptist sects, emphasizing the role of election obtained through grace, the rules of life, and especially the notion of predestination. First, he tried to find out what the connections were between specific denominational groups and social strata. Then he studied the Lutheran concept of vocation. Finally he dealt with professional ethics pertaining to Protestant asceticism.

As a reference point and a means of comparison, Weber largely used the concept of ideal-type. By emphasizing certain traits he obtained an experimental category, on which he could check the effects, weight, and impact of a hypothesis. This ideal-type worked as a methodological tool. Thus, using the Protestant ethic as a point of departure, he was able to establish an ideal-typical law, namely, that Protestantism favored the development of the specific phenomenon known as capitalism. However, this ideal-typical notion as a starting condition was neither absolute nor the only one possible. Other ideal-type conditions could be added for further studies.

Critical contributions to Weber's work have been and continue to be rather vast. Many scholars have dealt with the German sociologist's thought, among them Neurath, Kraus, Tawney, Parsons, Troeltsch, Jaspers, Schutz, Aron ([1955] 1977:447–523), Bendix, Freund, Runciman, Giddens, Rossi, Ferrarotti, and Cavalli (1968).

PROTESTANT ETHICS

The main point analyzed by Weber was "the influence of certain religious ideas on the development of an economic spirit, or the *ethos* of an economic system. In this case we are dealing with the connection of the spirit of modern economic life with the rational ethics of ascetic Protestantism" (1976b:27). This influence was demonstrable because of the "fact that business leaders and owners of capital, as well as the higher grades of skilled labour, and even more the higher technically and commercially trained personnel of modern enterprises, are overwhelmingly Protestant" (ibid.:35). In this regard, however, the father of the scientific nonjudgmental attitude made an extremely critical remark:

> The rule of Calvinism, on the other hand, as it was enforced in the sixteenth century in Geneva and in Scotland, at the turn of the sixteenth and seventeenth centuries in large parts of the Netherlands, in the seventeenth in New England, and for a time in England itself, would be for us the most absolutely unbearable form of ecclesiastical control of the individual which could possibly exist. (ibid.:37)

This evaluation, however, is useful in emphasizing the constraining character of the rationalist stance of the Calvinist faith. This rationalist stance developed an inner-worldly asceticism, maintaining the obvious contradiction between the importance of economic profit and an indifference to worldly goods. Weber went so far as to posit a direct link between a strong business sense and a rigid religious organization in one's everyday life, especially "among those sects whose otherworldliness is as proverbial as their wealth" (ibid.:44).

The "spirit of capitalism" was essentially characterized by four principles:

> Remember, that time is money.... Remember, that credit is money.... Remember, that money is of the prolific, generating nature.... Remember this saying, *The good paymaster is lord of another man's purse*. He that is known to pay punctually and exactly at the time he promises, may at any time, and on any occasion, raise all the money his friends can spare. (ibid.:48–49)

Everything seems to revolve around money. Benjamin Franklin had stated this idea in his aphorisms—quoted by Weber—published in two texts in 1736 and 1748, in which he developed the idea of the importance of increasing one's capital. This idea was in line with the ethics according to which to be honest was useful in order to obtain credit. According to the notion inherent in this ethic, earning money was viewed as an existential goal and not as an instrument for personal satisfaction. Moreover, professional success was a sign of divine election. Franklin remembered his Calvinist father saying that a successful worker was worthy of appearing in front of a king (Proverbs 22,29). Thus, he who was conscientious in his work was worthy of meeting the highest authorities (figuratively also

God), or at least of working for the king instead of for an anonymous employer.

Weber remarked that Pietists' religious education, which had Lutheran origins, was very individualistic but was based on an active faith, which somehow favored, more than other religions did, an economic attitude. In fact, Weber wrote:

> The ability of mental concentration, as well as the absolutely essential feeling of obligation to one's job, are here most often combined with a strict economy which calculates the possibility of high earnings, and a cool self-control and frugality which enormously increase performance. This provides the most favorable foundation for the conception of labor as an end in itself, as a calling which is necessary to capitalism: the chances of overcoming traditionalism are greatest on account of the religious upbringing. (ibid.:63)

According to Weber, from this it was easier to understand what the "modern spirit of capitalism" of a Western industrial kind was:

> that attitude which seeks profit rationally and systematically in the manner which we have illustrated by the example of Benjamin Franklin. This, however, is justified by the historical fact that that attitude of mind has on the one hand found its most suitable expression in capitalist enterprise, while, on the other, the enterprise has derived its most suitable motive force from the spirit of capitalism. (ibid.:65)

"Men who had grown up in the hard school of life" belong to this cogent logic. They were "calculating and daring at the same time, above all temperate and reliable, shrewd and completely devoted to their business, with strictly bourgeois opinions and principles" (ibid.:69). These were the clergymen of the capitalist spirit, completely dedicated to their work by vocation, the "elect" and those "predestined" who through earning demonstrated that God had chosen them. They lived in an ascetic way and they did not waste time or dissipate the profits of their labor.

THE PROFESSION AS VOCATION

The idea of vocation is a crucial concept.

> Now it is unmistakable that even in the German word *Beruf*, and perhaps still more clearly in the English calling, a religious conception, that of a task set by God, is at least suggested. The more emphasis is put upon the word in a concrete case, the more evident is the connotation. And if we trace the history of the word through the civilized languages, it appears that neither the

predominantly Catholic peoples nor those of classical antiquity have possessed any expression of similar connotation for what we know as a calling (in the sense of a life-task, a definite field in which to work), while one has existed for all predominantly Protestant peoples. (ibid.:79)

Vocation was also

the fulfillment of duty in worldly affairs as the highest form that the moral activity of the individual could assume. This it was which inevitably gave every-day worldly activity a religious significance, and which first created the conception of a calling in this sense. The conception of the calling thus brings out that central dogma of all Protestant denominations which the Catholic division of ethical precepts into *praecepta* and *consilia* discards. The only way of living acceptably to God was not to surpass worldly morality in monastic asceticism, but solely through the fulfillment of the obligations imposed upon the individual by his position in the world. That was his calling. (ibid.:80)

This would then be the Puritan's "acceptance of his life in the world as a task" (ibid.:88).

In order to prevent an overly determinist reading of the relationship between Protestantism and capitalism, Weber was, however, eager to delimit the scope of his interpretation.

In such a study, it may at once be definitely stated, no attempt is made to evaluate the ideas of the Reformation in any sense, whether it concern their social or their religious worth. We have continually to deal with aspects of the Reformation, which must appear to the truly religious consciousness as incidental and even superficial. For we are merely attempting to clarify the part which religious forces have played in forming the developing web of our specifically worldly modern culture, in the complex interaction of innumerable different historical factors. We are thus inquiring only to what extent certain characteristic features of this culture can be imputed to the influence of the Reformation. At the same time we must free ourselves from the idea that it is possible to deduce the Reformation, as a historically necessary result, from certain economic law, and are not susceptible of economic explanation of any sort, especially purely political processes, had to concur in order that the newly created Churches should survive at all. On the other hand, however, we have no intention whatever of maintaining such a foolish and doctrinaire thesis as that the spirit of capitalism (in the provisional sense of the term explained above) could only have arisen as the result of certain effects of the Reformation, or even that capitalism as an economic system is a creation of the Reformation. In itself, the fact that certain important forms of capitalistic business organization are known to be considerably older than the Reformation is a sufficient refutation of such a claim. On the contrary, we only wish to ascertain whether and to what extent religious forces have taken part in the qualitative formation and the quantitative expansion of that spirit over the world. (ibid.:90–91)

Thus the sociologist from Heidelberg anticipated his critics and clearly recognized that the capitalist phenomenon preceded the advent of Lutheranism and the Reformation. He wanted to underline the claim that the specific relation between capitalism and Protestantism occurred under particular conditions, specifically where there were clear religious conditions favorable to the expansion of capitalism. On the other hand, not all Protestantism was ascetic in the same way that seventeenth century Calvinism, Pietism, and the Baptist sects were. And "all types of moral conduct in which we are interested may be found in a similar manner among the adherents of the most various denominations, derived from any one of the four sources mentioned above, or a combination of several of them" (ibid.:96–97).

PREDESTINATION AND ASCETICISM

An important matter was the dogma of salvation, of being chosen through divine grace. The sinful man would not be capable of goodness, but God intervened and predestined some people to eternal life while others were condemned to eternal death. Sacraments as a means of salvation administered by the Catholic church were less relevant. God "likes" to perform his "call" to grace directly. If one were elected, then it would be indispensable to have God as one's only confidant, only confessor, with no one else acting as a go-between. Thus "the Calvinist's intercourse with his God was carried on in deep spiritual isolation" (ibid.:106–7). Consequently,

> The world exists to serve the glorification of God and for that purpose alone. The elected Christian is in the world only to increase this glory of God by fulfilling His commandments to the best of his ability. But God requires the social achievement of the Christian because He wills that social life shall be organized according to His commandments, in accordance with that purpose. The social activity of the Christian in the world is solely activity *ad majorem gloriam Dei*. This character is hence shared by labor in a calling which serves the mundane life of the community. (ibid.:108)

It was not easy to tell the elected individuals from the reprobate ones on the basis of their everyday actions. However, the elected person was called to prove his state of grace by showing self-assurance and an uninterrupted professional activity. Such an attitude erased religious doubt and provided the certainty of the state of grace. Thus, to carry out good deeds was not enough; rather, one should elevate the holiness of the good deeds, creating a new life system that realized itself in asceticism. This meant conducting a clear and conscious life and suppressing the unprincipled enjoyment of life. This behavior was approved both by Catholic monasticism and by Calvinism. It was not by chance that the keystone of the Protestant reformation lay in the transformation of each Christian into a monk, an ascetic. Calvinists added to this the importance of commitment to a profession.

As for Pietism, salvation could also be found in the lay world. According to the principles of Pietism, this led to a stricter control over one's professional life and a stronger religious basis regarding morality within professional activity (ibid.). Success on the job was a sign of divine election, of grace's beneficial action. Thus, one's profession was like a mission within the brotherhood of the community.

On the contrary, for the Methodists the *certitudo salutis* must be reached by right behavior. This had been the main focus in religious activity from its origins. The main objective was "sanctification." "However difficult this end is to attain, generally not until the end of one's life, it must be sought, because it finally guarantees the *certitudo salutis* and substitutes a serene confidence for the sullen worry of the Calvinist" (ibid.:141).

The situation differed for the Baptist movement, the Mennonites, and the Quakers. Some of these movements expressed a total rejection of some aspects of society; for instance, they were against any public appointment, any kind of political commitment, or any sort of compromise. In particular,

> For our purposes the decisive point was, to recapitulate, the conception of the state of religious grace, common to all the denominations, as a status which marks off its possessor from the degradation of the flesh, from the world. On the other hand, although the means by which it was attained differed for different doctrines, it could not be guaranteed by any magical sacraments, by relief in the confession, nor by individual good works. That was only possible by proof in a specific type of conduct unmistakably different from the way of life of the natural man. (ibid.:153)

Finally,

> Christian asceticism, at first fleeing from the world into solitude, had already ruled the world which it had renounced from the monastery and through the Church. But it had, on the whole, left the naturally spontaneous character of daily life in the world untouched. Now it strode into the market-place of life, slammed the door of the monastery behind it, and undertook to penetrate just that daily routine of life with its methodicalness, to fashion it into a life in the world, but neither of nor for this world. (ibid.:154)

However, there was an element that should be considered for its importance: "This asceticism turned with all its force against one thing: the spontaneous enjoyment of life and all it had to offer" (ibid.:166). Thus, the joy of life opposed asceticism, diverted from work and from religious conduct. Even going to the theatre became a reprehensible deed. Life must be linear and homogeneous. Also buying and possessing more and more goods did nothing but increase one's responsibility for their correct use in the face of God, for his honor and glory.

> The religious valuation of restless, continuous, systematic work in a worldly calling, as the highest means to asceticism, and at the same time the surest and most evident proof of rebirth and genuine faith, must have been the most powerful conceivable lever for the expansion of that attitude toward life which we have here called the spirit of capitalism. (ibid.:172)

Indeed, what was verified was the regular increase of capital through a marked tendency to saving and a strong desire to accumulate wealth.

CHURCHES AND SECTS

In 1893 the first Parliament of the World's Religions was held in Chicago. Weber attended the meeting and was very impressed by it. The event also represented the official entrance of Asian religions into North American popular culture. Weber was inspired by this impact and was probably already planning a huge and well-documented work on the *Sociology of Religion* (Weber [1920–21, 1922] 1976a). The decision to publish such a work was taken after the appearance of *The Protestant Ethic and the Spirit of Capitalism*. In this new work Weber wrote several book-length essays, each dedicated to a different religion: Confucianism, Taoism, Hinduism, Buddhism, and ancient Judaism (this last essay is incomplete), carrying out a comparative study of world religions according to an ethical outlook. He also wrote a few "intermediate considerations" (*Zwischenbetrachtung*) on "the religious rejection of the world" (ibid.:II, 583–625).

He started his work in 1913 and ended it in 1919. In 1915 Weber published the Introduction together with the essay on Confucianism. At the same time, he began to think about the major Eastern religions. Initially, Weber wanted to publish the essays within the volume *Wirtschaft und Gesellschaft* (1922) (*Economy and Society*), but they appeared separately in *Gesammelte Aufsätze zur Religionssoziologie* in 1920–21; the second edition came out in 1922–23. However, in 1922 the first of the three volumes containing *Protestant Ethic and the Spirit of Capitalism* had already appeared in the third edition.

Even before that, Weber (1906), after a journey to the United States in 1904, had started to work on an essay on the churches and the sects. He republished it in an expanded version in the first edition of *Gesammelte Aufsätze zur Religionssoziologie* with the title "Die protestantischen Sekten und der Geist des Kapitalismus" (*The Protestant Sects and the Spirit of Capitalism*). Thus, Weber revised the text and defined it as the sequel of *The Protestant Ethic and the Spirit of Capitalism*. He rediscussed the concepts of church and sect, which had also been extensively elaborated by Troeltsch ([1912] 1976).

As far as the situation of the sects in the United States was concerned, Weber offered a number of interesting details, presenting them in an informal way, halfway between a sociological descriptive style and a journalistic mode. He reported observations that he had made with the help of traveling companions. He added a few historical observations and concluded:

> It is crucial that sect membership meant a certificate of moral qualification and especially of business morals of the individual. This stands in contrast to membership in a "church" into which one is "born" and which lets grace shine over the righteous and the unrighteous alike. . . . Affiliation with the church is, in principle, obligatory and hence proves nothing with regard to the member's qualities. A sect, however, is a voluntary association of only those who, according to the principle, are religiously and morally qualified. If one finds voluntary reception of his membership, by virtue of religious probation, he joins the sect voluntarily. (Weber 1962b:305)

The difference between church and sect is an interesting one. Generally the sect imposes a tighter bond on the individual, a strong sense of belonging, a willing support, and a rigorous social control, which guarantee loyalty among the sect members and their ethical-economic fairness.

It is not by chance that

> In the past and up to the very present, it has been a characteristic precisely of the specifically American democracy that it did *not* constitute a formless sand heap of individuals, but rather a buzzing complex strictly exclusive, yet voluntary. . . . He who wished to be fully recognized in this democracy, in whatever position, had not only to conform to the conventions of bourgeois society, the very strict men's fashions included, but as a rule he had to be able to show that he had succeeded in gaining admission by ballot to one of the sects, clubs, or fraternal societies, no matter *what* kind, were it only recognized as sufficiently legitimate. And he had to maintain himself in the society by proving himself to be a gentleman. (ibid.:310–11)

Aside from the influence the sects had in the United States, Weber was also convinced that in Europe the religiosity of the sects had been widespread throughout many centuries (ibid.). Then, talking again about the Baptists, Pietists, and Methodists, Weber noticed how the discipline in the ascetic sects—which was very close to the discipline of the convents—was even more rigorous than that of the churches and, moreover, the sects defined the monastic principle of novitiate. In fact, before being accepted in a sect, a person had to undergo a trial period. However,

The member of the sect (or conventicle) had to have qualities of a certain kind in order to enter the community circle. Being endowed with these qualities was important for the development of rational modern capitalism, as has been shown in the first essay (*The Protestant Ethic and the Spirit of Capitalism*). In order to hold his own in this circle, the member had to prove repeatedly that he was endowed with these qualities. They were constantly and continuously bred in him. For, like his bliss in the beyond, his whole social existence in the here and now depended upon his "proving" himself. (ibid.:320)

THE UNIVERSE OF RELIGIONS

The period of time during which Weber worked on the relationships between religious ethics and socioeconomic processes was the most difficult one because of his psychophysical ailments. But he was still a strenuous worker and was able to produce keen observations and original insights. He was influenced by the Calvinist background of his mother, Hélène, and his maternal aunt, Ida Baumgarten. This explains in part his interest in the spiritual aspect of social action.

Weber was convinced that Calvinism was crucial for the spreading of the idea that financial success and resulting capital accumulation demonstrated the existence of divine election. Thus, worldly asceticism was a choice that favored the development of capitalism and made religious moral duties endurable.

Weber first presented his interpretation of Protestant ascetic morality in relation to the spirit of capitalism in the journal he edited, *Archiv für Sozialwissenschaft und Sozialpolitik*, and subsequently in other periodicals. However, in 1910, during the first meeting of the German Association of Sociology, which he founded together with Simmel and others, Weber discovered Russian mysticism. He set up Russian mysticism against asceticism, since for the latter everything was based on the individual's action as a divine instrument in the world, while the aim of Russian mysticism was the individual's identification with the divine.

Thus, after a first long Puritan phase, mysticism, asceticism, and eroticism (Whimster 1995; Whimster and Lash 1987; Mitzman 1985) were jointly combined in Weber's thought. This was directly linked to Weber's private life, in particular to an extramarital relationship that made him dwell on the religious rejection of the world (Weber 1976a:II, 583–625; 1962c).

In the realm of political sociology, Weber's distinction among charismatic, traditional, and legal authorities turned out to be crucial. Charismatic authority included both the religious element and prophetic connotation. Weber later employed these same categories in his long essays on Eastern religions (1962) and on Judaism.

Raymond Aron summarizes Weber's point of view:

At the outset of Weber's sociology of religion, I find an interpretation of primitive religion which is very close to Durkheim's conception in *Les Formes élémentaires de la vie religieuse*. . . . Weber retains as the major concept in primitive religions the notion of *charisma*, which is quite close to the Durkheimian notion of the *sacred*. Charisma is the quality of that which is outside the commonplace or, as Weber says, *ausseralltäglich* (outside the everyday), and which becomes attached to human beings, animals, plants and things. The world of the primitive contains a distinction between the commonplace and the exceptional, to paraphrase Weber, or between the profane and the sacred, to adopt Durkheimian terminology. If the point of departure for the religious history of humanity is a world peopled with the sacred, the point of arrival in our time is what Weber calls *Entzauberung der Welt*: the disenchantment of the world. The sacred, the exceptional quality which was attached to the things and creatures surrounding us at the dawn of the human adventure, has been banished. The capitalist's world—that is, the world we all live in, Soviets and Westerners alike—is composed of forces or creatures which offer themselves to us to be used, transformed, and consumed, but which no longer carry the charm of charisma. (Aron 1970:II, 271–72)

In the above-mentioned chapter on the different kind of religious communities, Max Weber discussed at length the birth of religions; roles like the sorcerer, the priest, and the prophet (the latter considered in distinction to the previous two); ethics, taboo, and totemism; but especially communities, preaching, the cure of souls, social stratification, and religion. Finally, he discussed the question of theodicy (the justification of God's ways to man) together with the problem of redemption. Weber also dealt with the previously discussed questions of the relationship between religion and capitalism and of the religious rejection of the world as they were treated by religious traditions such as Judaism, Catholicism, Puritanism, Islam, and Buddhism.

Weber easily shifted from one context to the other in his own peculiar way, providing the reader with an abundance of references, accurate details, distinguishing features, and convincing examples—a good instance was the distinction between "ascesis of the rejection of the world" and "intra-worldly ascesis."

The leitmotiv of his investigations remained the same—to grasp the links between economy and religion. A clear instance of this was provided by a few reflections by Weber on the role of religious art:

Mass religion in particular is frequently and directly dependent on artistic devices for the required potency of its effects, and it is inclined to make concessions to the needs of the masses, which everywhere tend toward magic and idolatry. Apart from this, organized mass religions have frequently had connections with art resulting from economic interests, as, for instance, in the case of the traffic in icons by the Byzantine monks, the most decisive opponents of the caesaropapist Imperial power which was supported by an army that was iconoclastic because it was recruited from the marginal provinces of Islam, still strongly spiritualistic at that time. The imperial power, in turn, attempted to cut off the monks from this source of income, hoping thus to destroy the economic strength of this most dangerous opponent to its plans for domination over the church. (Weber 1978:II, 609)

3

Religiosity and Religion in Simmel (1858–1918)

RELIGIOSITY AS THE MAKER OF RELIGION

As a scientific discipline, sociology has existed and has been developing for more than a century using theoretical approaches and empirical investigations that have favored the analysis of religious phenomena. As is well-known, all the previous major sociologists in this field have offered original insights and systematic expositions that are still useful today and that are employed at length by scholars who deal with old and new dynamics of religion and of religiosity.

The two concepts of religion and religiosity are the starting point for innumerable lively and fruitful debates among specialists. German sociologist Georg Simmel differentiates religiosity from religion in the following way: He defines religiosity as the inner form of human experience, which thus precedes religion. Religion then is nothing but the empirical transposition of religiosity, a realization at the organizational level through the various modalities of church, sect, denomination, and movement.

Simmel wrote that just as cognition does not create causality, but instead causality creates cognition, so religion does not create religiosity, but religiosity creates religion (Simmel [1906, 1912] 1997). There is, in fact, in human beings a special inner disposition, a peculiar state in which the individual finds himself, a religious orientation that is the precondition for the encounter with the divine. Religion, on the other hand, is a cultural product that comes into being after long interpersonal exchanges and through multiple interactive experiences, which find a social outlet in the church-as-institution or in other organized religious forms. A common belief underlies these institutions: a readiness of the person to feel religious, or to have religiosity.

A similar process is outlined in Simmel's concept of *Geselligkeit*, or sociability, conceived as the natural tendency people have to be together, to form a community, even if conflicts are present. From this tendency derives the ultimate cultural product—society itself, with its set of institutions, which are created to meet the needs of the individual and of various social subjects.

This is a central aspect in Simmel's sociological thought. There exists, in fact, a substantial parallel in the use of the two concepts *Religiosität* and *Geselligkeit*, also as far as time is concerned. In fact, Simmel's book *Soziologie* (1908), in which he deals with the concept of sociability, was published just two years after the publication of the first edition of the essay *Die Religion* (Simmel [1906] 1997). Indeed, Simmel preferred the term *Vergesellschaftung*, signifying chiefly a "growing socialization" or "societalization," rather than *Geselligkeit*, or sociability. However, the latter term was more widely used in later sociological works.

In Simmel's social-religious approach, the parallelism between religiosity and sociability is fairly clear. While religiosity is at the basis of religion, sociability is at the origin of society. Moreover, in the second edition of *Die Religion* (Simmel [1912] 1997), religious disposition and social disposition are interwoven to the point that it is possible to conceive a *religiöse Leben*, a religious life. This religious life represents the passage from the simple initial religious availability to the notion of the "absolute divine" as a final consequence. This outcome is possible because, as Simmel writes,

> Religion in its fully developed state, the entire spiritual complex associated with the transcendent sphere, presents itself as the absolute and unified form of the feelings and impulses that social life itself develops in a tentative and apparently experimental fashion, insofar as it is religiously oriented as a mood or function. (ibid.:151)

Moreover, religious life has two aspects: an intersubjective aspect based on social exchange, and a more concrete one exhibited in various ways—at the institutional level there is the church, while movements, groups, and other cohesive forms represent less formalized solutions. Simmel writes that these phenomena fit into an overall picture, insofar as "one of the most characteristic forms of social life, one of those fixed norms of life by which society ensures that its members behave in an appropriate and beneficial way, is that of custom—in less sophisticated cultures the only generally characteristic form of socially determined behavior" (ibid.:151–52).

RELIGIOSITY AND CULTURE

In order to have a better grasp of Simmel's approach, one should take into account his concept of culture as it is presented in a book seemingly very distant from purely religious concerns. In his *Philosophy of Money* (Simmel [1900] 1990), Simmel wrote:

If we define culture as the refinement, as the intellectualized forms of life, the accomplishment of mental and practical labor, then we place these values in a context to which they do not automatically belong by virtue of their own objective significance. They become manifestations of culture to us inasmuch as we interpret them as intensified displays of natural vitality and potential, intensified beyond the level of development, fullness and differentiation that would be achieved by their mere nature. A natural energy or allusion, which is necessary only in order that it may be surpassed by actual development, forms the presupposition for the concept of culture. From the standpoint of culture, the values of life are civilized *nature*; they do not have here the isolated significance that is measured from above, as it were, by the ideals of happiness, intelligence and beauty. Rather, they appear as developments of a basis that we call nature and whose power and intellectual content they surpass insofar as they become culture. (ibid.:446)

As for religion Simmel envisages the same perspective. At first religion is merely nature, then it becomes more spiritual until it completely develops into culture. Then the original predisposition becomes a cultural product; from a simple attitude it transforms itself into a concrete reality. Thus the transition from nature to culture matches in many aspects the passage from religiosity to religion.

Religiosity, on the other hand, provides vital substance to customs and habits. It is then appropriate to maintain that, as Simmel writes:

Custom, law, and individual morality are varying combinations of social elements, all of which can be based on the very same principles of behavior and which in fact occur in diverse forms among various peoples at different times in history. Among the social forms that allow the community to encourage the individual to act appropriately are religions. The religious character of social conditions has very often been one characteristic stage of their development. In a given period, an aspect of social life that previously and subsequently is represented by different forms of relationship between human beings will adopt a religious form. (Simmel [1906, 1912] 1997:152)

Essentially, one might argue that sociality creates society, through custom, and that religiosity, through religious life, creates religion.

Horst Jürgen Helle has rightly observed, in his introduction to the English edition of *Die Religion*, that Simmel precedes Durkheim in stressing the binding role of group membership for expressing religiosity as devotion toward a specific divinity of the group (ibid.).

In fact, for Durkheim the concept of religious life seems more important when it is conceived of as a totality of attitudes and behaviors connected with religious experience. Whenever we meet with an example of religious life, we can be sure to find at its basis a definite group of people (Durkheim [1912] 1995). The link between religious life and group membership is immediate and taken for granted. This emerges to the extent that "religious beliefs proper are always shared by a definite group that professes them and that practices the corresponding rites" (ibid.:41). Thus, religious beliefs need a collectivity and are not recognized at the level of the individual. The difference with Simmel is clear at this point—he gives much greater emphasis to the religious inclination of the individual.

At the same time Durkheim had a clear notion of religion as a group of beliefs and rituals that gives rise to a religious community or church: "a society whose members are united because they imagine the sacred world and its relations with the profane world in the same way, and because they translate this common representation into identical practices, is what is called a Church" (ibid.:41). The outcome of religious life, of religion *tout court*, into a church is taken as established. Indeed, Durkheim states that "in history we do not find religion without Church" (ibid.:41).

Durkheim then clearly makes a distinction between religion and magic, on the basis of the greater instrumental, individualistic use encountered in the magical worldview. Magic is something different with respect to church experience since practitioners of magic do not manage to have a religious life in common. Consequently, Durkheim declares that *"there is no Church of magic"* (ibid.:42, emphasis in original). While the faithful and their priests experience and share the same religious life, the same church, this is not so for magicians and their followers.

In particular, one might say that beliefs fall under Simmel's version of religiosity, whereas rituals might lie halfway between religiosity and religion, since they are based on beliefs, without which they would have no raison d'être. Furthermore, rituals would be inconceivable without some shadow of a structure, a specific place for their celebration, a normative network, a differentiation of roles, a predefined symbolic system, and thus a church organization, or something similar. From this comparison of Simmel and Durkheim it is possible to derive the following theoretical framework:

Phenomenal typology (Simmel):   religiosity⇒link⇒religion
Expressive typology (Durkheim):   beliefs⇒rituals⇒church

It must be made clear, however, that Simmel does not speak explicitly of a link. Perhaps the concept of religious life itself would better express the idea of a guiding thread leading from religious disposition to the objectivization of faith and finally to religion. In fact, Simmel writes that "one might thus enumerate three domains of life that exemplify this transposition into the religious key: the behavior of man toward the external, natural world around him" (Simmel [1906, 1912] 1997:144–45). This is how, according to Simmel, the religious element finds its own space: "Things gain religious significance and are raised to a transcendent level because and insofar as they have been subsumed under the religious category from the outset; this category has determined their constitution, even before they are fully recognized as religious phenomena" (ibid.:146).

Once more Simmel is consistent with his line of thought, which he developed further when he wrote: "Just as, from an epistemological stand-point, we draw our life-contents from a realm of objectively valid entities, so, viewed historically, we draw the major part of them from the stock of accumulated mental labour of the species. Here too we find preformed contents that are ready to be realized by individual minds" (Simmel [1900] 1990:452).

In this context, tradition takes on the characteristics of a transmission of preelaborated contents, which are then used by successive generations along the *continuum* of the human species. Culture is a form of historical objectivism that draws consistent elements from a patrimony of "truths" already considered valid and objectified. However, culture does not level itself out on its material forms, but preserves its separate nature in abstract form, although in one that is not empirically measurable. The high level of the "spirit" is not lowered in its empirical transposition but remains intangible, even sacred. Thus, from the potential to the act itself, from the possibility to the concrete realization, from virtuality to materialization, the transition is made feasible to the degree in which human beings are capable—and in fact they are—of managing their own world, of inheriting "the objectified spirit" by way of "words and deeds, organizations and traditions." Thus:

> By establishing this category of the objective mind as the historical manifestation of the valid intellectual content of things in general, it becomes clear how the cultural process that we recognize as a subjective development—the culture of things as a human culture—can be separated from its content. This content, by entering that category, acquires, as it were, another physical condition and thus provides the basis for the phenomenon of the separate development of objective and personal culture. This objectification of the mind provides the form that makes the conservation and accumulation of mental labor possible; it is the most significant and far-reaching of the historical categories of mankind. (ibid.:452–53)

Reverting now to the theoretical framework, reversing in practice the usual conception of starting from religion to arrive at religiosity, it thus seems that beliefs themselves are the initial crux, which is religiosity. Religiosity, then, becomes explicit through rituality—including, we must suppose, prayer. As the final, but closely connected and necessary, result, the institutional level rises and grows to become religion.

The double path that attempts to set Durkheim's and Simmel's insights along the same theoretical-analytical track may lead to interesting results, but because it is both determined and determining it must, from the outset, exclude any other possible alternative proposition not in line with the unidirectional path of this Simmel-Durkheimian trajectory. If we stand by this misleading line—which leads nowhere but to the single destination of the institution—we cannot fully analyze those specific characteristics of what is not included in what is already foretold and historically preordained.

In short, however stimulating and useful they may be, the references suggested by the two authors become an interpretative trap with characteristics of a *conventio ad excludendum,* and an agreement that allows neither parallel nor divergent paths.

4

Freud (1856–1939)

The Psychic Dimension of Religion

PSYCHE AND RELIGION

Sigmund Freud worked in a historical and cultural period that was particularly fertile for the study of religious phenomena. A physician of Jewish origins, the founder of psychoanalysis was born in 1856 in Moravia—today's Czech Republic—and studied medicine in Vienna, specializing in neurology. He later went to Paris to study neurology and got particularly interested in phenomena of hysteria. Through his "free association" technique, Freud enabled a patient with a specific symptom to remember past events that might be the cause of the symptom. Freud's "free association" technique is found in his text *The Interpretation of Dreams* ([1938–39] 1953a:vols. IV–V) and replaces hypnosis in the exploration and treatment of neurotic symptoms. Freud's scientific interest in religion started with the text *Obsessive Actions and Religious Practices* (1959:vol. IX). At the beginning of his career he deepened the knowledge of psychoanalytic issues through weekly meetings with other colleagues and scholars, which later led to the foundation of the Psychoanalytic Society of Vienna and to the International Psychoanalytic Association. In later years, Freud began to give sexual explanations for the origins of neurosis. He developed the notion of the Oedipus complex, which originated in the love for a parent of the opposite sex and in the consequent aggressive feelings toward the parent of the same sex. Then in the essay *Totem and Taboo* (1953b:vol. XIII), Freud examined questions concerning totemism. He analyzed the case of *A Demoniac Neurosis of the Seventeenth Century* (1961a). In the texts *The Future of an Illusion* (1961b:vol. XXI) and *A Religious Experience* (1961c:vol. XXI), Freud wrote about God and religion. In the last years of his life he published *Moses and Monotheism* (1964:vol. XXIII). When the Nazis occupied Vienna in 1938, Freud fled the country and went to London, where he died in 1939.

The religious and private character of the obsessive neurosis (Freud 1959:IX, 117) was one of the first hypotheses that caught Freud's interest. In fact, he felt that there was a meaningful similarity between "what are called obsessive actions in sufferers from nervous afflictions and the observances by means of which believers give expression to their piety." He has accurately described this similarity, which allows different kinds of readings:

> It is easy to see where the resemblance lies between neurotic ceremonials and the sacred acts of religious ritual: in the qualms of conscience brought on by their neglect, in their complete isolation from all other actions (shown in the prohibition against interruption) and in the conscientiousness with which they are carried out in every detail. But the differences are equally obvious, and a few of them are so glaring that they make the comparison a sacrilege: the greater individual variability of (neurotic) ceremonial actions in contrast to the stereotyped character of rituals (prayer, turning to the East, etc.), their private nature as opposed to the public and communal character of religious observances, above all, however, the fact that, while the *minutiae* of religious ceremonial are full of significance and have a symbolic meaning, those of neurotics seem foolish and senseless. (Freud 1959:IX, 119)

The symbolic dimension then is at the basis of religious practice.

Almost at the end of his essay, Freud tries to explain the relationship between obsessions and religiosity after examining a few specific clinical cases.

> The formation of a religion, too, seems to be based on the suppression, the renunciation, of certain instinctual impulses. These impulses, however, are not, as in the neuroses, exclusively components of the sexual instinct; they are self-seeking, socially harmful instincts, though, even so, they are usually not without a sexual component. A sense of guilt following upon continual temptation and an expectant anxiety in the form of fear of divine punishment have, after all, been familiar to us in the field of religion longer than in that of neurosis. Perhaps because of the admixture of sexual components, perhaps because of some general characteristics of the instincts, the suppression of instinct proves to be an inadequate and interminable process in religious life also. Indeed, complete backslidings into sin are more common among pious people than among neurotics and these give rise to a new form of religious activity, namely acts of penance, which have their counterpart in obsessional neurosis. (Freud 1959:IX, 125)

Indeed, the comparison between neurotic obsessions and religious practices cannot be completely plausible. As already mentioned, on the one hand, at the religious level there is the symbolic dimension, and on the other, the atonement for one's sins through an act of repentance. This means that obsessive actions and religious practices overlap only partially.

Nevertheless, the existing connections between the two are interesting and hold true to some extent. Freud utilizes these connections in order to hypothesize that obsessive neurosis would be a sort of personal religion, while religion would have the character of a universal obsessive neurosis (Freud 1959:vol. IX).

TOTEMISM AND INCEST

Totem and Taboo (Freud 1953b:vol. XIII) is a more mature and thoughtful work. Karl Kerényi has described how Freud had become extremely interested in the most recent publications of British anthropology. He avidly read the available volumes of monumental works by James Frazer: *Totemism and Exogamy* (1910) and many parts of *The Golden Bough* ([1907–15] 1994). Kerényi reminded the reader that *The Golden Bough* began with a description of the ancient rituals at the lake of Nemi, near Rome. In 1911–15 the book added up to twelve volumes and had already reached the third edition. Freud dedicated some time to the study of these books during his three stays in Rome, while working on *Totem and Taboo,* and it was during one of his stays in Rome that he wrote the introduction to his book *Totem and Taboo.* Freud also recognized the influence that the mountain environment of Tyrol had on the beginning of his work (from a letter of September 10, 1911, to Ludwig Binswanger). Freud wrote that the crucifixes throughout the Tyrol were so numerous that they sometimes even outnumbered the tourists. This induced him to study the psychology of religion (Kerényi 1969:10).

To be sure, *Totem and Taboo* was the outcome of an ambitious project and appeared after a long gestation. Freud himself could not completely hide his intentions: he wanted to build a theory of religion and of its origins that would replace the outmoded contributions of many contemporary scholars. This was not an easy task. More than once Freud was about to give it up and to dedicate himself more regularly to *Imago,* the journal he edited. But finally the book appeared. In his book Freud agreed with Frazer about the prior origin of matrilineal descent; Freud's intent was, however, to support the idea that totemic prohibitions concerned sons who had incestuous desires toward their mothers, and not fathers who had incestuous desires towards the daughters, as Frazer (1910) maintained. Indeed, Kerényi suggested that Freud was a more careful reader of *The Golden Bough* (Frazer [1907–15] 1994)—a less rigorous work—than of *Totemism and Exogamy* (Frazer 1910).

Frazer's approach held its influence for a long time, notwithstanding the somewhat simplistic and superficial interpretation of some of the facts he described. Indeed, Freud's observations on the similarities of the behavior of the "savages" and of the neurotics are more convincing. In this regard, Kerényi rightly observed that these similarities concerned the typical behavior one found in magic and in totemism and its resemblance to the behavior of neurotic individuals, independently of any theoretical explanation. The constant reference to these similarities defined as "common phenomena" of two separate human realms—the first pertaining to the ethnologist, the second belonging to the physician and the psychoanalyst—was the scientific worth of *Totem and Taboo* (Kerényi 1969:16–17).

This text by Freud is the most meaningful one in the social-religious perspective. The four essays that form the book deal with the behavior of primitive populations in relation to some traits that can be found in neurotic individuals. Thus these traits pertained to an unconscious basis common to all individuals. The subtitle of the book is clear—*Some Points of Agreement between the Mental Lives of Savages and Neurotics*. The declared objective was to find the origin of religion, within a perspective that completely separated Freud's thought from that of Jung.

The first essay deals with *The Horror of Incest*. The second one is concerned with *Taboo and Emotional Ambivalence*. The third is about *Animism, Magic and the Omnipotence of Thoughts*. The last one is *The Return of Totemism in Childhood*, which takes on a question discussed by Robertson Smith about the totemic meal and the Semitic religion.

In the introduction to the Hebrew edition of *Totem and Taboo*, which appeared in 1930, Freud declared that despite the fact that his book dealt with the origin of religion, he did not adopt a Jewish point of view. He did not take an especially favorable position as far as Jewish religion was concerned since he wanted to prove his nonjudgmental and scientific attitude.

In a letter (April 9, 1913) to his pupil and biographer Jones, he declared that this work was the hardest task on which he had ever embarked. Moreover, in *Totem and Taboo*, many of the topics previously treated by Freud reappeared, that is, incest, emotions, childhood fears of animals. As Cesare Musatti stressed:

> It was above all important for him to have found in the lives of the savages who worshipped a totem the two laws of totemism, that is, the same ones to be found in the Oedipal complex among neurotic people. The intimate connection between totemism and exogamy, which has been refuted by ethnologists and by Frazer himself in his later works, was fully accepted by Freud. Freud supported this connection not only because other scholars believed in it, but because he could verify it in his psychoanalytical experience with neurotic patients. (Freud 1953b:XIII, 6)

The two laws to which Musatti was referring concerned the prohibition against killing the totem and the interdiction against having sexual intercourse with a woman belonging to the same totem or clan (ibid.:11–15).

According to Freud, in the beginning totemism was an important social-religious institution that with time had been progressively neglected. In fact, in modern religions there is no trace of totemism. On the other hand, the taboo, which has a strong link with totemism, is still valid in today's religions.

The taboo regards first of all the totem itself, which cannot be destroyed. However, the taboo applies also to other objects and individuals. Indeed, today the past role of the taboo has been replaced by phobias. Through neurotic, obsessive forms of behavior, which are always linked to particular rites, it is possible to study the attitudes and the behaviors of primitive peoples. They develop a love-hate feeling for the totem, the same emotion they have for their fathers, thus reconstructing the typical situation of the oedipal complex.

"What is a totem?" Freud asks himself in the first essay.

> It is as a rule an animal (whether edible and harmless or dangerous and feared) and more rarely a plant or a natural phenomenon (such as rain or water), which stands in a peculiar relation to the whole clan. In the first place, the totem is the common ancestor of the clan; at the same time it is their guardian spirit and helper, which sends them oracles and, if dangerous to others, recognizes and spares its own children. Conversely, the clansmen are under a sacred obligation (subject to automatic sanctions) not to kill or destroy their totem and to avoid eating its flesh (or deriving benefit from it in other ways. (ibid.:2)

Aside from a few typical Freudian notions—such as the one concerning the abstinence from enjoyment—this definition of the totem does not add anything new to those existing at the time of the publication of *Totem and Taboo*. The totem was inherited through the maternal and later also through the paternal line. Then Freud dealt with the taboo: "Every place where we find totems we also find a law against persons of the same totem having sexual relations with one another and consequently against their marrying. This, then, is 'exogamy,' an institution related to totemism" (ibid.:4).

In the second essay one reads:

> "Taboo" is a Polynesian word. It is difficult for us to find a translation for it, since the concept connoted by it is one which we no longer possess. It was still current among the ancient Romans, whose *"sacer"* was the same as the Polynesian "taboo." . . . The meaning of "taboo," as we see it, diverges in two contrary directions. To us it means, on the one hand, "sacred," "consecrated," and on the other "uncanny," "dangerous," "forbidden," "unclean." . . . Thus, "taboo" has about it a sense of something unapproachable, and it is principally expressed in prohibitions and restrictions. Our collocation "holy dread" would often coincide in meaning with "taboo." (ibid.:18)

This "holy dread" in reality does not have a religious or moral origin. The interdiction is not enjoined by a divine entity. Rather, the origin of this prohibition remains unknown. It is through this crucial detail that taboos and obsessions are somehow linked:

> The most obvious and striking point of agreement between the obsessional prohibitions of neurotics and taboos is that these prohibitions are equally lacking in motive and equally puzzling in their origin. Having made their appearance at some unspecified moment, they are forcibly maintained by an irresistible fear. No external threat of punishment is required, for there is an internal certainty, a moral conviction, that any violation will lead to intolerable disaster. (ibid.:26)

Freud assumed that the essential issues regarding the link between taboos and obsessive neurosis were the substantial lack of grounds for the prohibitions and the interiorization of the taboo as a necessity. Moreover, there was also the possible contagion of the object of the taboo and the origins of the ceremonies that derived from the prohibitions. Then, Freud presented a long list of examples and specific cases concerning various instances of taboo forms.

The third essay dealt with animism. On this topic the founder of psychoanalysis argued:

> Animism is a system of thought. It does not merely give an explanation of a particular phenomenon, but allows us to grasp the whole universe as a single unity from a single point of view. The human race, if we are to follow the authorities, has in the course of ages developed three such systems of thought—three great pictures of the universe: animistic (or mythological), religious and scientific. (ibid.:77)

From this statement it is clear that Freud also referred to the ideas of Spencer, Wundt, and Tylor, which supported his notion of animism as a psychological theory. As far as the "omnipotence of thoughts" is concerned, Freud wrote:

> At the animistic stage men ascribe omnipotence to themselves. At the religious stage they transfer it to the gods but do not seriously abandon it themselves, for they reserve the power of influencing the gods in a variety of ways according to their wishes. The scientific view of the universe no longer affords any room to human omnipotence; men have acknowledged their smallness and submitted resignedly to death and to the other necessities of nature. (ibid.:88)

Moreover, magic was nothing but a technique of animism. After extensively quoting the "code of totemism in twelve articles" by S. Reinach, published in 1900, Freud paid his homage to Frazer, his inspirer, and then proceeded by commenting on various sociological and psychological theories that discussed whether exogamy preceded totemism or not. He believed that the psychoanalytical experience could solve this question. To this aim he discussed the fears children usually have of animals, the zoophobias. Also in this case the explanations resorted to sexuality and the Oedipal complex, for instance, in the story of young Hans, who "admired his father for possessing a big penis and feared him as threatening his own" (ibid.:130). Thus, by a number of motivated analogies, Freud assimilated the father to the animal. If the totemic animal was the father, then the totemic prohibitions became applicable and made sense—the father must not be killed and it was forbidden to have sexual intercourse with his woman. Oedipus violated the code when he killed his father and married his own mother. Thus, Freud (ibid.) assumed that the totemic system originated and developed from the Oedipal complex.

Subsequently, Freud closely examined the question of the totemic meal, in line with Robertson Smith ([1889] 1956), in order to emphasize the importance of eating and drinking together, especially the ritual of eating the totemic animal. Through this act the participants were linked by a sacred bond, by a "sacred cement," to use an expression of Robertson Smith that Freud reported in italics. Indeed, the sacred rite of the killing and of the collective eating of the totemic animal was a crucial trait of the totemic religion. Under normal circumstances the totemic animal could not be killed (Freud 1953b:XIII). Freud concluded that "the beginnings of religion, morals, society and art converge in the Oedipus complex. This is in complete agreement with the psychoanalytic finding that the same complex constitutes the nucleus of all neuroses, as far as our present knowledge goes" (ibid.:156–57). He also expressed a few doubts and reservations: "I must find room to point out that, though my arguments have led to a high degree of convergence upon a single comprehensive nexus of ideas, this fact cannot blind us to the uncertainties of my premises or the difficulties involved in my conclusion" (ibid.:157).

Freud was convinced that religion was a device to avoid neurosis. Religion would be the projection of the father figure, which was linked to a series of prohibitions. Moreover, religion seemed to provide a childlike feeling of security in the adult age, thus prolonging the length of childhood.

Freud conceived history as a fight between two instincts—the life instinct (*Eros*) and the death instinct (*Thanatos*).

Freud's analysis of *A Demoniac Neurosis of the Seventeenth Century* (Freud 1961a) was carried out from a historical perspective. He examined the documentation regarding an artist who was considered possessed. Freud stressed the strong character of the possessed person and how he resembled his father. At the same time Freud argued that being possessed could also be a device to free oneself from guilt feelings. Then, the demons could be viewed as the repudiated bad desires that originated from repressed drive impulses (ibid.).

RELIGION AS AN ILLUSION

In *The Future of an Illusion* (1961b:vol. XXI), Freud specifically dealt with religion, recognizing its usefulness for many people. However, he agreed that in the future religion would disappear due to the development of a more rational critical consciousness. In this essay Freud chose the form of the dialogue. He envisaged and wrote down the possible objections of his critical readers. On the relationship between civilization and religion, he answered a hypothetical interlocutor in this way: "Religious ideas have arisen from the same need as have all the other achievements of civilization: from the necessity of defending oneself against the crushingly superior force of nature" (ibid.:21).

But what are religious representations?

> Religious ideas are teachings and assertions about facts and conditions of external (or internal) reality which tell one something one has not discovered for oneself and which lay claim to one's belief. Since they give us information about what is most important and interesting to us in life, they are particularly highly prized. (ibid.:25)

However, religious doctrines appear to be illusions. Moreover,

> It is doubtful whether men were in general happier at a time when religious doctrines held unrestricted sway; more moral they certainly were not. They have always known how to externalize the precepts of religion and thus to nullify their intentions. The priests, whose duty it was to ensure obedience to religion, met them halfway in this. God's kindness must lay a restraining hand on His justice. One sinned, and then one made a sacrifice or did penance and then one was free to sin once more. (ibid.:37)

In his conclusion, Freud favored science, which was not at all an illusion. On the contrary, the alternative hypothesis to science was illusions in the full sense, since they pretended to offer what the scientific approach could not possibly provide.

In *A Religious Experience* Freud (1961c:vol. XXI) briefly examined a case of conversion from atheism to religious belief. It is the story of a North American physician who became a believer after seeing the face of a dead woman. Being himself a nonbeliever, Freud showed a certain amount of skepticism about this story. In the interpretation of this case Freud resorted once again to the Oedipus complex. The face of the dead woman reminded the doctor of his own mother and thus the Oedipal rivalry with his father. There was, moreover, a similarity between the paternal figure and God. At first, hate toward the father prevailed; this was the nonbelief phase. Later on, however,

> the conflict seems to have been unfolded in the form of a hallucinatory psychosis: inner voices were heard which uttered warnings against resistance to God. But the outcome of the struggle was displayed once again in the sphere of religion and it was of a kind predetermined by the fate of the Oedipus complex: complete submission to the will of God the Father. The young man became a believer and accepted everything he had been taught since his childhood about God and Jesus Christ. He had had a religious experience and had undergone a conversion. (ibid.:171)

Freud formulated this analytical hypothesis. It is clear, however, that a more in-depth discussion of this case would have required direct knowledge of many more details and especially of the person himself. In fact, a conversion does not result from simply seeing a face. The mechanisms involved in a case of conversion are usually much more articulated and difficult to work out.

The three essays forming the book on *Moses and Monotheism* (Freud 1964:vol. XXIII) deserve much more space than can be given in the present volume. Freud's stated intention was to write a "historical novel" about Moses. Especially in the first part of the book, Freud maintained a novelistic style, while the third part was rather long and teeming with reflections. In all three essays the Jewish and religious questions were growing even more intertwined. Moses' multifaceted character lent itself easily to the examination of various questions such as the cult of divinity, the meaning of the exile in Egypt, moral involvement, and the historical truth of religion. This last issue allowed Freud to reevaluate the religious experience.

The first essay dealt with "Moses as an Egyptian"; the second one dealt with the question of whether Moses was Egyptian; the third and last essay discussed "Moses, his people and the Monotheistic religion." The Egyptian Moses was a follower of the monotheistic religion to which he converted the Jewish people, who then decided to kill him. However, Jews later rehabilitated the figure of Moses through the so-called "return of the repressed." In fact, through doctrines and rites the past was reproduced. It is a device to avoid oblivion. Finally, Freud also discussed the Christian religion, which according to Freud derived from Saint Paul. Freud viewed it as a natural development of the Jewish religion.

5

Religion in William James's (1842–1910)
Psychosocial Perspective

PRAGMATISM AND RELIGION

William James offered a crucial contribution to the empirical analysis of the religious phenomenon. James's interests embraced many different fields. He was a pragmatist (James [1902] 1961) and was influenced greatly by the philosopher and logician Charles Sanders Peirce (1839–1914). James focussed his attention mainly on the outcomes and the effects of ideas more than on the ideas themselves. Being a radical empiricist, James attacked body-soul dualism. He first dealt with general studies concerning psychology (James [1890] 1912), then moved on to research on the psychology of religion with an empirical outlook (James [1902] 1961). His father was a Protestant theologian, while his brother was the novelist Henry James. With such a stimulating background, William James had many different experiences. He led an expedition to Brazil in 1865–66; he became an instructor of anatomy; later he taught psychology, physiology, and then philosophy.

Notwithstanding the angina pectoris that progressively wore him out, James was an indefatigable scholar and plunged himself into studies and research on the relationships between science and faith, on belief, and on the "specious present," which contained in itself both the future and the past. According to his theory, emotions derived from physical, bodily sensations. Thus, the whole emotional process originates from sensorial impressions that at first produce changes in bodily activity and later provoke the emotions. This theory, which was reintroduced by the Danish physicist Carl George Lange (1834–1900) as far as changes in the circulatory systems are concerned, is known as the James-Lange theory of emotions. Moreover, James viewed religious belief as a path that went beyond simple evidence, as a genuine and strong will to believe so that even an indecisive stance as far as believing was concerned revealed a negative attitude toward belief itself.

James was grateful to Peirce because he

> rendered thought a service by disentangling it from the particulars of its
> application to the principle. . . . He calls it the principle of *pragmatism*, and he
> defends it somewhat as follows: "Thought in movement has for its only con-
> ceivable motive the attainment of belief, or thought at rest. Only when our
> thought about a subject has found its rest in belief can our action on the sub-
> ject firmly and safely begin. Beliefs, in short, are rules for action; and the
> whole function of thinking is but one step in the production of active habits."
> (James [1902] 1961:347)

By assuming Peirce's point of view it is possible to overcome the meta-
physical-deductive approach and to reach a more dialectical and less
"theological" reflection. It is possible then to imagine a "critical science of
religions" that "would depend for its original material on facts of personal
experience, and would have to square itself with personal experience
through all its critical reconstruction. It could never get away from concrete life, or work in a conceptual vacuum" (ibid.:356).

Indeed James based his approach more on empirical data than on philosophical considerations. He utilized a large number of examples by referring to concrete experience; he criticized religion but agreed with its
essential dictates. He was an incredibly learned man, but instead of dogmas and theories he preferred to study "mental states" through which he
was able to grasp the functional powers of religion, by working essentially
on the individual.

James was attracted by the varieties of religious forms, which included
both mystic figures and simple believers at the same time. He held to a pluralistic rather than a monistic approach. In fact, the reality of religious life
did not seem homologous to him. On the contrary, it is rich with meanings
and ideas, whose worth is given both by theoretical and concrete support.

James's classical study on religious experience (ibid.) was defined in
1961 by H. Richard Niebuhr as a milestone of religious thought. Indeed, it
is a text teeming with original and fruitful ideas. First of all, the fundamental distinction between "institutional religion" and "personal religion" must be stressed.

> At the outset we are struck by one great partition which divides the religious
> field. On the one side of it lies institutional, on the other personal religion. As
> M. P. Sabatier says, one branch of religion keeps the divinity, another keeps
> man mostly in view. Worship and sacrifice, procedures for working on the
> dispositions of the deity, theology and ceremony and ecclesiastical organi-
> zation, are the essentials of religion in the institutional branch. Were we to
> limit our view of it, we should have to define religion as an external art, the
> art of winning the favor of the gods. In the more personal branch of religion
> it is on the contrary the inner disposition of man himself, which form[s] the

center of interest, his conscience, his desert, his helplessness, his incompleteness. And although the favor of the gods, as forfeited or gained, is still an essential feature of the story, and theology plays a vital part therein, yet the acts to which this sort of religion prompts are personal not ritual acts, the individual transacts the business by himself alone, and the ecclesiastical organization, with its priests and sacraments and other go-betweens, sinks to an altogether secondary place. The relation goes direct from heart to heart, from soul to soul, between man and his maker. (James [1902] 1961:41)

James obviously strongly preferred the analysis of personal religion. This brought him close to the position of a well-known and criticized scholar, an expert in the life of Saint Francis of Assisi, the theologian and historian Paul Sabatier (1858–1928). Hence, James went beyond the typically institutional scope in order to highlight "the field of pure and simple personal religion."

The discussion at this point became rather lively:

In one sense at least the personal religion will prove itself more fundamental than either theology or ecclesiasticism. Churches, when once established, live at second-hand upon tradition; but the founders of every church owed their power originally to the fact of their direct personal communion with the divine. Not only the superhuman founders, Christ, Buddha and Mahomet, but all the originators of Christian sects have been in this case;— so personal religion should still seem the primordial thing, even to those who continue to esteem it incomplete. (James [1902] 1961:42)

Later, the topic is summed up in this fashion:

In critically judging of the value of religious phenomena, it is very important to insist on the distinction between religion as an individual personal function, and religion as an institutional, corporate, or tribal product. . . . The word "religion," as ordinarily used, is equivocal. A survey of history shows us that, as a rule, religious geniuses attract disciples, and produce groups of sympathizers. When these groups get strong enough to "organize" themselves, they become ecclesiastical institutions with corporate ambitions of their own. The spirit of politics and the lust of dogmatic rule are then apt to enter and to contaminate the originally innocent thing; so that when we hear the word "religion" nowadays, we think inevitably of some "church" or other; and to some persons the word "church" suggests so much hypocrisy and tyranny and meanness and tenacity of superstition that in a wholesale undiscerning way they glory in saying that they are "down" on religion altogether. Even we who belong to churches do not exempt other churches than our own from the general condemnation. (ibid.:267)

As I have stated earlier, James's main interest was not institutional religion:

The religious experience which we are studying is that which lives itself out within the private breast. First-hand individual experience of this kind has always appeared as a heretical sort of innovation to those who witnessed its birth. Naked it comes into the world and lonely; and it has always, for a time at least, driven him who had it into the wilderness, often into the literal wilderness out of doors, where Buddha, Jesus, Mohammed, St. Francis, George Fox, and so many others had to go. (ibid.:267)

RELIGION AS PERSONAL EXPERIENCE

The personal dimension is in any case prevalent; it cannot be disregarded. In fact, James defined religion as *"the feelings, acts, and experiences of individual men in their solitude, so far as they apprehend themselves to stand in relation to whatever they may consider the divine"* (ibid.:42; emphasis in the original). On the other hand, he was convinced that personal religious experience was rooted in the mystical states of consciousness (ibid.:299).

To the objection regarding the existence of other prereligious forms, James confirmed the preeminence of personal religion:

> There are, it is true, other things in religion chronologically more primordial than personal devoutness in the moral sense. . . . But, quite apart from the fact that many anthropologists—for instance, Jevons and Frazer—expressly oppose "religion" and "magic" to each other, it is certain that the whole system of thought which leads to magic, fetishism, and the lower superstitions may just as well be called primitive science as called primitive religion. The question thus becomes a verbal one again; and our knowledge of all these early stages of thought and feeling is in any case so conjectural and imperfect that farther discussion would not be worth the while. (ibid.:42)

The question of primitive religion was treated here in a rather perfunctory manner.

The discussion on the relationship between religion and neuropathology—an interesting field also for Freud—appears less superficial. James recognized that the origin of a few religious experiences could lie in pathological situations. However, he denied the sexual origin of religion and in particular the reinterpretation of religion as a sexual perversion (ibid.). James instead recognized that melancholy, happiness, and also ecstasy could hold an important role in the development of religious belief (ibid.). However, he criticized a few excessive stances:

> First of all let us take Devoutness. When unbalanced, one of its vices is called Fanaticism. Fanaticism (when not a mere expression of ecclesiastical ambition) is only loyalty carried to a convulsive extreme. When an intensely loyal and narrow mind is once grasped by the feeling that a certain superhuman

person is worthy of its exclusive devotion, one of the first things that happens is that it idealizes the devotion itself. (ibid.:271)

Then James dealt with the notions of sacrifice, confession and prayer. On the latter he was especially acute and precise. He thought that prayer was "every kind of inward communion or conversion with the power recognized as divine. . . . Prayer in this wider sense is the very soul and essence of religion" (ibid.:361).

James derived from Starbuck (1899) the importance of empirical data concerning the growth of the religious consciousness and conversion during adolescence. James valued Starbuck's (1866–1947) use of the questionnaire. However, in his own research James preferred to resort to biographical and autobiographical data, which he called the "human document," because it offered many illuminating instances on the meaning of existence.

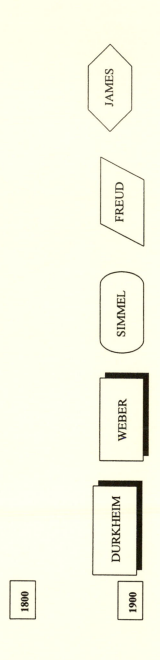

Synoptic Table 2:   From Durkheim to James

PART III

———◦•◦———

The Contemporaries

1

Religion as Universal

LÉVY-BRUHL (1857–1939): SUPERNATURAL FOR PRIMITIVE PEOPLES

Lucien Lévy-Bruhl was an atypical expert in the realm of the social sciences. He was a philosopher like Comte and shared with him the same interests in ethics. This interest brought him close also to Durkheim. A scholar of Jewish origin, Lévy-Bruhl could be defined a philosopher as well as an anthropologist. He undertook various interdisciplinary experiences and participated in the first debates about the issues of the individual and society. He supported Durkheim's positions regarding the central role of collective representations, which were also present in many primitive peoples' mentality.

Lévy-Bruhl, however, advised us against possible misunderstanding concerning his expression "collective representations." It should not be interpreted, as it would be today, as a cognitive fact (an idea, an image, or a concept of an object). Rather, it is a more complex phenomenon, characterized by emotional elements, which involve a completely different attitude toward reality. Such collective representations are, for example, the beliefs in spirits present in the natural environment, myths, rites, and magic practices. However, instead of meeting the intellectual need to learn and explain the various phenomena, collective representations express collective emotional expectations (cf. the introduction to Lévy-Bruhl 1973:10–11). Emotions, then, acquire a scientific relevance.

Lévy-Bruhl lived till almost the beginning of the Second World War. He published a long series of works concerning primitive tribes, their mentality, their notions of nature and supernatural, and their mythology, following a mystical conception of existence (Lévy-Bruhl 1938). He could well be defined as an anthropologist who was also interested in sociological issues. He chose not to carry out fieldwork, but he worked mainly through secondary sources—other scholars' researches, and ethnologists' and missionaries' reports. Moreover, he traveled a great deal and continuously compared the data he gathered.

Carlo Prandi (1989:7) has provided a good background interpretation of the anthropologist:

> Lévy-Bruhl's clearly oriented vocation underwent a progressive radical change. This change led him from the study of theoretical thought, typical of Western philosophical tradition, to the study of instinctive thought of the cultural tradition pertaining to those peoples that, because of their non-literate tradition, are improperly called "primitives."

Lucien Lévy-Bruhl ([1931] 1935, 1973) wrote a number of studies on primitive populations. He was well-known for his book *Le surnaturel et la nature dans la mentalité primitive,* published in 1931, which emphasized the mystic, prelogical, and intuitive character of primitive thought. Thus we can see continuity between the visible and the invisible, between sensible reality and the other world. Hence, it appeared logical for primitive populations to search in the over-sensible world the explanations for the phenomena that occurred in the sensible one. Sorokin (1957), however, objected to this idea by stating that primitive mentality was able to attribute to sensible reality the possibility of providing explanations through acquired experience. This would be done by finding a connection among phenomena and by searching each time for characteristics and potentialities of the factors in action.

According to Lévy-Bruhl, myth and rite were two elements that strengthened each other. In fact, myth could explain ritual; the rite, in turn, legitimated the myth. Moreover, the latter was an atemporal aspect that is part of the rite, that is, the cult, in which the meeting between the origin of time and its end occurred.

A few reflections by Lévy-Bruhl around the mystic virtues of blood were original and interesting:

> We regard it—blood—as a liquid that circulates in the arteries and veins in accordance with the impulse given to it by the heart. That it coagulates and forms clots when it leaves the body is well-known to us but this property is not an important part of our current ideas about blood; as a rule, it scarcely occurs to us; while to the primitives, who know nothing about the functioning of the heart, or the circulation, the coagulation of the blood, its drying, and forming clots are an essential characteristic of blood. They vaguely imagine it as existing thus inside the body, and it is its liquid aspect that to them seems to be momentary and of secondary importance.

Various ritual modalities enacted by the primitives originated from this different perspective:

> Accordingly, when natives who are going to take part in a ceremony smear their bodies with red ochre, it is not a costume they are donning in which to

play their role. They actually believe that they are rubbing their bodies with blood, and just as sick people, by rubbing red ochre all over them, believe that they are renewing their vital powers, the actors in the ceremony feel that the ochre is endowing them with the same mystic virtue as blood would do. (Lévy-Bruhl [1931] 1935:268–69)

EDWARD EVANS-PRITCHARD (1902–1973)

Edward Evans-Pritchard is another scholar who, like Lévy-Bruhl, worked a great deal on the origins of primitive religion. He was professor of social anthropology at Oxford University. He was the author of *Theories of Primitive Religion* (Evans-Pritchard 1965), in which he devoted an entire section to Lévy-Bruhl, whom he compared to Pareto, when the latter was dealing with nonlogical actions. Evans- Pritchard argued that Lévy-Bruhl

always refused to identify himself with the Durkheimian group; so it is only in a formal sense that he can be called . . . one of Durkheim's collaborators. He remained more of the philosopher pure and simple; hence his interest in primitive systems of thought rather than in primitive institutions. He held that one might legitimately begin a study of social life by analysing ways of thought as well as behaviour. Perhaps one should say that he studied them primarily as a logician, for the question of logic is a crucial one in his books, as indeed in a study of systems of thought it should be. (ibid.:78–79)

Evans-Pritchard wrote further clarifying reflections on Lévy-Bruhl, who "was one of the first, if not the first, to emphasize that primitive ideas, which seem so strange to us, and indeed sometimes idiotic, when considered as isolated facts, are meaningful when seen as parts of patterns of ideas and behaviour, each part having an intelligible relationship to the others" (ibid.:86). This relationship is then of basic importance.

Evans-Pritchard was opposed to an evolutionist vision of reality; he was closer to Radcliffe-Brown than to Malinowski. Moreover, he strongly believed in the necessity of carrying out empirical research to exploit the direct experience of fieldwork.

Another crucial question was the importance Evans-Pritchard placed on the use of the historical perspective. Anthropology could not possibly exist without history (Evans-Pritchard 1965:14). The decisive issue of Evans-Pritchard's perspective was the problem of the "effects" of religion on the individual and social life. He proposed a "relational" theory by which religion must be studied and understood through its effects, that is, in relation with the other aspects of life and culture. Perhaps this position was an effect or a development of Malinowski's functionalism. One can, however, disagree with Evans-Pritchard's claim that one must be a believer in order to understand religion, and indeed Evans-Pritchard has been attacked on this point.

Evans-Pritchard's (1956) attempt to assimilate the religion of the Nuer, a population of Nilotic origin, to Judaism, because of its monotheistic character, is a rather weak one. Indeed, it is true that in the Nuer religion there is a god, called *kwoth*, and some other gods, called *kuth*, which means spirits. In Hebrew *ruah* signifies a strong "breath" of extraordinary nature. Evans-Pritchard's research on the idea of a similarity between the two religions started from this element.

However, the essential point remains stable and is of a different nature: "Science deals with relations, not with origins and essences. In so far as it can be said that the facts of primitive religions can be sociologically explained at all, it must be in relation to other facts, both those with which it forms a system of ideas and practices and other social phenomena associated with it" (Evans-Pritchard 1965:111).

PHENOMENOLOGICAL ANALYSIS BY
VAN DER LEEUW (1890–1950)

The Dutch theologian and historian Gerardus van der Leeuw ([1933] 1986) was influenced by Husserl and Dilthey, above all in his ideas on religion. He developed, however, a personal and autonomous scientific point of view. He appeared to be mainly concerned about what religion manifests of itself, religion conceived as a phenomenological occurrence, an object in relation to a subject that acknowledges it. Phenomenology is usually understood as the approach to an object on the part of a subject.

Giovanni Filoramo formulated a good synthesis of the three phases of van der Leeuw's methodology:

1. The lived experience, or *Erlebnis*, of the religious phenomenon taken into consideration; 2. The understanding, or *Verstehen*, of the religious phenomenon; 3. The evidence, or *Bezeugung*. Points 1. and 2. are the inclusion within the phenomenological paradigm of two fundamental aspects of the Diltheyan hermeneutics of understanding. (Filoramo 1984:38–39)

The first thing that a researcher of religious phenomena must do is to feel empathy (*Einfühlung*) for the object in question. This is a crucial and inescapable aspect for defining the researched object itself. And it is the only way to resuscitate the object amidst the chaotic mass of data. Thus— as Filoramo explained—the object transfers itself into the subject according to the same etymology of the *Verstehen*. All of this aimed at reexperimenting and reliving (*Er-leben*) the object, according to the consti-

tutive modalities of Dilthey's description of *Erlebnis*. This second fundamental moment involved, according to van der Leeuw, two logically distinct operations, which were, however, complementary aspects of a
process. The first operation was a static-phenomenological understanding
of the object; it aimed at defining the object as it was but according its separate elements. The second operation was of a genetic-structural kind; it
established the structural connections between these elements, which
were known, experienced, and lived as living wholes. From this phenomenology of the *"Verstehende Religion,"* or "comprehending religion" (Filoramo 1985:280–83) there is the passage to a theological outcome that unites
understanding and evidence, casting full light on van der Leeuw's personal option for Christianity. This choice can be found both in his work
and his status as a minister. Thus, the possibility of a value-free phenomenology of religion was fading.

More attentive to the developments of German sociological thought
than other scholars, van der Leeuw resumed and elaborated Weber's concept of ideal-type. He linked this concept to that of structure in order to
grasp the "essence of religion." In effect, van der Leeuw considered the
"structure" or "level" of what could be found in reality and that was
described by phenomenology in a static form. The structure had a unitary
character, which could not be subdivided into different parts, since the
structure, as van der Leeuw wrote, was an organic whole that cannot be
divided but should be understood through its parts. It was a texture of different elements that could not be added together nor subtracted, but taken
as a whole was to be understood as such. In other words, the structure was
experienced but not immediately; it was built but not abstracted from
causal logic. The structure was reality organized according to a meaning
(van der Leeuw [1933] 1986).

Also, van der Leeuw's examination of rite and myth was included in a
traditional research trend that, as we have seen already, attracted many
different scholars. Through the study of sacred phenomena, van der
Leeuw stressed the exceptionality of the power connected to the religious
experience. He talked about a science of religions in dealing with human
behavior in relation to that power. Unlike William James, he did not separate the institutional level from the personal one; in this regard he maintained that everything was personal but nothing was only personal. Then,
too, he had an eschatological outlook of reality: his thought was concerned
about the "extreme things," the last meaning of the religious experience.

Unlike most preceding scholars' aims, van der Leeuw gave up the idea
of searching for the original religion. He limited himself to examining concrete situations, definite historical religions, and organized denominations. He attempted to see what a religion showed of itself. Indeed, at the
personal level religion acquired different modalities for each subject

considered. This held true also for van der Leeuw himself; he recognized a strictly personal religion that differed from the religious forms belonging to a concrete, historical religion. At this point, the need emerged to resort to ideal-types in order to analyze the different organized religious expressions, and hence the necessity to study the general and specific forms of religion, from Christianity to Buddhism. The historical datum and phenomenological understanding were thus linked. However, in order to study the content of a particular religious faith, van der Leeuw chose not to use the phenomenological approach. He decided, instead, to see the relationship that the human subject established with the content of a religious faith and what he had to say about it. In this way, phenomenology gathered the power that the individual needed to give sense to his existence and to worship a superior being. The presence of such a superior power provided a meaning to life, and life itself was organized around it. This meaning, in turn, had a preeminent place in the construction of the existential path. Above all, salvation helped to guide life to a special direction. Religion itself aimed at making sense of the difficulties of both the past and present life. In the end, according to van der Leeuw, every religion strove for redemption conceived as an improvement, a liberation and a re-creation that derived, however, from something else, which was placed somewhere else.

2

The Macrosociological Approach

TALCOTT PARSONS (1902–1979): RELIGION AS AN INTEGRATED WHOLE

According to Parsons (1972b), who shared Durkheim's perspective (Parsons 1978), religion is a more or less integrated whole of beliefs about sacred or supernatural entities, which are extraordinary and thus can be manipulated. Beliefs are mutually related to the practices and the institutions that develop in each society. Life itself finds its meaning within such beliefs, which allow us to face existential problems. Unpredictable and uncontrollable events stimulate the need for a religious faith. This need usually becomes evident when an individual has to face exceptional works or engagements in order to reach an established objective. Religion is thus used as a device to relieve the frustration and to comfort the dissatisfied individual who is not able to realize his aspirations.

It should be made clear, however, that for Parsons the division of labor within complex societies attributes a well-defined role to each function. Hence, the religious dimension does not significantly influence the other social spheres and variables. The single subjects influence the context in which they live through their values and religious beliefs.

Talcott Parsons did not publish any book on the specific themes dealing with the sociology of religion. However, from time to time he made comments on this subject with regard to some important themes. First of all, Parsons dissociated himself from Sorokin and his ideational pattern by stating that the worldly dimension of religiosity should direct reality in the name of religious values. The institutionalization of religion aimed at the realization of asserted values would derive from this.

Also, according to Parsons, the internal side of religion is different from its external aspect. Thus religion carries out various functions that allow for the integration of society, strengthening solidarity, and maintaining a close tie between religion itself and the social structure to which it refers. Durkheim (Parsons 1978) and Malinowski had already stressed these functions of religion (Parsons studied with Malinowski at the London School of Economics). Thus, this was the structural-functional framework as applied to religious data. This also confirmed Weber's hypothesis concerning the relationship between the religious perspective pertaining to a specific culture and the existence of norms and aims linked to that religion and also present in the social world.

The critical exchange between Parsons and Sorokin occupied a central place in the development of the sociology of religion, even though today many contemporary scholars do not recognize the importance of this scientific discussion between the two scholars. Parsons dedicated a long part of an essay (Parsons 1963; Zadra 1969) to the differences between his vision of reality and Sorokin's. He considered his essay a homage to Sorokin and viewed him as an author who belonged to the Western tradition of sociological thought (Zadra 1969:301).

Parsons emphasized the progressive functional differentiation of society and thus of religiosity. The latter, however, remained an active element of society both in the case of its being a hegemonic perspective of a transcendental kind, and in the case of a religion that aimed at dominating the world in the name of religious values. For Parsons Christianity had a strong intraworldly character, whereas Sorokin viewed Christianity in an extraworldly position.

The following quotation makes this even more explicit:

> I think of religion as an aspect of human action. Like all other aspects, in the course of social, cultural, and personality development it undergoes processes of differentiation in a double sense. The first of these concerns differentiation within religious systems themselves, the second the differentiation of the religious element from non-religious elements in the more general system of action. In the latter context the general developmental trend may be said to be from fusion of religious and non-religious components in the same action structure, to increasingly clear differentiation between multiple spheres of action. (Parsons 1963:37)

Moreover, for Parsons differentiation implies the homogeneous definition of a particular historical phase. In fact, even if there were the same dominant basic perspective, there could exist dissimilar and heterogeneous parts. The "degree of religiosity" did not stay the same forever, but underwent continuous variations in line with the progressive differentiation of society. Hence, "the degree of religiousness of Christian society clearly suffered a progressive decline by the mere fact that the society had become functionally a more highly differentiated system of action than was the early 'primitive' church" (ibid.:39).

Parsons then provided the reader with a historical instance of differentiation:

The conception of the church, which implied the fundamental break with the Jewish law which Paul made final, constituted the *differentiation* of Christianity as a religious system (a cultural system) from a conception of a "people" as a social system. Given the Roman ascendancy in the secular society of the time, this differentiation was expressed in the famous formula "Render unto Caesar the things that are Caesar's"—i.e., the church did not claim jurisdiction over secular society as such. At the same time this church was a solidary collectivity. The keynote here was the conception of "brothers of Christ." (ibid.:40)

Talcott Parsons did not fail to emphasize that the church itself was, from the beginning, a peculiar social organization: "It had in its own social structure institutionalized a set of values" (ibid.:48), giving support to the lay world through the work and teachings of the clergy. Moreover, there was an internal differentiation in the church between a sacramental system and an administrative one. At the same time the differentiation from the secular society took place. A further instance of differentiation was given by the "religious 'enfranchisement' of the individual" (ibid.:50). All these differentiations occurred throughout a long time span that started with the primitive Christian church and went through the medieval church up to the Protestant Reformation. Parsons dwelt more on the latter, inspired by Weber's thought. Later he opposed Troeltsch's ideas, who saw in Catholicism, Lutheranism, and Calvinism many "authentic versions of the conception of a Christian society in Western history" (ibid.:60). In fact, Parsons believed that there was a substantial continuity in the North American "denominational pluralism" in consonance with the institutionalization of Christianity and with the Protestant Reformation.

In agreement, but also in disagreement with Weber and Troeltsch, the avatar of the structural-functionalist current in sociology saw the "denomination" as a third possibility with respect to the traditional church-sect dichotomy. In fact, the denomination

shares with the church type the *differentiation* between religious and secular spheres of interest. . . . On the other hand, the denomination shares with the sect type its character as a voluntary association where the individual member is bound only by a responsible personal commitment, not by *any* factor of ascription. . . . The denomination can thus accept secular society as a legitimate field of action for the Christian individual in which he acts on his own responsibility without organizational control by religious authority. But precisely because he is a Christian, he will not simply accept everything he finds there; he will attempt to shape the situation in the direction of better conformity with Christian values. (ibid.:61)

The denominational phase was the fourth stage, which came after the primitive church, the medieval church, and, successively, the Protestant

Reformation. The denomination was a voluntary association with a plurality of affiliation models. Its pluralistic character, which was typically North American, was based on tolerance and freedom.

PITIRIM SOROKIN (1889–1968): ASCETICISM AND ACTIVISM

Parsons outlined Sorokin's threefold model on cultural orientation:

> The ideational is one which gives unquestioned primacy to transcendental and other-worldly interests in the religious sense. Reality itself is defined as ultimately beyond the reach of the senses, as transcendental. The goal of life must be to reach the closest possible accord with the nature of transcendent reality, and the path to this must involve renunciation of all worldly interests. Broadly speaking, other worldly asceticism and mysticism are the paths to it. . . . The opposite extreme to the ideational pattern is the sensate. Here the empirical, in the last analysis the "material," aspect of reality is taken as ultimately real or predominant. In practical conduct the implication of a sensate view of the world is to make the most of the opportunities of the here and now, to be concerned with world success, power, and—in the last analysis—to put hedonistic gratifications first of all. The idealistic pattern is conceived as intermediate between the two, not in the sense of a simple "compromise," but rather of a synthesis which can achieve a harmonious balance between the two principal components. This basic classification is then used as the framework for outlining a developmental pattern leading, in the history of civilization, from ideational to idealistic predominance and in turn from idealistic to sensate. (Parsons 1963:34–35)

Within ideational culture there emerged the "active ideational culture mentality" that derived from the "ideational asceticism." Indeed:

> As soon as the Ascetic initiators attract the attention of other men, they begin to acquire followers. As the number of followers increases, an organization appears; and with it the pure Ascetic attitude—the attitude of complete indifference toward, and non-interference in, the affairs of the empirical world—becomes impossible. An "organization" or an "institution" is a phenomenon of this world. It requires management, direction, guidance, and the administration of many needs and relationships which are purely empirical. Thus, any Ascetic current, as soon as it grows in influence, becomes an organization; as soon as it becomes an organization, it necessarily becomes more and more Active Ideational; and the more Active, the more rapidly it grows. Such is the inevitable chain of transformation. (Sorokin 1957:46)

A typical example of this, among others, was Francis of Assisi. As soon as he attracted quite a number of followers, he found himself in the middle of an organized formation, full of worldly concrete problems. Hence, asceticism began to lose its original purity and started to mingle with the things of the world. Activism thus began to prevail.

According to Sorokin, the passage from asceticism to activism marked a loss of strength on the part of religion, which found itself compelled to maintain its principles even by resorting to constrained forms. Hence it suffered a certain decline leading to the sensate model: "until they become demoralized and lose their vigor and spirituality, and fall into the snares of the Sensate mentality" (ibid.:47).

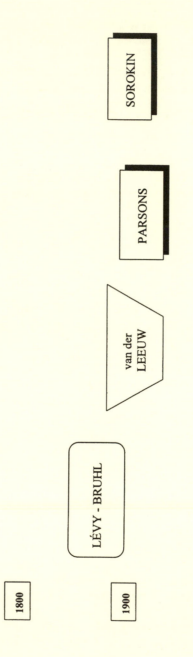

Synoptic Table 3:   From Lévy-Bruhl to Sorokin

3

The Historical-Cultural Dynamics

CHURCH AND SECT IN THE ANALYSIS OF
ERNST TROELTSCH (1865–1923)

Lutheran theologian and sociologist Ernst Troeltsch, who had been influenced by Dilthey (1833–1911), developed a typology of church and sects (Troeltsch [1912] 1976). In his opinion, one usually belongs to a church because of birth. Moreover, individuals belonging to a church are not compelled to follow rigid norms. But, one decides to join a sect—a concept used by Weber also—on the basis of a personal choice. Differently from the church, the behavior of individual members is controlled in a much more rigid fashion. Troeltsch saw in mysticism, or in spiritual religion, another category that was close to church and sect.

A church is usually conservative and adapts itself to worldly demands by aiming at mass support rather than at an elitist kind of loyalty. On the contrary, the sect is characterized by a more rigorous stance in that its members show a stronger and more direct commitment. Generally speaking, the sect is characterized by a certain amount of isolation from society. Society itself is an object of hostility. Whoever does not belong to the sect is discriminated against in varying degrees. While the church searches for society support, the sect moves away from society with the aim of protecting those members who do not have much power in society itself. Since a sect is less institutionalized than a church, it has a tendency to be less formal. It is a more spontaneous community organization.

Troeltsch's third category, mystic, spiritual religion, has a more individual character and consequently the interaction among its members is generally not emphasized. Moreover, it is indifferent to some of the typical elements of the church such as sacraments, dogmas, moral principles, and the organizational dimension. In addition, differently from the church, mysticism does not aim at transforming the world.

It should be mentioned at this point that it was not easy to discover pure kinds of church and sect at the empirical level. In fact, in many instances

123

the traits of the church and the sect tended to overlap making it difficult to discern the two. There existed, then, the risk of defining a church or a sect by means of a subjective interpretation of social reality.

Some scholars (Becker 1932) have incorporated Troeltsch's category of mysticism into the concept of cult because of the loose and weak bonds existing among its members, and because of the low level of institutionalization and rather tolerant religiosity that characterize cults.

However, Troeltsch's definitions undoubtedly revolved mainly around the dichotomy between church and sect. This led to a debate among scholars on whether it was Weber who had influenced Troeltsch on this matter. Alfred Dumais (1997), for instance, supported the opposite thesis, according to which Troeltsch had influenced Weber.

It is useful at this point to read Troeltsch's text directly in order to show the content of what differentiates the two categories of church and sect, which correspond, in many aspects, to those described by Weber. Also, the date of publication of the works of both authors was not of great help in determining who influenced whom. Troeltsch published his book in 1912. Weber, however, conceived a systematic work on religions many years before; in 1906 he published the definitions of "churches" and "sects" in *Christliche Welt* and *Frankfurter Zeitung* (Weber 1906). As already mentioned in this volume, Weber argued that the sect called for a more rigorous morality, securing for its members a strong sense of belonging of an almost elitist kind, like a "conventicle" (Weber 1962b:320).

As far as Troeltsch was concerned,

> At the outset the actual differences are quite clear. The Church is that type of organization which is overwhelmingly conservative, and which to a certain extent accepts the secular order, and dominates the masses; in principle, therefore, it is universal, i.e., it desires to cover the whole life of humanity. The sects, on the other hand, are comparatively small groups; they aspire towards inner personal perfection, and they aim at a direct personal fellowship among the members of each group. From the very beginning, therefore, they are forced to organize themselves in small groups, and to renounce the idea of dominating the world. Their attitude towards the world, the State, and Society may be indifferent, tolerant, or hostile, since they have no desire to control and incorporate these forms of social life; on the contrary, they tend to avoid them; their aim is usually either to tolerate their presence alongside of their own body, or even to replace these social institutions by their own society. (Troeltsch [1912] 1976:331)

From this general picture a set of outcomes may be derived:

> The Church is forced to dominate Society, compelling all the members of Society to come under its sphere and influence; but, on the other hand, her stability is entirely unaffected by the fact of the extent to which her influence

over all individuals is actually attained. The Church is the great educator of the nations, and like all educators she knows how to allow for various degrees of capacity and maturity, and how to attain her end only by a process of adaptation and compromise. Compared with this institutional principle of an objective organism, however, the sect is a voluntary community whose members join it of their own free will. The very life of the sect, therefore, depends on actual personal service and co-operation; as an independent member each individual has his part within the fellowship; the bond of union has not been indirectly imparted through the common possession of Divine grace, but it is directly realized in the personal relationships of life. (ibid.:338–39)

Like Weber, Troeltsch looked beyond Christianity and the so-called world religions, thus contributing to the social science of religion with a more open, pluralistic approach (Gisel 1992).

RUDOLF OTTO (1869–1937): THE SACRED BETWEEN IRRATIONALITY AND RATIONALITY

The German theologian, philosopher, and historian Rudolf Otto investigated the question of the sacred in a more systematic way than other authors. His most important text, *The Idea of the Holy* (Otto [1917] 1958), is viewed as a masterpiece by scholars interested in religion. It appeared just after the publication of the major classics of sociology of religion, and acknowledged the influence that Schleiermacher and other German scholars had on Otto. Apart from Schleiermacher, Otto was also influenced by William James.

It was Otto's conviction that religion sprang from the confluence of rational and irrational forces, which allowed the sacred to be isolated as a separate category, a mysterious, fascinating, and "wholly other" element. Otto thought that only someone endowed with religious sensitivity could grasp the notion of sacred; this would leave out those people who had never had a "religious emotion." At this point once again the question emerged about who could carry out an analysis of religious facts. In Chapter 3 of his book, Otto went so far as to warn his readers that "whoever cannot do this, whoever knows no such moments in his experience, is requested to read no further" (ibid.:8).

Otto began by saying:

It is essential to every theistic conception of God, and most of all to the Christian, that it designates and precisely characterizes deity by the attributes spirit, reason, purpose, good will, supreme power, unity, selfhood. The nature of God is thus thought of by analogy with our human nature of reason and personality; only, whereas in ourselves we are aware of this as qualified by restriction and limitation, as applied to God the attributes we use are "completed," i.e., thought as absolute and unqualified. Now all these attributes constitute clear and definite *concepts*: they can be grasped by the intellect; they can be analyzed by thought; they even admit of definition. An object that can thus be thought conceptually may be termed *rational*. The nature of deity described in the attributes above mentioned is, then, a rational nature; and a religion which recognizes and maintains such a view of God is in so far a "rational" religion. (ibid.:1)

Rationality became the criterion by which to recognize a religious dimension constructed for people. The divine was perfection, which was present within man, but in an imperfect form. A religion could be considered rational that allows us to imagine the divine on the same wavelength of definite human characteristics, intensified to the maximum level in divinity.

This first level of rationality was neither the only way nor was it sufficient to define the divine. The divine must have also traits of nonrationality not comparable to that of humans, for otherwise its superiority would be erased. In this regard, Otto was rather clear when he stated:

In all these cases the "rational" element occupies the foreground, and often nothing else seems to be present at all. . . . For so far are these "rational" attributes from exhausting the idea of deity, that they in fact imply a non-rational or supra-rational Subject of which they are predicates. They are "essential" (and not merely "accidental") attributes of that subject, but they are also, it is important to notice, *synthetic* essential attributes. That is to say, we have to predicate them of a subject which they qualify, but which in its deeper essence is not, nor indeed can be, comprehended in them; which rather requires comprehension of a quite different kind. (ibid.:2)

By virtue of its traits, which were similar to those of human beings, the divine was at the same time expressible but also *arreton*, inexpressible, since it rose above the human dimension. Otto acutely observed:

Yet, though it eludes the conceptual way of understanding, it must be in some way or other within our grasp, else absolutely nothing could be asserted of it. And even mysticism, in speaking of it as *arreton*, the ineffable, does not really mean to imply that absolutely nothing can be asserted of the object of the religious consciousness; otherwise, mysticism could exist only in unbroken silence, whereas what has generally been a characteristic of the mystics is their copious eloquence. (ibid.:2)

The dialectic between rationality and irrationality became a methodology suitable for research in the field of religion. In such research, in fact, it was not possible to merely analyze rational expressions without placing them within a broader picture of interactions.

In this regard, the most meaningful instance was obviously provided by the category of the sacred itself:

> "Holiness"—"the holy"—is a category of interpretation and valuation peculiar to the sphere of religion. It is, indeed, applied by transference to another sphere—that of ethics—but it is not itself derived from this. While it is complex, it contains a quite specific element or "moment," which sets it apart from "the rational" in the meaning we gave to that word above, and which remains inexpressible—an *arreton* or *ineffabile*—in the sense that it completely eludes apprehension in terms of concepts (ibid.:5)

According to Otto, the sacred is the core of every religion. He conceived it as "numinous," deriving from the *noumen,* from the "Spirit." As a consequence, the sacred produces the "creature" feeling of dependency—an element that clearly derives from Schleiermacher ([1799] 1988)—this is the so-called first numinous.

The same numinous was also something else. Indeed, during ritual celebration and in the places filled with religiosity "there is only one appropriate expression, *'mysterium tremendum'*"—the awful mystery (Otto [1917] 1958:12). Now we are dealing with the "second numinous." It has multiple forms and expressions—meditation, transport, spasm, ecstasy, and horror. "It will be felt at once that there is yet a further element which must be added, that, namely, of 'might,' 'power,' 'absolute overpoweringness.' We will take the term *majestas,* majesty, to represent this" (ibid.:19).

Otto singled out a further element:

> There is, finally, a third element comprised in those of *tremendum* and *majestas,* awefulness [*sic*] and majesty, and this I venture to call the "urgency" or "energy" of the numinous object. It is particularly vividly perceptible in the *orghé* or "wrath"; and it everywhere clothes itself in symbolic expressions— vitality, passion, emotional temper, will, force, movement, excitement, activity, impetus. These features are typical and recur again and again from the daemonic level up to the idea of the "living" God. (ibid.:23)

But that is not all. The mystery is also marvelous, "mirific"; it is something that is "wholly other" (ibid.:25). It is glorified with numinous hymns that represent the "third numinous." Moreover, it possesses "fascination," it is attractive—the "fourth numinous"—and it is prodigious, which is the "fifth numinous."

Otto then examined the direct and indirect forms of expressions of the numinous. He talked about art and discussed the numinous in the Old and New Testament and also the numinous present in Luther's theology.

We then get to the definition of the sacred as a "composite category" (ibid.) characterized by an articulated historical process.

Rational parts and irrational aspects constitute the sacred. However, we have to sustain—against every sensualism and evolutionism—that the sacred constitutes a purely a priori category. On the one hand, there are absoluteness, completeness, necessity, and substantiality as rational ideas of the good, which is an absolute and binding value. These rational ideas do not "evolve" from any sensitive perception. On the other hand, aspects of the numinous and the corresponding feelings are absolutely pure, precisely like rational ideas and feelings. Here the criteria suggested by Kant regarding "pure" notions and the "pure" feeling of respect find their proper application (ibid.).

Otto then recapitulated:

> Not only the rational but also the non-rational elements of the complex category of "holiness" are *a priori* elements and each in the same degree. Religion is not in vassalage either to morality or teleology, *ethos* or *telos*, and does not draw its life from postulates; and its non-rational content has, no less than its rational, its own independent roots in the hidden depths of the spirit itself. (ibid.:136)

The link between irrationality and rationality came into being through the "moralizing of the divine" (ibid.), that is, the development among human subjects of norms, rules, morality, and justice criteria that depend on the divine, the keeper of all goodness and justice.

It must be remembered, however, that the sacred has also its exterior manifestations. An example of this is the link between myth and ritual, which has also been studied by the French scholar Arnold van Gennep (1873–1957). (Van Gennep had also been critical of Durkheim's theory of totemism.) The tie was expressed through the narration and the r ythm of the dances, between the narrative and the gestures of the dance. Both the celebrant and the onlooker directly participated, forming a wholeness that is an essential element for the dramatization of the myth (van Gennep [1909] 1981).

The "ritual meaning" remained beyond its momentary enactment. A ritual could be celebrated without direct reference to myths; however, the complementary nexus with the original myth was somehow kept. But if a separation between myth and ritual occurred, then one must rather talk about legend.

RELIGION AND CAPITALISM IN R. H. TAWNEY (1880–1962)

Religion and the Rise of Capitalism, by the historian R. H. Tawney [1926] (1977), necessarily referred to Max Weber's classic study *The Protestant Ethic and the Spirit of Capitalism* (Weber [1904–5] 1976b).

Franco Ferrarotti clarified the basic differences between the two authors' perspectives:

> Differently from Weber, Tawney thinks that English Puritanism, which at the beginning had certain traits, like collectivism, rigor, and discipline in the social sense, was then influenced by the development of capitalism and has bent its own ethics to capitalism's demands of development. Indeed, this new "adapted" form has had a noteworthy influence on the development of capitalism itself. Tawney attacks Weber for having ignored the influence of the economic and social condition of Puritanism. Moreover, Tawney emphasizes the specific "character" formed by religion which was more important for the development of capitalism than its specific rules, like the ascetic method of life. (Tawney 1975:21)

In this regard, Ferrarotti made reference to Parsons's position (1962). According to Tawney the influence of Protestantism on capitalism had been totally permissive, a weakening of resistance to the presumed amoralism of capitalism; whereas for Weber the development from Calvin to later Puritanism was neither only nor essentially an adaptation to a change in external circumstances. It involved a "clarifying" of the latent implication of the religious position. In the last analysis, Tawney was favorable to the ethical discipline that runs counter to economic individualism (Tawney 1975:14–15).

Otherwise said, Tawney's study was based on English historical experience and partly overturned Weber's thesis by emphasizing the original influence of capitalism on Puritanism rather than the reverse. However, Tawney later recognized a great adaptability to the needs of capitalism in Puritan religion. From this new situation would derive the Puritan's competence to influence capitalist development.

After having recognized, among other inspirers, Troeltsch's and Weber's influence on his work, Tawney moved along a threefold path of political, ecclesiastical, and economic reconstruction:

> through which England passed between the Armada and the Revolution, every ingredient in the cauldron worked a subtle change in every other. There was action and reaction. *"L'ésprit calviniste,"* and *"l'ésprit des hommes nouveaux que la révolution économique du temps introduit dans la vie des affaires,"* if in theory distinct, were in practice intertwined. Puritanism helped to mould the social order, but it was also itself increasingly moulded by it. (Tawney [1926] 1977:xii–xiii)

In his work Tawney preferred to keep to an historical approach, but his historical reconstruction did not go beyond the chronological limit of the sixteenth and seventeenth centuries. He also investigated the Middle

Ages, by dealing with the problems of earnings, avarice, and usury, and also the Reformation in continental Europe, focusing on Luther and Calvin. He later examined the role of the Church of England and of the Puritan movement.

Tawney criticized Weber for having undervalued the influence of Calvinism. However, in the reprint of his 1936 book, while substantially maintaining his point, Tawney seemed to attenuate the tone of his attack:

> Puritanism was the schoolmaster of the English middle-classes. It heightened their virtues, sanctified, without eradicating, their convenient vices, and gave them an inexpugnable assurance that, behind virtues and vices alike, stood the majestic and inexorable laws of an omnipotent Providence, without whose foreknowledge not a hammer could beat upon the forge, not a figure could be added to the ledger. But it is a strange school which does not teach more than one lesson, and the social reactions of Puritanism, trenchant, permanent and profound, are not to be summarized in the simple formula that it fostered individualism. Weber, in his celebrated articles, expounded the thesis that Calvinism, it its English version, was the parent of capitalism, and Troeltsch, Schulze-Gaevernitz, and Cunningham have lent to the same interpretation the weight of their considerable authority. (Tawney [1926, 1936] 1977:211)

H. RICHARD NIEBUHR (1894–1962) AND NORTH AMERICAN DENOMINATIONALISM

H. Richard Niebuhr could also be viewed as a nonsociologist who dealt with sociological issues. His most important book, *The Social Sources of Denominationalism* (Niebuhr 1972), first published in 1929, could be considered a theological text. However, since Niebuhr carefully dealt in his volume with socioreligious dynamics and with authors like Weber, Troeltsch, and Tawney, the book could also be included among the sociological studies on religion, with special reference to the North American context and to the themes dealing with Denominationalism.

Niebuhr's main concern seemed to be the division of the churches, their tendency to "factionalism," which represented a real "ethical failure." Also, there would be different doctrinal and moral effects if a religious group became a church or a sect.

Niebuhr—whose older brother Reinhold, a theologian and a scholar of social ethics, wrote a noteworthy book on social ethics (Niebuhr 1932)—complained about the lack of a common ethics within the Christian churches. These churches usually differed on important issues and rarely agreed upon common objectives. He clearly stated that "denominationalism thus represents the moral failure of Christianity" (Niebuhr [1929] 1972:25).

This failure had roots far back in the past. Even the Reformation was not able to meet the needs of the destitute (ibid.:34). Later on, the individualistic interests of the middle class emerged. From here it was not a long way to nationalism and "sectionalism."

Niebuhr noticed that the majority of the various Christian religious confessions originated and developed in the United States. Also those confessions of European origin had developed in various ways outside Europe. The consequence of this has been that the conflicts among the different religious confessions have created deep and insuperable divisions. The result was the existence of nationalistic, "sectionalist," and schismatic churches. Even the divisions between east and west, north and south somehow influenced different forms of religious affiliation. The various experiences of the frontier, of different social classes, of immigration, of linguistic and ethnic differences in the various churches have had a deep influence on their basic attitudes. For instance, big religious organizations like the National Baptist Convention, the African Methodist Episcopal, the African Methodist Episcopal Zion, and the Colored Methodist Episcopal churches are totally black denominations. Niebuhr noticed also the existence of other smaller black associations (ibid.:239).

It should be remembered that we owe the concept of denomination to Niebuhr himself. Denomination is rather close to church, but it lacks the latter's tendency to dominate the world.

Niebuhr was also interested in the transformation of the sects after their collision with the world, and he registered their inner weakening, which led them to change into denominations.

Schismatic tendencies were the expression of cultural division and of the various interests that derived from it. The development of the denominations followed world disintegration. That is why Christianity, "following the leadership of nationalism and capitalism, . . . cannot but continue the process of schism which has marked its entire past history" (ibid.:270).

Niebuhr's last appeal was for a less sectarian church, which would transcend divisions and would overcome personal interests. There would be only one path to follow—repentance and sacrifice. At this point, however, Niebuhr spoke as a theologian and not as a social scientist.

MYTHS AND SYMBOLS IN ELIADE (1907–1986)

When the name of Rumanian scholar Mircea Eliade is mentioned, one immediately thinks of the "myth of the eternal return," to which he dedicated a book (Eliade [1949] 1991) with the intention of accurately analyz-

ing collective rituals performed at irregular intervals that entailed the construction of a cult house and the solemn recitation of the original myths
concerning the cosmogonic structure. Eliade wrote:

> The beneficiary is the whole community, including both the living and the
> dead. On the occasion of the re-presentation of the myths the entire commu-
> nity is renewed; it rediscovers its "sources", relives its "origins." The idea of
> a universal renewal brought about by the religious re-presentations of a cos-
> mogonic myth is documented in many traditional societies. . . . For the
> mythico-ritual scenario of the periodic renewal of the World can show us one
> of the most significant functions of myth, both in archaic cultures and in the
> earliest civilizations of the East. (Eliade 1998:35–36)

Once this was clarified, there emerged the cultural relativistic orientation, which a great deal of weight on the context pertaining to the myths:
"To be sure, the symbolism is the same; but the context differs, and it is the
intention shown by the context that gives us the true meaning in each
case" (Eliade 1998:82). The old conceptions that established once and for
all the forms of a social phenomenon appeared to have been overcome. In
fact, Eliade was convinced that today it is no longer possible to talk in general terms about myths and rituals. Also, it is quite difficult for us today to
realize the unity that primitive people experienced between themselves
and nature. Such general considerations were purely abstract and the
same was true with regard to the notion of "primitive men" in general. The
most concrete and specific datum was given by the religious phenomenon
that revealed itself in history and through history (ibid.).

Eliade wrote that the ways in which we return to the past differ and give
rise to several situations: first of all, the direct reintegration of the primordial situation (Chaos, or the pre-cosmogonic state, or Creation time); second, the progressive return all the way back to the "origin," from the
present back to the absolute beginning (Eliade [1952] 1991).

Among the various symbols studied by Eliade, aside from those of time,
those dealing with the "center" and the "bond" are worth mentioning. As
Dumézil stressed in his introduction to *Images et symboles. Essais sur le sym-
bolisme magico-religieux* (ibid.), there were basic representations that are
largely employed; for instance, the "center" with its third-dimensional
variant, the "zenith," according to which all the divisions and values
within a society are ordered following hierarchical criteria. The "bond"
expressed, first of all, the fact that every physiological, collective, and
intellectual life form is a tangle of relations. In only a few pages, but with
a great amount of appropriate examples, Eliade illustrated the richness of
variations of these two themes—the "center" and the "bond"—and helped
us perceive their unitary character.

An important variation concerning the center and the bond was given by the *mandala* :

> The term itself means "a circle"; translations from the Tibetan sometimes render it by "centre" and sometimes by "that which surrounds." In fact a *mandala* represents a whole series of circles, concentric or otherwise, inscribed within a square; and in this diagram, drawn on the ground by means of coloured threads or coloured rice powder, the various divinities of the Tantric pantheon are arranged in order. The *mandala* thus represents an *imago mundi* and at the same time a symbolic pantheon. . . . Any Indian temple is, like a *mandala*, a microcosm and at the same time a pantheon. . . . The *mandala* can be used in support, either at the same time or successively, of a concrete ritual or an act of spiritual concentration or, again, of a technique of mystical physiology. This multivalency, this applicability to multiple symbolism of the Centre in general, is easily understandable, since every human being tends, even unconsciously, towards the Centre, and towards his own centre where he can find integral reality—sacredness. (ibid.:50–54)

It is as if everyone tried to maintain a bond both with the center and with himself.

Eliade talked at length about the Indian god Varuna, the "Terrible Sovereign" of the Indo-European myths, who ruled the world through the use of strings, knots, and bonds. He then discussed the case of the "binding," particularly used in ancient Italy and especially in popular medical practices as a magic device when dealing with disease and death, which were believed to be controlled with strings by funerary divinities and demons. On these issues Eliade proposed a new interpretative perspective:

> All these beliefs and all these rites certainly lead us into the domain of the *magical* mentality. Yet, from the fact that these popular practices derive from magic, have we the right to regard the general symbolism of "tying" as exclusively a creation of the magical mentality? I think not. Even if, among the Indo-Europeans, the rites and symbols of "binding" include chthonic and lunar elements, and therefore betray strong magical influences—which is not certain—we still have to explain other documents which not only express authentic religious experience but also a general conception of man and of the world which is, in itself, truly *religious* and not magical. (ibid.:112–13)

Briefly, the existence of elements connected with underground gods, for example, those of the chthonic world or of the moon goddess, were proof of a possible use of the symbol of the "binding" also in religion. An instance of this presence was provided by the ancient Mithraic temples (dedicated to the god Mithras). The churches of San Clemente and San

Stefano Rotondo in Rome were built over Mithraic temples. In San Stefano Rotondo there is a well-preserved image of the lunar divinity. Indeed, religion is itself a bond *par excellence*; in fact, the etymology of the word religion—*re-ligare*—means to unite, to link. Finally, it is possible to affirm that the whole is linked up, either through magic, myth or religion (ibid.).

Finally, Eliade accused Tylor and Frazer of "confusionism" because

> in their anthropological and ethnological researches, [they] accumulated examples which had no geographical or historical contiguity, and would cite an Australian myth together with one from Siberia, Africa or North America, persuaded as they were always and everywhere they were dealing with the same "uniform reaction of the human mind before the phenomena of Nature." (ibid.:175)

Eliade's main contribution was his *Traité d'histoire des religions*, first published in Paris in 1948. It had an articulated structure and touched upon different topics employing at the same time a cosmological, biological, mythological, and symbolic outlook. The themes Eliade treated in his masterpiece were the sacred and the profane; celestial divinities; solar and lunar cults; water, stones, earth, and vegetarian symbolism; fertility cults; sacred space and time; the functions of myths; and the structure of symbols. This long list showed the broadness of the book's contents and testified to Eliade's immense and many-sided erudition.

Briefly, in introducing his text, Eliade ([1948] 1976) tackled specific problems: (1) What is religion? (2) To what extent can one speak of a history of religions? Eliade was skeptical about the usefulness of a preliminary definition of religious phenomena. For this reason, he seemed to be satisfied with the description of *hierophanies* (by which he meant anything that showed the "sacred").

A meaningful conclusion reached by the author concerned the "complexity of 'primitive' religion" (Eliade [1958] 1996:30):

> (1) The sacred is qualitatively different from the profane, yet it may manifest itself no matter how or where. . . . (2) This dialectic of the sacred belongs to all religions, not only to the supposedly "primitive" forms. . . . (3) Nowhere do you find only elementary hierophanies (the kratophanies of the unusual, the extraordinary and the novel, mana, etc.). . . . (4) We find everywhere, even apart from these traces of higher religious forms, a system into which the elementary hierophanies fit. (ibid.)

Other conclusions dealt with the persistence of the sacred celestial symbolism; the coherence of the religious purifying function of the waters; the exploitation of the earth as a producer of fruits; the renewal of a "nostalgia for eternity" expressed through myths and rites belonging to sacred times and spaces.

Finally, "the dialectic of hierophanies allows for the spontaneous and complete rediscovery of all religious values, whatever they may be and at whatever historical stage may be the society or individual who rediscovers them" (ibid.:465).

THE QUESTION OF MAGIC: ERNESTO DE MARTINO (1908–1965)

The Italian anthropologist Ernesto de Martino was not at all in agreement with Eliade's interpretative stance. De Martino commented on an article by Eliade published in 1957 in the appendix of the second edition of *Il mondo magico*:

> I decided to include in this appendix the observations by Mircea Eliade for a set of reasons. Firstly, they bring to the extreme consequences—even with a caricature touch—a laying out of flaws that inevitably unsettles the book's structure; secondly, Eliade's remarks are a meaningful example of particular currents called historical-religious irrationality and cultural relativism that I reject down the line. These two perspectives ignore the complexities of the problems and the importance of the tasks that are linked to the historicist trend of Western thought. (de Martino 1973:313)

The theoretical and ideological distance between de Martino and Eliade was thus evident. Even though the Italian ethnoanthropologist was a student of Benedetto Croce's idealism, he chose a historicist perspective (de Martino 1941), with some Marxist influence, with the aim of detecting the historical origins of phenomena. His research was multifaceted; it dealt with recurring themes typical of the social sciences concerning religion. These themes were magic (de Martino 1960, 1975, 1976), symbolism (de Martino 1962), tarantism (de Martino 1961), funeral laments (de Martino 1958), and the apocalypse (de Martino 1977).

His study on magic (de Martino 1973) probably remained his most significant work. It revolved around a concept that de Martino employed on various occasions (de Martino 1958, 1973): the "crisis of presence" as an "anguish" that, as de Martino writes, expressed the willingness to exist as a presence in the face of the risk of nonexistence. Then transitoriness became a problem and as such stimulated defense and redemption. The individual tried to reestablish his own endangered presence (de Martino 1973:95). Especially in the world of magic there were two recurrent elements: "the risk of losing one's soul and, as a consequence, losing at the same time its possible redemption" (ibid.:96). In sum, the personal presence risks losing itself. The risk is overcome through forms of redemption, of rescue of presence. The resort to magic was one of the most frequent forms for overcoming the crisis of presence.

De Martino (ibid.) explained that the fight of the menaced presence, with the consequent resort to magic, generally occurs when the person is undergoing a difficult existential period and is forced to make an extra effort to solve a problem. A person might resort to magic even to solve a minor difficulty in everyday life. De Martino went on to say that: "In general, the weakening of presence, of a being, is closely connected to the weakening of the world in which a being is necessarily immersed. Then there are magic techniques that are mainly aimed at fighting the world as "other" that more and more emerges in the consciousness" (ibid.:111). Thus, the spell, the "counterspell" and other redemptive forms became part of the existential drama of the magic world, whose roots

> go back to a fundamental experience—the endangered presence, which is a defense form against a risk. Presence does not put up with the effort of being there. Presence runs away, it empties itself, undergoes malign influences, gets stolen, eaten and so on. . . . Then magic intervenes, overcoming these difficulties, and fights against the disintegrating process. Through magic the danger is signaled and then it is faced. (ibid.:195)

De Martino (1958) later wrote further on the loss of presence, especially after criticism formulated in particular by Croce. De Martino reiterated his ideas, stating that the risk of the loss of the presence and the consequent danger of being wiped out was a given fact both for primitive civilizations as well as for contemporary societies. In today's societies the menace concerns the risk of being left out from one's cultural context, from the ongoing processes, thus of not being there.

In particular, de Martino underlined the "dehistoricization" of the negative, of evil, which was linked to the crisis of presence in that the concrete historical roots of events were no longer recognized. Institutionalized religion could be viewed as another form of dehistoricization. It was based on a metahistorical order, the myth, that could deal with a metahistorical order of behavior, the rite (ibid.:37). Religious life for de Martino thus became a protective technique that produced values that were able through culture to reshape individual fears deriving from the loss of presence.

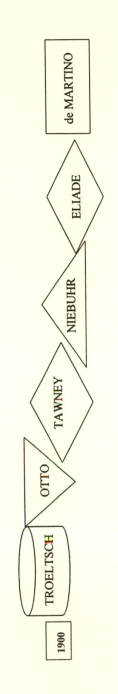

Synoptic Table 4: From Troeltsch to de Martino

4

The Frankfurt School and Religion

The scholars of the Frankfurt school did not seem to favor the study of the religious factor of twentieth-century society, particularly after their "critical theory of society" and the "negative dialectic."

Nevertheless, Adorno (1903–69) and especially Horkheimer (1895–1973) provide us with stimulating and original readings on religion. Their reflections began with the Marxist perspective of the Frankfurt school, and reached a position charged either with theological implications or, at least, dialogically open toward the most attentive intellectuals of our century. Among them there are Paul Tillich (1886–1965)—especially in the case of Horkheimer—Karl Barth (1886–1968), Martin Buber (1878–1965), and Ernst Bloch (1885–1977), who has been studied by Jürgen Habermas (1929–).

The sociologists belonging to the *Institut für Sozialforschung* maintained an aversion toward metaphysics and consequently toward any religious ideology. They were convinced that the churches made instrumental use of reason in order to enslave and tame the social subject in the name of supposedly higher motivations that have little to do with the actual individual's desires.

According to Horkheimer and Adorno ([1947] 1997), even though the Enlightenment actively contributed to conquering theocracy, it nevertheless favored the advent of antidemocratic and despotic solutions in the name of absolute rationalization.

Horkheimer, in particular, was convinced about the impenetrability of some sectors pertaining to human behavior. His attitude toward religion "is not of mere negation but, rather, reveals a cautious, unforeseen approach. He examines the various aspects of religious phenomena and freely expresses his opinion about them also employing, as is common for him, irony and sarcasm. He is convinced, however, of the relevant social role of various movements and religious beliefs" (Cipriani 1986:12).

There is in Horkheimer a "nostalgia for the Other," which remains unexpressed or at least suspended. However, what he expressed on the occasion of the death of his friend and colleague Adorno remains unambiguous.

Horkheimer wrote that Adorno always talked about the "nostalgia for the Other," but he never used words such as heaven, eternity, or beauty. However, Horkheimer laid stress on the fact that while Adorno questioned himself about the world, in the last analysis, he perceived the "Other." At the same time, he was convinced that it is impossible to understand this "Other" through a mere description. Rather, it is possible only through interpretation of the world as it is, also hinting that the world is not the only place, the only destination in which our thoughts might rest (Horkheimer 1969:108–9).

Horkheimer himself (1970), while showing some interest in Judaism and Christianity (without however abandoning his initial Marxist positions), talked explicitly and at length about a "nostalgia for the totally Other."

He argued that the religious factor did not always act as a distraction from worldly matters, but rather that it had probably contributed to the development of energies that today stigmatize disengagement. It is also for this reason that social research is called upon to investigate religion as a phenomenon that can be understood *only* in connection with people's social life and their material and spiritual culture. Such a guideline is present in the initial program of the Institute for Social Research (Horkheimer 1931).

According to Adorno, death did not represent the globality of existence. Moreover, Adorno was convinced that the impossibility of thinking deeply about death did not protect thought from the unreliability of every metaphysical experience (Adorno [1966] 1990). Briefly, the other world was denied as a reality but continued to bear weight in philosophical and sociological reflection. Besides, metaphysical categories, now secularized, still act within the impulse called "the question of the sense of life" (ibid.).

In *Minima moralia* ([1951] 1993) Adorno attacked knowledge dominated by economic interests.

> The same thing occurs for religion. Adorno did not attack religion in the light of its primary essence, but criticized ideology that was available for uses of a capitalist kind. The violent criticism shown by Adorno against religion should be viewed as an attitude within the general picture of his vigorous attack against the whole of bourgeois society. In fact, this approach was understandable within the general framework of Marxist analysis; moreover, Adorno did not spare Marxist analysis from some criticism. The final outcome was a rather pessimistic one. Adorno talked about hope but only within the historical dimension. As for salvation, he hinted that it represented an opening toward hope but of a utopian kind. (Cipriani 1986:21)

The search for the "Other" through the world, according to Horkheimer's interpretation of Adorno, was a final objective that could not be given up. In Adorno's *Negative Dialectics* ([1966] 1990) there emerged a question about what could happen after Auschwitz. The main question was whether the death of innocent people should require a critical reflection, and redemption as a last need for justice. If justice could not be found in the human world, the absence of any further hope—a divine justice that would give order to every element—would seem like an unexplainable monstrosity.

It is worth mentioning a work by Adorno (1975) on horoscopes. Adorno defined astrology as "secondhand superstition." The work was the result of three months of research in the *Los Angeles Times* in 1952–53. Adorno carried out a content analysis of the horoscope in the newspaper. At the same time, he checked the reference to biblical commandments and to the logic of a highly competitive society. In sum, he concluded that astrology itself is an ideological instrument directly linked to the status quo.

Erich Fromm (1900–80) was another representative of the Frankfurt school. However, after his departure for the United States, he moved away from the positions of his German colleagues. Fromm too devoted part of his production to spiritual themes, developing the relationship between psychoanalysis and religion. Indeed, *Psychoanalysis and Religion* ([1950] 1958) was the title of a short book Fromm published in 1950. Fromm wrote in his text that

> the former viewpoint has been expressed both by psychoanalysts and by representatives of the church. . . . The fact that a considerable number of ministers study psychoanalysis indicates how far this belief in the blending of psychoanalysis and religion has penetrated the field of ministerial practice. If I undertake to discuss the problem of religion and psychoanalysis afresh in these chapters it is because I want to show that to set up alternatives of either irreconcilable opposition or identity of interest is fallacious; a thorough and dispassionate discussion can demonstrate that the relation between religion and psychoanalysis is too complex to be forced into either one of these simple and convenient attitudes. (ibid.:8–9)

First, it should be noted that Fromm's reference to religion as a scientific discipline appeared to be rather problematic. Even before him, in 1938, Carl G. Jung (1865–1961) had attempted to bring the two realms together. In fact, he published *Psychology and Religion* (1958), in which he gathered the lectures he had given on the topic. A few years later, in 1942, he published a book on the symbolism of the Mass (Jung [1942] 1954). In this text, Jung paid attention to the transformation that occurred during the Eucharistic celebration, which he considered to be an anthropomorphic symbol of an otherworldly state going beyond rational understanding (ibid.).

After mentioning Freud's ideas in *The Future of an Illusion*, Fromm went on to discuss Jung, whose ideas appeared to him to be opposite to Freud's.

Jung would have limited himself to the observation of facts without elaborating either metaphysical or philosophical considerations, as Jung himself suggested in *Psychology and Religion* (1958:2). Fromm quoted another passage from Jung's text, in which religion was defined as "a careful and scrupulous observation of what Rudolph Otto aptly termed the "numinosum," that is, a dynamic existence or effect, not caused by an act of will. On the contrary, *"it seizes and controls the human subject which is always rather its victim than its creator"* (Fromm [1950] 1958:17; emphasis in the original). Fromm then draws a summary of the different points of view of the two colleagues: "Summing up the respective positions of Freud and Jung we may say that Freud opposes religion in the name of ethics—an attitude which can be termed "religious." On the other hand, Jung reduces religion to a psychological phenomenon and at the same time elevates the unconscious to a religious phenomenon" (ibid.:20). Indeed, there is in Freud a negation of God but not of ethical ideals, while in Jung the unconscious level is emphasized to the point that in the end it acquires a religious dimension.

As for Fromm, he too formulated, with some difficulty, his own personal definition of religion: "any system of thought and action shared by a group which gives the individual a frame of orientation and an object of devotion" (ibid.:21). If it were not for the word "devotion" this broad definition could be used to define very different kinds of social phenomena. However, Fromm was convinced that his description sufficed for the purpose. In fact, in his opinion all societies, even the past ones, always had a religion, and a society without religion was inconceivable (ibid.). Moreover, psychoanalysis functions as a "cure of the soul" (ibid.:65) since it provides the patient with the "art of loving" (ibid.).

5

The New European Perspectives

THE SOCIOLOGY OF RELIGION OF JOACHIM WACH (1898–1955)

In the history of socioreligious thought, sociologist Joachim Wach has been undervalued. This is probably because he dealt with different disciplines at the same time. He started to work within the area of the *Religions-wissenschaft*, the science of religion, as it had been developed within the German current, which was one of the best traditions in these studies. After moving to the United States in 1935 as an exile from Nazi Germany, like his colleagues of the Frankfurt School, Wach wrote an essay on the sociology of religion.

In order to understand thoroughly Wach's point of view, one must take into account Wach's strong interest in hermeneutics, in the wake of Dilthey's theory of *Verstehen*. Indeed, Wach devoted a huge work in three volumes published respectively in 1926, 1929, and 1933 in Tübingen to the understanding of social reality.

Wach's encounter with Friedrich Heiler, the great German phenomenologist, and with Rudolf Otto, a leading member of the not so appropriately called "Marburg school," was crucial for the development of Wach's sociology of religion.

Thus, the initial inputs into Wach's work were hermeneutics and phenomenology. He associated with noteworthy scholars and philosophers such as Weber, Troeltsch, Husserl, and Simmel. The work of Friedrich Schleiermacher was even more influential, especially with his emphasis on the experience and autonomy of religion as a feeling with respect to the religious institution.

Wach employed a method—*Verstehen*—through which one could penetrate to the innermost feelings of the individual as the vital nucleus from which the world of expressions and the objectivation of the spirit took form. From religion as an object to be studied, Wach became more and more interested in religion as it was lived by people, through the experience of religiosity. Also for Wach, as for Otto and Schleiermacher before

143

him, religion was essentially an experience, the *Erlebnis,* which is the source of religious life. At this point Simmel's distinction between religiosity and religion reemerged, as did James's distinction between the individual and institutional religion.

Wach attributed a noteworthy importance to research method, to religion's influence on society, to the identity of social groups and religion, and to the influence of society on religion.

As far as methodology was concerned, Wach preferred hermeneutics as a theory of interpretation. He held (Wach 1944) that the science of religion needed precise definitions and comprehensive discussions (like the ones that took place in the great theological, philosophical, and legal hermeneutic systems) dealing with the presuppositions, the methods, and the limits of the interpretation. One must note, however, that here the reference framework was not the sociology of religion but, rather, *Religionswissenschaft.*

Wach added that he employed a descriptive and interpretative method in order to understand the complexity of the exchanges between society and religion. He was careful about the risk of a "Christian sociology" (ibid.:7), because "it is a mistake to assume, as was frequently done at the high tide of the promulgation of the "social gospel," that the sociology of religion should be identical with definite programs of social reform. Such a conception of sociology would be a betrayal of its true character as a descriptive science" (ibid.:7–8).

Another important requirement was neutrality, and scientific and cognitive openness toward different forms of religious experience. In fact, one should not limit oneself to the study of one's own religion. Moreover, one should hold a sympathetic attitude, which is useful for *Verstehen,* that is, an understanding and an appreciation of the nature and meaning of religious phenomena as understood by the believers themselves.

Joachim Wach taught both in Germany, at Leipzig, and then in the United States, at Brown University and the University of Chicago. He had belonged to the Lutheran church, but once in the United States he joined the Episcopal church. He got very interested in the interactions between religion and society and formulated a number of working hypotheses starting from the fundamental notion provided by Otto that dealt with religion as an experience of the sacred. According to Wach, the theoretical expression of religion is the doctrine, the practical is represented by the cult, while the sociological is the communion that manifests itself through social relations.

Wach too was in line with Marx's and Horkheimer's theses concerning the ambivalence of religion whose influence, he wrote, "is twofold: there is a positive or cohesive integrating influence, and there is a negative, destructive, disintegrating influence" (ibid.:35). The experience of the sacred and the role played by tradition are fundamental both for the group and the individual.

Wach's typology of cults is multifaceted. There are family cults and parental, local, racial, national, and other cults connected to associative forms according to sex and age. Another important classification is the founded religion (which is linked to inspired leaders and promoters of new communities), and the "brotherhood" kind of religion, which usually develops after the death of the founder. The next step is the evolution toward the formation of an ecclesiastical body, namely a church that substitutes the chief's charisma, as far as the founded religion—that is, the religion derived by human experience—is concerned, and the role carried out by the brotherhood.

However, it was within the field of the reactions against the ecclesiastic body that the various schisms and separations originated. Besides, there exists a modality of internal rebellion:

> The groups which are formed *within* the ecclesiastical body itself to protest against its policies, against "compromise" and "laxity" which it considers pernicious. These criticisms, generally mild, may be directed against doctrinal tenets, elements in the cult, or organization. The last is the primary subject of censure among those desirous of raising the religious and ethical standards of the body without provoking a split. (ibid.:173)

Philipp Spener, the founder of German Pietism designated the *collegia pietatis* of this religious current as *ecclesiolae in ecclesia*. The *collegium pietatis* was a "loosely organized group, limited in numbers and united in a common enthusiasm, peculiar convictions, intense devotion, and rigid discipline, which is striving to attain higher spiritual and moral perfection than can be realized under prevailing conditions" (ibid.:175). Another modality was provided by the *fraternitas*, which produced "a 'liberal' and critical attitude toward doctrine, cult, and practice of the main groups, manifesting either indifference or a tendency to adhere to peculiar, if not heretical, views" (ibid.:180). Finally there could be the monastic kind of order with "a stricter and more rigid conception of the new community within the main body" (ibid.:181). In the event of a more rigid separation, there emerged the "independent group" with its own organizational principles. The "sect", on the other hand, was much more rigorous, with "bizarre and fantastic features" (ibid.:199). Briefly, "we can safely conclude that characteristic attitudes . . . determine the sociological type of the sect or, in instances, of the independent group" (ibid.:202).

Wach's analysis dealt with different times and places and demonstrated an ability to use available materials and sources correctly. Wach distinguished between the "religions of the warrior," present in Mexico, in the cult of Mithras, and in Zen Buddhism, and the "religions of the merchant," which prevail in Japanese, Chinese, Jain, and Parsi religions. Finally, there were the religions of the peasants in Asia.

The author concluded his book by providing a description of various typical religious personae, such as the founder, the reformer, the prophet, the soothsayer, the wizard, the clairvoyant, the saint, the priest, and the "religiosus."

Together with Friedrich Heiler, who influenced Wach, Gustav Mensching (1901–78) must also be mentioned. A noteworthy member of the Marburg school, Mensching was a *Verstehen* phenomenologist of religion and author of *Religious Sociology* (1951). Some of his reflections, however, are obsolete, especially according to the observations by Widengren (1969). Nevertheless, his critical remarks on Durkheim are worth mentioning. Mensching affirmed that sociocultural conditions were not the decisive influence on religion. In this regard, other characteristics should be examined whose interpretation through *Verstehen* tended to confute both Durkheim's assumptions and North American functionalistic perspectives, which were based on the assumption that religion is necessary as an answer to collective and individual needs. Mensching did not deny the relevance of the relationship between the social and the religious factors; however, he preferred to deal with them in a double perspective by studying the social phenomena within the realm of religion and the social relations of religion themselves. Moreover, he conceived a general sociology of religion that analyzed the basic and universal features of the social relations within the various historical religions, instead of a particular sociology of religion, which would deal exclusively with one specific religion. According to Mensching, an instance of this type of study was Troeltsch's research on the social doctrines of the Christian churches.

RELIGION AND RELIGIOUS PRACTICE: GABRIEL LE BRAS (1891–1970)

Gabriel Le Bras, professor of canon law, promoted "religious sociology" in France and elsewhere. He had a crucial role in the passage from a classical sociology of religion to a better-implemented methodological approach, especially regarding the statistical dimension. In 1954 he founded the *Group for the Sociology of Religion* in Paris.

He has been criticized for his exclusive attention to religious demography, to the data regarding religious practice, the number of religious believers who regularly attended Mass, who attended the Easter services, and who confessed and took communion at least once a year. Actually, he explicitly affirmed that researching religious practices alone did not provide enough data on "religious vitality." Notwithstanding this conviction, Le Bras's research developed more in the direction of a census of the multifaceted religious population rather than toward the sociological survey. He carried out his research mostly in France.

In 1926 Le Bras completed his first investigation in England. His intentions were clear as far as the pastoral application of the results of the field-work are concerned, even though he thought that other specialists must carry out this task. Le Bras clearly stated in many of his essays his affiliation to Catholicism. His writings were published but always for Catholic journals, and in scientific symposiums in disciplines such as archaeology, history, and geography, as well as sociology.

It was Le Bras's conviction that research on religious practice was more accessible but was also more superficial. The scholar was well aware of the need for investigations into "the soul," more in-depth themes like the reasons for faith and religious feeling. In his view, such investigations should also deal with the content and the intensity of beliefs within a specific environment, such as the parish, school, or workshop. "Patient and discreet researchers who do not neglect the complexities of individual and social elements must carry out the investigations" (Le Bras 1955–56). Le Bras's language (he talks about "souls" instead of social individuals) revealed the perspective within which he moved. He was honest, however, about his intention to consider other important factors, besides mere practice, as religious indicators. Moreover, from the sociology of Catholicism he wanted to shift to a broader and more comprehensive sociology of religion (ibid.) in order to prevent possible attacks on the part of the clerical world. Le Bras wrote that he was conscious of the fact that sociology could stir feelings of enthusiasm as well as a great deal of suspicion among men of the church whether Catholic or Islamic. Le Bras then attempted to find out what the clergy was alarmed about. He thought that first of all they were afraid of the researcher's indiscretion; then they feared that upsetting revelations might discourage people; finally, they were concerned that the religious phenomenon could be described as and reduced to a profane mechanism. Le Bras tackled each of these three points in an effort to undermine their foundation. As far as the first point was concerned, he observed that the researcher's indiscretion was limited, since what he observed was public. As for the second point, the fear of unpleasant revelations betrayed a lack of trust in God and in the reactions of his servants. The last point was the most serious objection since it derived from a sincere religious fear. In fact, to explain the state of souls as a result of purely human causes and to expect some remedies to come from these explanations would be placing little importance on God's action. Even the most spiritual among the mystics could observe that the spirit of goodness as well as the spirit of evil is present in men, who are made of flesh. We can perceive the effectiveness of the spirit exclusively by observing the visible world (ibid.). It seems that Le Bras's discussion was worked out with a reasoning that was deeply rooted within the church's problematic. Le Bras, however, was determined to defend academic work and its plausibility even from within a religious perspective.

This was typical in Le Bras. His shortcomings were mostly due to his confessional allegiances, which he sometimes used as a way to overcome ideological difficulties. These difficulties pertained to his preconceptions of real phenomena that ran contrary to sociological analyses. This eminent scholar of canon law was, however, able to obtain relevant scientific results as documented by a number of his contributions. In his essays he made extensive use of local studies, diocesan researches, university theses, and historical and sociological research projects. He was the organizer of so many scientific enterprises that his reservations about science seemed to fade away. Nevertheless, he tended more toward a religious sociology than to a sociology of religion or religions. Le Bras, however, sometimes showed a broader attitude also toward the sociology of religion (ibid.).

Finally, Le Bras was still attached to a positivistic approach in order to offer empirical behavioral evidence to ecclesiastical pastoral practice. This practice was usually devoid of any specific knowledge of empirical phenomena. Le Bras thought that research should now be carried out in the "extraparish" field rather than within the ecclesiastical experience. In the parish it was only possible to find the existence of tradition but not the evolution of religion.

Le Bras was aware of faith as an interior phenomenon that escaped the possibility of research as such. He wrote that while it would be useless to attempt to establish a mathematical relation between external acts and consciousness, it would be senseless to deny a relationship that existed (ibid.).

Le Bras also established precise norms and methodological instructions aiming at a neutral research approach. He made suggestions on statistical procedures and warned against improper generalizations; stock statements must be carefully verified on the basis of concrete facts. Then Le Bras established some data typologies. He talked about "seasonal conformists" to describe those people who only go to church on special occasions such as baptism, weddings, funerals, and first communions. The "practitioners" went to church and took Holy Communion at Easter. The "pious and zealous people" took part in religious associations and often took Holy Communion. There were also the baptized who did not take part in any religious activity and those who belonged to other religions. Other people did not belong to any religion at all (ibid.). Finally, Le Bras defined religious life as characterized by "beliefs, conducts and practices" (ibid.).

One of Le Bras's objectives was to draw up maps, diagrams, and charts representing the index of the religious life for all the French regions (ibid.). This ambitious task was not carried out by Le Bras himself but, at least in part, by F. Boulard. In 1947 Boulard published a map of religious practice in the French countryside. Other scholars later accomplished the useful task of a geography of French religiosity (Isambert and Terrenoire 1980).

In conclusion, Le Bras wrote that "practice is an interesting phenomenon for a descriptive science. However, research into the causes turns out to be even more interesting." He asked what the cause of normal religious practice might be. Apparently it would be faith, just as the avoidance of practice seemed due to indifference toward religion. "Faith, however, implies for different people various representations, different dispositions and degrees in intensity" (Le Bras 1955–56). The terminology employed by Le Bras tended to describe the causes instead of the trends. It was rather outdated and betrayed its tie with positivistic tradition.

A PIONEER AND FOUNDER: JACQUES LECLERCQ (1891–1971)

The history and the success of a social science discipline are not necessarily or exclusively linked to scholarly publication or to the amount and quality of research. Important or even more determining and contributing to the shaping and development of a discipline are factors such as scholar associations, changes in university regulations, the introduction of new teaching subjects, the setting up of research centers, the beginning of wide-ranging studies, the founding of journals, and publishing. All of these provided the new discipline with importance, visibility, and recognition both within and outside the university communities. They also brought in money and people, thus favoring the difficult task of establishing a new area of social science. It was well-known that, at least at the beginning, a new discipline is surrounded by doubts concerning its reliability and effectiveness.

This could well have been the case with sociology. Notwithstanding the large number of sociological works produced at the end of the nineteenth century and at the start of the twentieth, in many countries and universities sociology did not have an easy life. These difficulties were not exclusively due to political reasons, as in the case of Italy.

Sociology arrived rather late in Belgium, notwithstanding its presence in neighboring countries like France, Germany, and England. In the Catholic University of Louvain, sociology was introduced in 1938, thanks to Jacques Leclercq. An open-minded philosopher, Leclercq actively contributed to the overcoming of prejudices surrounding sociology's presumably positivistic orientation.

After the Second World War, Leclercq's aid to the development of sociology and of the sociology of religion was crucial both in Belgium and elsewhere. In 1948 he founded the CISR—the *Conférence Internationale de Sociologie Religieuse*—of which he became the president. The membership of CISR consists of both European and non-European sociologists, who meet every two years at a symposium to compare theories and research within the socioreligious realm. At first the CISR was ruled by a Catholic orientation. However, later the name was changed into the SISR—*Société Internationale de Sociologie des Religions*—thus losing its confessional connotations.

In 1948 Leclercq (1948) published an introductory book on sociology. The appearance of the volume further contributed to the recognition of the discipline.

In the end, though, Leclercq's aim was to provide a useful tool for evangelization. His approach was a rather empirical one as he was influenced by the North American sociological tradition, which favored a less speculative and less philosophical stance. In this Leclercq was close to Le Bras. However, he differed from the French scholar when he tried to unite theology and sociology, thus sociologizing theology. His intention was formulated on the occasion of the fourth International Conference of Sociology of Religion. Leclercq wrote that he was not totally enthusiastic about the theology of sociology. He argued that it might be too soon to try this sort of synthesis. In the end, religious sociology as a method or field of investigation was just beginning (Leclercq 1955:167): Leclercq was not giving up his task, but was only postponing it.

HENRI DESROCHE (1914–94):
THE OPERATIONAL SOCIOLOGY OF RELIGION

It is not uncommonly the case that a sociologist of religion has been or is still working as a religious minister within a church, a denomination, or another kind of confessional group. One wonders if this constitutes an obstacle or, rather, an advantage for the scholar's work and whether or not he can be objective. Weber himself was aware of this question, especially when he wondered if one has to have a good ear for music to be able to discuss it. Indeed, there is more than one answer, since the question is not as clear-cut as one would be apt to believe. There are advantages and disadvantages. A priest can be a sound sociologist, just as a lay scholar can express himself in ecclesiastical terms or, on the contrary, assume an anti-institutional stance.

Le Bras influenced Henri Desroche, who had a good grasp of Marxist literature and had been one of the first scholars to establish a link between socialism and religious sociology (Desroche 1965). His case offers a good example of the weight that an ecclesiastic education could have on a person's effective field of studies and social commitment.

Desroche wrote *Sociologies religieuses* (Desroche 1968), in which he took a pluralistic perspective, which led him to discuss religions—note the plural—(Desroche 1962, 1972), socialism (Desroche 1965), religious sociology (Desroche 1968), religious phenomena (Desroche 1974), and messianisms and millenarianisms (Desroche 1969).

Desroche was never a Marxist and did not seem to follow any particular ideology. Perhaps for this reason also he appeared to be a loner, although he could show at times a degree of solidarity by practicing a "sociology of hope" (Séguy 1994:11). The Christian education and background testified to his great interest in innovative and utopian movements. By following this path he was led to study the American Shakers sect—who were well-known for their complex ritual dances (Desroche 1955). Moreover, he was a zealous reader of Troeltsch ([1912] 1976).

Desroche was always open to interdisciplinary exchanges. He took various paths and, by following his natural tendency to be active, in 1954 contributed to the start of the Group of Sociology of Religion in Paris. In 1956 he was one of the founders of the *Archives de Sociologie des Religions*, which today is called *Archives de Sciences Sociales des Religions*. Desroche drew a distinction between sociotheology, just as Leclercq did (Desroche and Séguy 1970:186–92), and nontheological sociology (ibid.:197). For the latter he was inspired by the classics of the sociology of religion. He criticized Leclercq by claiming that sociology must be freed of theological, confessional, clerical, and ecclesiastical influences. This could be done by eliminating any form of dogmatism. Desroche theorized a religious sociology in its empirical phase; this was necessary to get rid of its doctrinal, ideological, and apologetic bases (ibid.:198).

Being very sensitive about the problems concerning development and cooperation questions of the Third World, Desroche started the IRD—*Intergroupe Religion-Développement* and the *Collège Coopératif.*

A MISSIONARY SOCIOLOGIST OF RELIGION: FRANÇOIS HOUTART (1925–)

François Houtart's intellectual approach was very similar to Desroche's from many points of view. He too was an unusual kind of scholar within the realm of the sociology of religion. He became very interested in difficult political and economic situations, while differentiating himself from Leclercq's perspectives; he developed an almost missionary passion for the sociology of religion to the point that he created a research center. The

latter became at first a university center for research, but then it was closed
down when its founder retired. He became an internationally known
scholar also for his frequent trips to South America and Asia and for the
international journal of sociology of religion he directed, *Social Compass*,
published by the *Fédération Internationale des Instituts de Recherches Sociales
et Socio-Religieuses (FERES)*.

Although a consultant for the Second Vatican Council, Houtart has
been critical toward the Catholic hierarchy. Houtart has been very close to
Latin American revolutionary movements, the Vietnam liberation movements, and the groups working for liberation in the Portuguese colonies.
His contacts with people in Indian and Sri Lankan societies brought him
closer to the problem of religion as an institutional and cultural factor in
its relations with politics and with problems such as the development and
structural dependence linked to neocolonialism (Houtart and Rémy 1969).

In most of his writings Houtart has dealt with the question of the role of
the ecclesiastic organization during times of upheaval and in revolutionary movements. Houtart was concerned about whether the church was an
antirevolutionary force. Through various research, Houtart tried to detect
the social conditions under which a religious institution establishes a relationship with the political field. He concluded that the content of the social
relationships within the religious realm is closely linked to the position of
those who work in this field, and to what extent these social relationships
are involved in political events (Houtart and Rousseau 1973:123).

Houtart's theoretical stance was rather clear. It was obvious to him that
religion has a role within societies and groups. He wrote, however, that
this role is not necessarily "functional," but could also be dysfunctional.
The variables pertaining to this role are both external, belonging, that is, to
society or the group, and internal to religion itself, especially in its consti-
tutive elements, that is, doctrine, moral, cult, community, and pastoral
(Houtart and Rémy 1969).

6

The Socioanthropological Perspectives

RELIGION AS IDENTITY IN THE UNITED STATES: WILL HERBERG (1901–1977)

If one considers attentively the so-called American way of life, it is possible to perceive its parareligious character, since it provides relevant references for the individual's existential behavior. Will Herberg (1955) suggested the triple distinction of American religions: Protestants, Catholics, and Jews. The three religions used to comprise the largest religious affiliations in the United States. To be sure, this is no longer true in present-day North American society. Massive immigration has contributed a great deal to sociocultural and religious change and differentiation.

In Herberg's view, affiliation with a specific religious denomination somehow established a way of life by directing many individual and collective actions and interactions. Being Protestant, Catholic, or Jew entailed having special relationships with subjects who shared the same religious creed.

On the one hand, religious affiliation was a defense and protective mechanism against external reality; on the other hand, the religious group provided a connected network, with a great number of intersubjective relationships. Thus, schools, businesses, interpersonal relationships, as well as social alliances were almost always developing through channels of the established religious organizations. These organizations were neither officially nor formally confessional, but they did in fact operate as if they were more or less religious bodies. Therefore, the choice of a rather visible affiliation created appointments that otherwise would not be available.

Indeed, the immigrant's country of origin was less important than her or his religion as far as social influence was concerned. Thus, to be Italian or Irish was less important than being Catholic. Moreover, as time went by, national origin tended to fade until it disappeared completely, whereas religious affiliation grew in importance.

It must be made clear that this process was not directly connected to any particular proof of faith or religious practice. What was crucial was the identification process with the religious groups that in the United States worked as an anchor one had to cling to with all one's strength. Briefly, Will Herberg believed that religion prevailed over national identities due to the North American multicultural jumble. The importance of religion was confirmed independently of a concrete practice commitment.

At first Will Herberg followed Marxist theories, then became interested in theology under the influence of Reinhold Niebuhr (1932), the younger brother of H. Richard Niebuhr ([1929] 1972). Herberg passed through North American sociology of religion, leaving a significant mark with his book *Protestant, Catholic, Jew* (Herberg 1955), whose basic proposition seemed to anticipate Bellah's (1967) "civil religion." Indeed, Herberg's anticipation of civil religion has been rather widely recognized. Among others, José Casanova (1994) wrote that in the mid-1950s the three religions—Protestant, Catholic, and Jewish—became the three denominational forms of a new civil American religion. The doctrinal and moral nucleus of this religion resided in the Protestant ethic and in the faith of a millenarian role for the United States (ibid.). We might add that these three religions also represented the three ways of becoming American in all respects.

Many scholars agreed with Herberg's basic idea theoretically and through empirical data. Aside from having paved the way for the American civil religion, Herberg's ideas allowed further developments within the realm of public religion and religious deprivatization (ibid.). His thought also contributed to the "rational choice" theories applied to religion.

J. MILTON YINGER (1916–):
RELIGION, SOCIETY, AND INDIVIDUAL

J. Milton Yinger's best-known work, *Religion, Society, and the Individual*, appeared in 1957. Yinger went on to publish *The Scientific Study of Religion* (1970). Here Yinger defined religion as a system of beliefs and practices through which a group of people deal with the ultimate problems of humanity.

It was Yinger's conviction that in studying religion one should also consider social and cultural questions. This broader perspective must be applied also when dealing with the individual and the group. Sociology of religion, that is, should consider problems within a global perspective without, however, going beyond its own boundaries. Thus strictly psychological, sociopsychological, and pedagogic questions were to be left out of the sociological field, even though interdisciplinary exchanges would not be totally eliminated.

According to Yinger, sociology of religion must have a highly scientific character in examining the different ways the religious experience—its origins, theologies, cultural expressions, and ideological evolution—can be influenced by society, cultures, and individual personalities (Yinger 1957). Such a notion was already clear from the title of the book.

Yinger also made the point that this analysis should not be limited to the relation between society and religion with the latter acting as a dependent variable. The dialectic between the two elements could also be inverted so as to view religion as the independent variable and society—and/or culture, and/or personality—as the receiver of religious influence.

Moreover, Yinger drew a distinction between what a religion could ideally do and what it actually did through its structure, operators, and believers.

Yinger maintained that it is impossible to apply one single theory to all specific cases. Interreligious differences are such that it would be useless to try to assimilate the various religions into a single theoretical perspective. Hence, he suggested an intermediate solution according to which there could be comprehensive theoretical propositions together with a specific theoretical project that could evidence the peculiar characteristics of individual cultural contexts and of particular religions.

In the interaction involving religion, society, culture, and the individual, every change must be considered important and influential even though it may exclusively pertain to one of the four elements. In fact, the other elements would also be affected by the change (ibid.).

Yinger agreed with the idea of a comparative study of religions. However, he was aware of the methodological and practical difficulties that could then make such a study ineffectual for acquiring new scientific information.

Yinger defined religion through a functional approach, i.e., religion should be considered according to what it does but not for its essence. The manifest function of religion is to provide an objective in life and to give meaning to such events as death, pain, and injustice, and to whatever is evil within existence. "Religion is the attempt to relativize the individual's desires, as well as his fears, by subordinating them to a conception of absolute good more in harmony with the shared and often mutually contradictory needs and desires of human groups" (Yinger 1970:17). Shared rites and beliefs are important for awareness itself, which is going to define a strategy for the final victory. Organized groups help to increase the awareness of the human condition and to maintain and teach the same rites and beliefs (ibid.).

As far as the difference between church and sect is concerned, Yinger considered three variables: the degree of exclusivism, or openness of a group; whether the group accepted secular values; and the group's level of integration within a national structure, with the creation of special kinds of professions and of a bureaucratic organization.

Moreover, Yinger discussed the notion of the "established sect" (ibid.), which defined a sufficiently organized group, jealous of its prerogatives. These prerogatives are protected thanks to a shrewd self-sufficient management of community life, which is based on stability and on the exclusion of external interventions.

At the theoretical level, Yinger attempted an integration of the functional approach with the conflictual and with the structural-functional outlooks. He suggested considering the three approaches simultaneously by using the field theory of religion (Yinger 1965). According to this perspective, the structure influences the individual, who in turn is going to show this influence through specific actions. In the meantime, both the structure and the individual undergo changes. Also other external factors, however, can influence the structure and the individuals.

Finally, religion is a dynamic and changing process whose outcome can also satisfy the needs of the social system.

GERHARD E. LENSKI'S (1924–) RESEARCH ON THE RELIGIOUS FACTOR

Gerhard E. Lenski became well-known in sociology of religion thanks to fieldwork research on the religious factor that he conducted in 1957–58. Thanks to this research, some hypotheses, which had previously been expressed theoretically but never empirically, were verified.

Lenski's research approach concerned several religious and ethnic groups, thereby confirming what Herberg (1955) had suggested on the importance of religious affiliation. Lenski's study can be defined as a multidimensional investigation because it tackled its subject on several analytical levels. Moreover, it was methodologically up to date and in this way it demonstrated the feasibility of conducting rigorous research on religion.

Dario Zadra (1969:38–39) observed that according to Lenski there are "community bonds," which unite individuals in religious groups, and "associational bindings," which unite individuals in associations. For this reason, the study of the cohesion of religious groups and of the function that these very groups develop cannot be reduced to the formal relationships connected with associations (for instance, the relationship between parish and parishioners). Therefore, the study of religious groups must be extended to the whole network of those community relationships that develop inside the religious group. Lenski also (1961:17–21) remarked that religious groups are at the same time communitarian and associational.

This was why he took into account both the religious communities and the religious associations.

Lenski's research was conducted in the metropolitan area of Detroit, where the major groups were, respectively, white Protestant (41 percent), white Catholic (35 percent), black Protestant (15 percent), and Jewish (4 percent). The author was aware that Detroit Protestant groups were no longer self-enclosed as in the past, whereas the ethnic groups were still rather self-enclosed. There was a clear-cut separation among Detroit Protestants on the basis of "race." Participation in religious services took place separately also. On the contrary, within the same ethnic groups there was a multiplicity of exchanges and relationships. The data showed that among the Protestant sects there were very small differences except as regards social conditions and the geographic origin of the individual members. Larger contrasts emerged among Catholics and Jews.

If one looks at association and community bindings, it becomes apparent that white Protestants had average bonds both in associations and in communities. The white Catholics maintained bonds that were strong in the associations and average in the communities. Black Protestants showed average bonds in the associations but strong ones in the community. On the contrary, Jews appeared weak at the association level but strong in the community one.

Lenski found that Catholics were less disposed toward commitments of an economic nature than were Protestant and Jews, and also showed mixed attitudes toward science and scientific activity. According to Lenski, these tendencies derived from the tight primary family bonds and from the emphasis attached to obedience. Both these factors would impair the secondary relationships, the predisposition toward scientific careers and economic activities.

CLIFFORD GEERTZ (1926–):
THE COMPARATIVE SOCIOLOGY OF RELIGION

A student of Talcott Parsons, Clifford Geertz has studied religion as a social-cultural phenomenon with great continuity, showing originality and persuasive empirical evidence. From his first study of Java (Geertz 1960) he looked at religion essentially as a cultural system based on village, market, and government bureaucracy. The traits of religion as a cultural system were later spelled out in a specific essay (Geertz 1966; Geertz cited in Zadra 1969:85).

First of all, Geertz made clear that, in his view, religious symbols are the basis of an agreement between a special lifestyle and a specific (often implicit) metaphysics. The concept that religion puts human action on the

same wavelength as an imagined cosmic order and projects the images of
the cosmic order on the level of human experience was far from new. This
concept, however, has never been carefully analyzed (Geertz 1966; Geertz
cited in Zadra 1969:85). Geertz put forward, at this point, his own "functional" definition of religion: (1) A system of symbols that aims at (2) establishing among men dispositions and motivations that are powerful,
pervasive, and lasting, through (3) the formulation of conceptions defining a general order of existence and (4) the definitions of these conceptions
in a frame of factualities such that (5) modes and motivations appear realistic in a unique manner (Geertz 1966; Geertz cited in Zadra 1969:86). On
the basis of his detailed analysis, Geertz maintained that for cultural patterns, that is, for the system of complexes of symbols, the generic trait that
is of primary importance for the anthropologist is that they are external
sources of information. With the term "external" Geertz meant that—differently, for instance, from the genes—cultural patterns are placed outside
the individual organism as such, and that they are to be found in the subjective world of common sense in which all human individuals are born,
make their career, and that remain after they are dead (Geertz 1966; Geertz
cited in Zadra 1969:87). In other words, the problem consisted in including
ideals and reasons for acting inside a more comprehensive system. As time
elapsed, what was complex differentiated itself more and more, and gave
rise to a variety of religious experiences. An instance of such an evolution
was provided by changes in Islam in Morocco and Indonesia. This change
was directly observed by the author through lengthy field researches.
Dario Zadra emphasized the significance of Geertz's concept of the "intentional nucleus." This is located at the crossroads of various differentiated
structural formations (symbolic and institutional, individual and collective). This intentional nucleus constitutes a specific modality of fusion
within the specificity of an action or of an institution. Something similar
can already be found in the research on Java (Geertz 1960) through the
identification of three different levels in Islam. In the case of Morocco and
Indonesia, religion was even more important as an object of study insofar
as it was an institution, a cult, and a faith. In order to be able to follow the
various Islamic trends in Morocco and Indonesia, the author used two
charismatic figures who interpreted the reality of their time and had a significant impact on their respective social and religious cultures. The historical period being analyzed was the premodern one, but the approach
did not lose its social and anthropological character; it has proven valid for
the present-day situation.

For Indonesia Geertz used the figures of Sunan Kalidjaga, who
belonged to the centralizing tradition of the Hindu court of Java and verified a threefold connotation: the doctrine of the "exemplary center" (king,
court, and state capital); the doctrine of "graduated spirituality" (with the

king at the top of the religious stratification); the doctrine of the "theatre-state" (with the court liturgy, which became exemplary for the cultural themes). At the same time, secularism tended to deny the centrality of the court, while written culture defended tradition and the doctrinal complex. The synthesis of these conceptions emerged with Sukarno, who recovered the symbol of centrality and the model of the theatre-state; he also smuggled in the idea of spiritual leadership. In Morocco the initial key figure was Sidi Lahsen Lyusi, who combined warlike and spiritual virtues in a single person. Lyusi succeeded in mixing together institutional charisma and spirituality. This conjunction of opposites was made possible, among other factors, also by the contribution of sufism, a mystical Islamic group. The written culture of Morocco, called Salafyyia, on the contrary, went against such mediation. Finally, King Mohammed V succeeded in fusing the institutional charismatic traits with those of holiness.

Whereas in Morocco the charismatic pattern prevailed, in Indonesia the centralizing structure was dominant. This was the most important finding in one of the most successful studies in the field of comparative religion. On the other hand, Geertz is not at all satisfied with what was achieved earlier by other scholars:

> What is in those thick volumes on totemic myths, initiation rites, witchcraft beliefs, shamanistic performances, and so on, which ethnographers have been compiling with such astonishing industry for over a century? . . . Do they not contain our subject matter? The answer is, quite simply, no. . . . The aim of the systematic study of religion is, or anyway ought to be, not just to describe ideas, acts, and institutions, but to determine just how and in what way particular ideas, acts, and institutions sustain, fail to sustain or even inhibit religious faith. (Geertz 1968:1–2)

In particular: "Religion may be a stone thrown into the world; but it must be a palpable stone and someone must throw it" (ibid.:3). For this reason one cannot understand Christianity without Jesus, Islam without Mohammed, or Hinduism without the Vedas; but neither can one understand Christianity without Gregory the Great, Islam without the *ulama* (Islamic scholars), Hinduism without the caste system.

The influences of Durkheim and Weber, Malinowski and Parsons, but also of Eliade, Schutz, and Bellah on Geertz are quite evident.

Here is one example of his critical attitude:

> If Durkheim's famous statement that God is the symbol of society is incorrect, as I think it is, it remains true that particular kinds of faith (as well as particular kinds of doubt) flourish in particular kinds of societies, and the contribution of the comparative sociology of religion to the general understanding of the spiritual dimensions of human existence both begins and

ends in an uncovering of the nature of these empirical, that is to say lawful, interconnections. The material reasons why Moroccan Islam became activist, rigorous, dogmatic and more than a little anthropolatrous and why Indonesian Islam became syncretistic, reflective, multifarious, and strikingly phenomenological lie, in part anyway, in the sort of collective life within which and along with which they evolved. (ibid.:20)

The last statement sounds imbued with cultural relativism to the extent that it would attribute the origin of attitudes and behavioral patterns to local characteristics. Actually, Geertz's position was much more theoretically articulated. It did not indulge in gross simplifications. In fact, the orientation "toward a scientific comprehension of religious phenomena is to reduce their diversity by assimilating them to a limited number of general types" (ibid.:24).

Another critical aspect concerns the question of "primitive thought": whether it should be considered pragmatic in the manner of Malinowski, or mystical according to Lévy-Bruhl's interpretation. Geertz offered a solomonic solution to this issue: "The conclusion that the dichotomy is a false one and that any man, civilized or not, is prudent and passionate by turns arises virtually of itself" (ibid.:91). Something similar can be detected regarding the more recent debate between the supporters of rational choice (Young 1997) and interpretations in an emotional key (Hervieu-Léger, with Champion, 1986, 1989).

Geertz's idea of religion (Geertz 1968) was based on the fact that sacred symbols formulate for those who believe in them an image of the construction of the world and a program for human behavior, which is a direct reciprocal reflection (ibid.:97).

Symbols, therefore, while constituting an expression of social reality, are also capable of influencing it, that is, they are patterns *of* reality and patterns *for* reality. Moreover, one can easily read a statement by Geertz that is obviously connected to Schutz (1962): "When men turn to everyday living they see things in everyday terms. If they are religious men, those everyday terms will in some way be influenced by their religious convictions, for it is in the nature of faith, even the most unworldly and least ethical, to claim effective sovereignty over human behavior" (Geertz 1968:110).

RELIGIOUS FUNCTIONS AND MOTIVATIONS: THE PSYCHO-CULTURAL VARIABLES OF MELFORD E. SPIRO (1920–)

Melford Spiro is another supporter of the sociocultural approach. To his researches in Burma, Micronesia, and Israel, he added a psychoanalytic approach. His basic formation, however, remained an anthropological one.

He followed a theoretical tradition no longer common at present: the centrality of human needs that would give rise to emotional behaviors. Religion would be one of these behavioral patterns and would have its basis especially in the family group.

Burmese Supernaturalisms ([1978] 1996) is Spiro's most well-known study. It examined popular religiosity in Burma from a subjective, structural, and beliefs-oriented point of view. Among these three dimensions there exists a tight interaction that marks out various religious modalities.

An essay published by Spiro in a collective work (Banton 1966:85–126) is also rather well known. The question of religion in *The Issue of Religion: Problems of Definition and Explanation* is discussed in detail in order to reach a solution according to which religion, in the end, is a cultural institution. As each institution is an instrument for satisfying human needs, religion can be defined as an institution based on a cultural interaction in relation with supernatural beings that are culturally postulated (ibid.:96). According to Spiro, the difference between religion and the other cultural institutions consists in the fact that only in the case of religion are the systems of action, of belief, and of value connected with supernatural beings.

Spiro tried to explain to what an extent the practice of religious beliefs is connected with needs and functions. He described the functions of religion according to a fourfold typology: intentional-recognized functions, nonintentional-nonrecognized functions, intentional-nonrecognized functions, and nonintentional-recognized functions. He then separated the apparent functions from the real ones, and finally he described the wishes that are satisfied by religion at the cognitive, substantive, and expressive levels through the respective function of adjustment, adaptation, and integration.

The explanations of religion were provided not only in a functional key but also in causal terms. Spiro, in fact, wrote:

> I have suggested that the acquisition of religious beliefs is to be explained causally, and that the practice of these beliefs is to be explained in terms of motivation—which means that it is explained both causally and functionally. Religion persists because it has functions—It does, or is believed to, satisfy desires, but religion persists because it has causes—it is caused by the expectation of satisfying these desires. Both are necessary, neither is sufficient, together they are necessary and sufficient. The causes of religious behavior are to be found in the desires by which it is motivated, and its functions consist in the satisfaction of those desires which constitute its motivation. (ibid.:117)

It is evident that Spiro used both psychological and sociological variables. The cognitive basis of religion lies in childhood experiences, but its explanation is to be found in social structural variables, especially in family ones. As far as family variables are concerned, the religious dimension appears as a dependent variable. The reasons for the persistence of religion are psychological and motivational; these variables are therefore to be regarded as independent variables. In this connection once more the family plays a strategic role. For this reason, one can say that religion must be explained on the basis of an approach that includes society and personality.

SYMBOLS AND RELIGION IN THE WORK OF MARY DOUGLAS (1921–)

It is impossible to study the work of Mary Douglas concerning symbols without making reference to Victor Turner (1920–83), author of studies of the rituals of the Ndembu in Zambia (Turner 1967, 1969) and of pilgrimages (Turner and Turner 1978). Through symbolic analysis, Turner looked at ritual as a dynamic process characterized by the comparison between structure (organizations active in a given society) and antistructure (redefinition of the collective human meaning without the support of the institutions) and elements of liminality (transition).

Mary Douglas brought to her work a sensitivity to Christianity, the influence of her teacher Edward Evans-Pritchard, and the influence of Emile Durkheim. At first she studied the Lele, a population living in Zaire (Douglas 1975, 1982). In her study *Purity and Danger* (1966) Douglas tackled the problem of ascertaining the reasons for the difference between more or less rigorous religions. The two essays *Social and Religious Symbolism of the Lele* and *The Animals of the Religious Symbolism of the Lele* showed that the rules governing hygiene and etiquette, sexuality and eating, derived from the Lele's conception of the universe. The Lele were not capable of providing a rational and explicit justification of these rules. Reasoning of this type would immediately call into question some principles and criteria on which their conception of the world and of life was based. For this reason such information was automatically denied.

Douglas wrote that the Lele did not have any systematic theology, not even a doctrinal body through which one could study their religion. If one considered their religious practices, their religion seemed to amount purely and simply to an amazing variety of prohibitions that usually concerned everybody, but at times only a few individuals. The rituals—like all rituals—were symbolic, but their meaning remained obscure. They emerged in the everyday situations in which the same series of symbols were used; it was rather similar to a religion in which the liturgical language, through the use of metaphor and poetical allusion, could excite a deep reaction but never defined its own terms because it used a vocabulary that was well understood in the nonritualistic rules (Douglas 1975, 1982).

The Lele were organized on the basis of cult groups. Only one of these cults was dedicated to an animal—the pangolin, some sort of anteater. It gave birth to one progeny at a time. From this point of view, at least, the pangolin seemed rather similar to human beings. As was well-known, twin births were rare; therefore, among the Lele the parents of twins obtained some advantages. In the same way the pangolin enjoyed the privilege of being the only animal that was a cult object. Douglas's analytical approach was very close to the structuralist approach of Lévi-Strauss (Cipriani 1988a). She recognized, however, that not everything could be explained on the basis of neostructuralist analysis (Douglas 1975, 1982).

One of the most important points of her work *Natural Symbols* (Douglas 1970) was the proposal of a *grid/group*. The *grid* checks the power of the social norms that influence the individual. The *group* establishes to what extent the individual social acting depends on social belonging. Moreover, the group sensitivity could be either *strong* or *weak*; the same could be said for the grid, that is, for the social regulations. By combining grid and group with strong and weak, one could obtain four possibilities: weak grid and weak group, strong grid and strong group, weak grid and strong group, strong grid and weak group. The consequence, for example, was that social contexts with a strong grid and a strong group showed a proclivity for rituals; social contexts with weak grid and weak group tended to collective enthusiasm; finally, those with weak grid and strong group were rather sectarian.

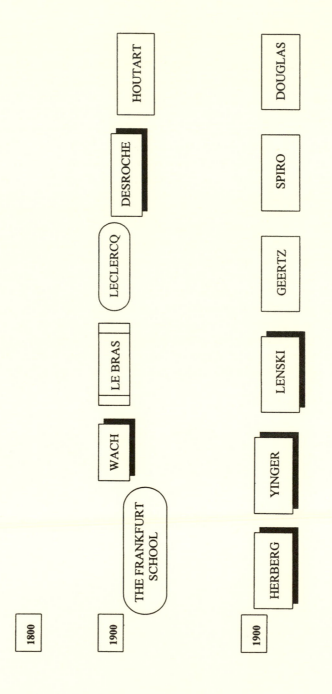

Synoptic Table 5:   From the Frankfurt School to Douglas

PART IV

Recent Developments

1

Secularization

Sabino Acquaviva, a sociologist at the University of Padua, was among the first social scientists to write, in 1961, about the crisis of the sacred, using a statistical documentation of religious practice at the international level. From an early idea concerning the probable survival of religion in the future, the author of *L'eclissi del sacro nella civiltà industriale* (*The Eclipse of the Holy in Industrial Society*, 1976) has been gradually modifying his own statements, until he himself recognized in his book *Fine di un'ideologia: la secolarizzazione* (*The End of an Ideology: Secularization*): "Roughly speaking the crisis of practice and the crisis of religion were almost coincidental: hence, the theory of the eclipse of the sacred in industrial civiliza-tion. . . . This theory was based on indicators used to measure the initial symptoms and the emergence of the crisis since the 16th century" (Acqua-viva and Stella 1989:7). However, "secularization as a process can by itself give rise to new ways of being religious. It is evident that if religion is robbed of its exterior forms, it allows in the end new ways of living the experience of the sacred precisely because the rules of the game change" (ibid.:9). Such an argument concerning the posteclipse phase aims at emphasizing that "with secularization, religiosity, as well as religion, changes in quality and diminishes in intensity" (ibid.:11). In order to prove his point, Acquaviva created a neologism: He wrote that more than about secularization, we could talk of "demagicalization" (ibid.:11). One could argue therefore that the eclipse of the sacred corresponded to the end of a magical use of the sacred. This interpretation of the socioreligious reality is not new, since in an earlier work he had written: "The magical use of the sacred is often tied up with popular and pagan religion, which in a Catholic milieu belongs to our past; this pagan religion somehow dis-solves after the decay of indulgences, of the use of sanctuaries and saints, and of the mythical image of the miracle as a potential factor of great turn-ing points in our lives" (Acquaviva 1979:33).

Acquaviva formulated a further hypothesis, namely, "the biopsychology (anthropology) of religion." This notion postulated that "religion, through religious practice but especially through experience, is helpful in order to overcome completely, or partially, the stress deriving from the limitations to the satisfaction of a whole series of needs" (Acquaviva and Stella 1989:21). These needs concern what follows: the "biogrammatic need for 'amortality,' of 'non-death,'" "the unfulfilled need to love and to be physically and psychologically loved, and consequently the sublimation of eros and libido." For this reason "I concentrate my love in God or towards his abstract ideal substitutes of religious character." "The need or instinct to explore leads, through the neocortical elaboration, to the need to know, to explain everything: God, being omniscient and the cause of everything, satisfies this need. The need to manipulate things, to dominate them, leads to the development of magic, which through time and secularization, transforms itself progressively in science," "The hunting and killing of animals generate a sense of guilt, and this guilt feeling is sublimated and controlled through the ritual sacrifice and meal"; "religion and religiosity are also tightly connected to the 'psychological need' of attributing meanings to things and facts"; "the ritual behavior partly has a biogrammatic origin" (ibid.:21–27). These topics were reconsidered in Acquaviva's book *Eros, morte ed esperienza religiosa* (1990).

Having completed this psychological foundation of religion as an instrument for satisfying "biogrammatical" needs, Acquaviva again tackled his initial theme of desacralization: "Religious crisis comes more from the inside than from the outside of the churches" (Acquaviva and Stella 1989:56).

It is necessary to say that the concept of desacralization had previously been defined "as a reduction, in intensity and diffusion of the experience of the sacred, as a psychological experience of the totally other," whereas secularization concerns the structures, the attribution of sacred meaning or of a magic value to persons and things as well as the attribution of sacred meaning to morality (Acquaviva 1971:67).

However, the conclusion of *The Eclipse of the Holy in Industrial Society* (1976) is still open to verification. Acquaviva wrote, in fact: "This is certain: the eclipse of the sacred is connected with a change in the development of human society and psychology; as such it cannot be considered contingent but it will determine the temporary or definitive decline of a series of traditions, cultures and religious values" (ibid.:306). Elsewhere, however, the author expressed some doubts: "I do not know what is going to occur in the near future. . . . One can be sure only of one thing: a long time will elapse before the new reality takes its shape and a new civilization will tell us how, specifically, the eternal problems will be posited: life, death, the meaning of the universe" (Acquaviva 1990:238).

In a more recent edition of *The Eclipse of the Holy in Industrial Society* (Acquaviva 1976), the author sharpened his 1961 argument without however changing its substance. He maintained that it was not completely true that religion was in crisis. But that was the basic thesis of his book (Acquaviva 1971, 1992:13). Frankly, these concluding remarks add further complexity, while mentioning existential uncertainty. Indeed, Acquaviva stated:

> From the religious point of view mankind has "entered into a long night" that with every new generation becomes more obscure and of which we do not seem to be able to see the end. A night in which it seems that there is no place for God or for the sacred; hence, a traditional way of giving meaning to our existence, of facing life and death becomes weakened. Even if motives of religious behavior persist—the need to explain anguish, the sense of precariousness, we ourselves and all that surrounds us. Individuals move progressively away from a religious presence in themselves or around themselves: often they wonder if somewhere there truly exists or has ever existed something other than uncertainty, doubt, [and] existential insecurity. (Acquaviva 1971, 1992:261)

DAVID MARTIN (1929–):
THE PROS AND CONS OF THE CONCEPT OF SECULARIZATION

David Martin, a British sociologist at the London School of Economics, has taken an openly polemical attitude to the concept of secularization: "I propose to consider the uses to which the term 'secularization' has been put, and to show that those uses (or perhaps, more accurately, misuses) are a barrier to progress in the sociology of religion" (Martin 1969:9).

His radical critique (Martin 1967:11) was expressed with strong persuasion and passion. By comparing optimistic rationalism, Marxism, and existentialism, Martin reached the conclusion that the concept of secularization was subject to many ideological biases that led to superficial generalizations. This was why he suggested deleting the idea of secularization from the sociological vocabulary. He examined the forms of secularization that have interested Christianity in connection with the development of scientific thought and proletarian alienation.

Martin has contested the utopian uses of secularization and stated the necessity of its correct use on the basis of classical sociological thinking from Durkheim to Parsons, from Weber to Berger. In fact, he has insisted that a wider critical approach be reached with contribution from the sociological community.

Martin again tackled the question of secularization in his book *A*

General Theory of Secularization (1978a), in which he suggested a survey of such phenomena, especially in Europe, and proposed his own theory. In his view, religion means the acceptance of a level of reality that goes beyond the knowledge of the world through science and also beyond the human dimension. At the same time, instead of insisting upon the rejection of the term secularization, he maintained that it has a wide scope. His general theory of secularization was influenced also by authors such as Durkheim, Parsons, and Wilson. At the outset Martin clarified that it was not an abstract but an empirical theory, based on research data. Unfortunately, it had an ethnocentric outlook, as it concerned only the West; the author, however, was quite aware of this shortcoming.

Martin conceived a stratification of the various types of societies: monopolistic, typical of Catholic nations; "duopolistic," with a Protestant church as a majority partner; pluralistic as in England, with a state religion and other fragmentary forms of dissent; pluralistic in the American sense, without a state religion and with various confessional denominations; pluralistic in the Scandinavian sense, with a central role for the Protestant Lutheran churches; monopolistic in the sense of Christian orthodoxy, with a strong convergence between state and church in Eastern Europe. There are, however, exceptions both in the Catholic religion as well as in other confessions. A mixed model, formed by competitive religions in a specific context, for example, in the Swiss cantons, is also indicated. On the opposite side, Martin analyzed the model of the secular monopoly exemplified by the Soviet Union. In another chapter he addressed the model of reactive organicism, especially in postwar Spain with its cultural Catholicism, limited dissent, high religious practice (with some differences: it was very low in Andalusia). A sociological remark was devoted to the crisis of the priesthood. In essence Martin's general theory of secularization was constructed on the basis of analytical categories derived from various cultural contexts.

The possible ambiguities of this sociologist of religion can be overcome if one accepts the interpretation provided by Oliver Tschannen (1992:293). Tschannen wrote that Martin's position with regard to secularization has its own coherence if one takes into consideration his opposition to the notion of secularization as a unilinear and irreversible process. However, he accepted the notion of secularization as a complex and ambiguous process. Martin's book *The Dilemmas of Contemporary Religion* (1978b) seemed to confirm this interpretation.

More recent studies of the same author (Martin 1990) concern the diffusion of Protestantism in Latin America in connection with his general theory of secularization (Martin 1978a) and the relation between Christianity and war (Martin 1997).

SECTS AND SECULARIZATION:
THE STUDIES OF BRYAN WILSON (1926–)

Together with David Martin, but even before him, Bryan Wilson must be considered a pioneer of English sociology of religion. He tackled a wide variety of topics with an unusual commitment.

His best-known work dealt with sects (Wilson 1961), and one of his preferred topics was secularization (Wilson 1976).

The phenomenon of sects is a well-researched subject, which, however, is often affected by conceptual limitations and value judgments. For this reason Wilson tried to define rigorously the concept of sects and the typology that he derived from it. He criticized Troeltsch for his arbitrary classification of the types of sect. In his view Troeltsch paid too much attention to a millenarian point of view, which was not present in all models of sects. Moreover, the contemporary conception of the religious phenomenon cannot overlook the fact that many sects are not small groups but involve vast numbers of people in various parts of the world. Wilson especially avoided opposing church and sect, in the sense that the church no longer represents a central institution for gaining access to metaphysical truth.

According to Wilson, sects are voluntary organizations in the sense that freedom to choose to join them is almost total. Equally free, however, is the will on the part of the older members to accept or reject new applicants. A prospective applicant must pass a test in order to be part of the "we" with which the sect identifies itself, as it considers itself an elite and imposes specific rules for its members. The individual who does not obey is expelled. From this, a strong awareness of one's commitment to the sect becomes apparent. An ideological legitimization covers each member and each activity. The ways in which sects interact with the world are numerous: some sects accept the world, while other sects reject it. The various attitudes and reactions toward the world can be classified as follows:

1. Conversion: the aim is an inner personal change because the world is bad.
2. Revolution: a supernatural change can transform the world, which is wicked.
3. Introversion: salvation is outside society and for this reason it is necessary to withdraw from it.
4. Manipulation: salvation is possible in the world, but to achieve it the use of unusual instruments such as occultism, esotericism, physical strength, and money is necessary.
5. Thaumaturgy: the world is full of evils; supernatural forces are necessary to escape the world and its normal laws.

6.   Reformation: the evil is here, but one can remedy it with adequate interventions, to be suggested at a divine level.

7.   Utopia: the world must be totally reshaped on the basis of religious principle.

This complex typology does not exhaust all the possible forms of "unorthodox reaction to the world," but it is certainly useful for a sociological understanding and interpretation of the contemporary development of sects.

The map of the American sects in Europe and Latin America described by Wilson is also very helpful. These sects are characterized by a strong proselytism, e.g., with the Mormons, Jehovah's Witnesses, and Pentecostals. Wilson studied their developments from their birth in the United States, and showed, for instance, how the Jehovah's Witnesses have been able to transform themselves since World War II from a type of traditional sect into a genuine mass movement. The statistical data provided by the author are very interesting. His work was completed by two studies on the sects of South Africa and Japan. Finally, despite external appearances, according to Wilson sects are communities of love. They live with the tensions of their conditions. As soon as these tensions decline, the desire to join other confessional groups is to be expected.

The relationship between religion and society presents itself as crucial when dealing with secularization. In Wilson's view, secularization is not only a change *in* society, but also a change *of* society in its basic organization (Wilson 1982). In particular, this change conveys a reduction of the power of religions and an expropriation of ecclesiastical properties. The reference to the supernatural also diminishes, and in this way religion itself loses importance. For Wilson as for Martin, secularization is a lengthy process, which is subject to changes that took many of religion's functions away. Wilson concludes:

> Traditional religion, in the West and in other fully modernized countries, has succumbed to the transformation of social organizations. Nowhere in the modern world does traditional faith influence more than residually and incidentally the operation of society, or even, for the generality of men, the quality of everyday life experience.... [In fact,] it is difficult to see how the otherwise irrevocable pattern of societal order could be reinfused with religious inspiration. As yet, only at the margins and in the interstices, and principally in the domain of private life, has such religious endeavor been effective. (ibid.:179)

Secularization is not only a factual condition, but it is part of the profound beliefs of the social agents: "Not only are men disposed to give less credence to the supernatural, and particularly in its conventionally received Christian formulations, but they are now—and this is a relatively recent change—strongly convinced that religion has diminishing importance in the social order" (Wilson 1976:15). The data on religious practice confirm this orientation. The decline appears evident: conventional faith is no longer the same. Wilson's final prediction was: "Religions are always dying. In the modern world it is not clear that they have any prospect of rebirth" (ibid.:116).

Together with Karel Dobbelaere, Wilson was carrying out research with questionnaires on Sokka Gakkai, a Japanese Buddhist organization that also has members in England and in the rest of Europe (Wilson and Dobbelaere 1994).

THE TRILOGY OF FRANCO FERRAROTTI (1926–)

Franco Ferrarotti has analyzed the contemporary dynamics of secularization. He stated explicitly in *A Theology for Non-Believers*: "The present book is concerned with some of the discussions on which sociological discourse has concentrated in recent years with important, sociological if controversial, results: from Robert N. Bellah's "civil religion" to Thomas Luckmann's "invisible religion" and finally to the somewhat myth-making theory of "secularization" by Peter L. Berger" (Ferrarotti 1987:v). This statement from the preface reflects Ferrarotti's previous approach in *Toward the Social Production of the Sacred* (1970) and his contribution to *Culturology of the Sacred and of the Profane* (1965).

However, an incentive to discussion comes from the Italian context also, especially regarding the hypothesis of the "eclipse of the sacred." Ferrarotti states his intent as follows:

> Far from witnessing an utter eclipse of the sacred, as some have incautiously announced, we are seeing a return to the sacred, experienced as a renunciation of human reason, which has disappointed, and as a reversion to the irrational, to pure feeling as a source of satisfaction and to the primacy of absurdity, misty and suggestive at one and the same time. . . . [Moreover] the need is to rebuild a postrationalist rationality: one no longer dichotomous, based on the rational-irrational dilemma, but instead one able to take into account the arational and metarational impulses that are part of and even enter as decisive elements into human experience. (Ferrarotti 1987:22)

Ferrarotti's interests are not confined to the field of sociology of religion but extend to philosophy as well as sociology, from Kant, Marx, and Nietzsche to Comte, Durkheim, and Weber. In this respect, Chapter 7 of a *Theology for Non-Believers* is particularly relevant. Here Ferrarotti formulated a bold proposal for a sociology capable of reversing, as it were, theology, in such a way as to become "the basic instrument for linking ethical principles and social practice, or as the essential bearer of a historically rooted ethic, not merely abstractly, sterilely, preached" (ibid.:161). It seems that the author went beyond a purely sociological analysis or, to put it more precisely, he used sociological insights in order to elaborate a far-reaching project that become apparent in his concluding remarks: "Not God, therefore, but the mystery of God: the awareness and respect for the shadowy area that makes man—every man, every woman—inexhaustible, cognizant of the fascination of the irrational, recalling the movable horizon of the possible; beyond the push toward acquisition and utilitarian logic—a calm scrutiny of men and things" (ibid.:169).

In 1983 Ferrarotti made a further development in his studies of the relationship between religion and technology in *The Paradox of the Sacred* (Ferrarotti 1984). While *A Theology for Non-Believers* faced philosophical and theological thinking about present-day issues, in his new book the author returned to philosophical considerations. This is the reason why the research began with observations concerning the crisis of rationality, the hunger for the sacred, the presence of the devil, and the industrial world. The character of the second volume of the trilogy was strongly critical and paved the way for the third volume, which was initially entitled *After the Christianity of Constantine,* but was finally entitled *A Faith Without Dogma* (Ferrarotti 1993), which was adapted from a statement by Simon Weil that "dogmas should never be affirmed" (Ferrarotti 1993).

In *The Paradox of the Sacred* Ferrarotti argued that it was a mistake on the part of sociologists of religion to fail to draw a distinction between religion and religiosity:

> The confusion between church religion and religiosity as a deep, debureaucratized personal experience hindered a recognition that not only was the supposed "eclipse of the sacred" not taking place, but that there was, rather, an undoubted growth of the need for religion and community, and that now we are witnessing the flourishing and growing "social production of the sacred." (Ferrarotti 1984:19)

After stating that the "eclipse of the sacred" was an "unfounded" (ibid.:19) hypothesis, the author then presented his own perspective:

> Religion, the sacred, and the divine do not point to the same realities. They move on different levels and obey incompatible logics. In its hierocratic form, religion is the expression of the administration of the sacred. The sacred is contrasted to the profane, but it does not necessarily have need of the divine. One might say that the more religion gains as a structure of power and center of economic interests and socio-political influence, the more the area of the sacred contracts. The field of the religious and the field of the sacred do not necessarily coincide. With good evidence, one probably could maintain that when the need, or the "hunger," for the sacred increases,

then organized religion declines. The paradox is that *organized religion is intimately desacralizing* and that the pure experience of the sacred, even in its relation with the divine, is blocked rather than helped by the religious hierocracy. One would need hypothetically to conclude that there is not an eclipse of the sacred but of religion, more precisely of church religion. (ibid.:37)

There is, however, another paradox that must be considered: "The "sacred" is the metahuman, which is required most of all for human coexistence, to avoid the flattening-out of living, the obscuring of the parameter or point of reference against which to measure oneself, the loss of the "sense of the problem," the risk of the loss of what is really uniquely human in man" (ibid.:83).

In *A Faith Without Dogma* (Ferrarotti 1993) many of the notions and suggestions appearing in the first two books are rediscussed and further deepened. From the "wind of the spirit" to the problems of theology, from the myth of development as a good in itself to the excesses of mechanistic rationalism, from the ambivalence of the sacred to Satanism and to the sociology of evil. In this work Ferrarotti took stock and used the empirical evidence from fieldwork conducted and dealt with in previous works, especially in *Toward a Social Production of the Sacred,* and Comte and Durkheim dealing with the issue of religion. He was skeptical about the possibility of civil religion (Bellah 1967) in Italy. In that country

> The weakness of the theoretical, conceptual apparatus of Italian positivism is obvious, but the difficulties for "civil religion" in Italy, did not arise only from philosophical deficiencies. From its unification in 1860, Italy lacked a profound national experience, shared by all citizens, which would consolidate its basic cohesion. . . . [In Italy] "civil religion" seems destined to have a difficult life and little capacity for obtaining that "interior disposition" to service for the common good that today seems to present itself as a basic precondition for the orderly progress of civil society. (Ferrarotti 1993:118–20)

These remarks are not incompatible with the positions elaborated by other scholars of secularization:

> The sacred points to and presupposes a community link. In its external, ritualistic aspect, this link is the religious bond, the community of the faithful, the Church. But precisely for this reason, sacred and religious must not be confused. They are two realities that should not be hastily conjoined, even if in everyday language they are often used as synonyms. The fact is that the idea of the sacred precedes the very idea of God, and that the religious is probably none other than the administrative arm of the sacred, a power structure that continually runs the risk—diabolically—of replacing the sacred while proclaiming itself at its service. (ibid.:144–45)

SECULARIZATION AS A MULTIDIMENSIONAL PHENOMENON:
DOBBELAERE (1933–)

Karel Dobbelaere, a Flemish sociologist at the Catholic University of Louvain, belongs to the tradition inaugurated by Leclercq, that is, a Catholic orientation coupled with a wide variety of polemical positions. This leads Dobbelaere to confront official church doctrine and to prefer some of the approaches of the Anglican church. He has also studied Buddhism (Wilson and Dobbelaere 1994). Moreover, Dobbelaere is engaged in various empirical research, especially in Belgium (Voyé, Dobbelaere, Rémy, and Billiet 1985; Voyé, Dobbelaere, Rémy, and Billiet 1992).

Dobbelaere's participation in various academic milieux has given him an extensive knowledge of emerging trends at the international level. His book on secularization, a concept that he defined as multidimensional (Dobbelaere 1981), documents his international experience. Secularization, according to Dobbelaere, can be subdivided into three levels: the societal as a lay level (with institutional differentiation, whereby religion loses its universal character and simply becomes one institution among others); the institutional, which is represented by religious change (with the modernization and worldliness of religion); and the individual, which is given by religious involvement (together with the decrease of formal religious practice). Only the first level directly concerns the phenomenon of secularization. Actually, Dobbelaere is so convinced on this matter that he would rather use the ambiguous term "lay" than the more specific word "secularization."

Tschannen (1992:310) sums up Dobbelaere's point of view: secularization is neither the equivalent of the fall, nor a form of religious pathology, nor a unilinear evolutionary process. The term "fall" stands for the collapse of a religious society such as medieval society was wrongly thought to be.

Having resolved the issue of secularization in this way, Dobbelaere goes deeper into the definition of religion, by choosing those of a substantive type, because even the functional definitions seem to him substantive. He then examines the relationship between society and religion from the point of view of integration. He is severely critical regarding "civil religion" (Bellah 1967), stating very clearly that civil religion is not even a religion. Quite persuasively Dobbelaere remarks that civil religion leads to a forced homologation that suffocates cultural and religious minorities by imposing upon them a fictitious integration. In this sense civil religion amounts to a factor of social disintegration. Dobbelaere criticizes the unilinear character of the secularization process and finally he draws a distinction between two analytic trends, the first stemming from Durkheim (and Parsons, among others) and the second characterized by a Weberian orientation represented by Bryan Wilson.

Dobbelaere's conclusion amounts to an invitation to choose the study of religion as a meaning system that operates at the social and individual level.

2

Religious Pluralism

THE "MODERN RELIGIOUS THEMES" PROPOSED BY THOMAS LUCKMANN (1927–)

Thomas Luckmann is interested both in the sociology of knowledge (Berger and Luckmann 1966) and in the sociology of religion. He offers data and reflections that usually go beyond a contingent interest and that show a lasting value. His best-known book is *The Invisible Religion* (Luckmann [1963] 1967), which, despite a controversial concept of religion, has the merit of indicating new directions. He states:

> A unifying perspective on the problem of individual existence in society is to be found in the sociological theory of religion. This insight must be attributed, within the sociological tradition, to Emile Durkheim and Max Weber. . . . Different as their theories are, it is remarkable that both Weber and Durkheim sought the key to an understanding of the social location of the individual in the study of religion. (ibid.:12)

It is important to specify that Luckmann deals with religion in a different manner than did Durkheim and Weber. In his view, the connection between these two classical authors is based on the fact that "both Weber and Durkheim recognized what is presupposed in the present essay: that the problem of individual existence in society is a 'religious' problem" (ibid.:12). Any reference to the supernatural is simply omitted. It is not by chance that he uses the adjective *religious* only in quotation marks. He does the same when he speaks of "hypotheses about the 'religious' components of the relation of individuals in contemporary societies" (ibid.:17).

Luckmann is especially critical of the kind of sociology of religion that is completely absorbed in minute descriptions of the decline of ecclesiastical institutions by using generally a narrow-gauged point of view. On the contrary, in his judgment the problem of personal existence in society is essentially a problem concerning the social form of religion (ibid.).

This social form is given by the overcoming of ecclesiastically oriented religion, which is then condemned to the margins of modern society.

Luckmann's approach has been variously influenced, in particular by the pragmatist social psychologist George Herbert Mead (1863–1931) and by his academic mentor, the phenomenologist and sociologist Alfred Schutz (1962). Hence, the outcome of Luckmann's thinking becomes perspicacious: "The world view, as an 'objective' and historical social reality, performs an essentially religious function and defines it as an *elementary social form of religion*. This social form is universal in human society" (Luckmann 1967:53). Moreover, Luckmann writes that both the "ultimate" meaning of everyday life and the significance of extraordinary experiences are located in this "different" and "sacred" side of reality (ibid.).

Luckmann proceeds to examine the character and the scope of ecclesiastical religiosity as opposed to a typically individual one. He aptly states that the "theoretical" character of the "official" model of religion contributes to a potential divergence between such a model and the subjective system of "ultimate" significance for the typical members of a given society (ibid.).

In addition,

> The fact that the sacred cosmos rests primarily on the "private sphere" and the secondary institutions catering to the latter, combined with the thematic heterogeneity of the sacred cosmos, has important consequences for the nature of individual religiosity in modern society. In the absence of an "official" model the individual may select from a variety of themes of "ultimate" significance. (ibid.:105)

Among these "modern religious themes," that of the "autonomous individual" comes to stand for the absence of external restraints and traditional taboos in the private search for identity (ibid.:110). In this connection, "the prevalent mobility ethos can be considered a specific expression of the theme of self-realization. . . . Another, peculiarly modern, articulation of the themes of self-expression and self-realization is sexuality. . . . Another theme which occupies an important place in the sacred cosmos of modern industrial societies is 'familism'" (ibid.:111–12). Families and sexuality are for Luckmann strongly united and are to be considered religious themes. These themes together with self-expression and self-realization form a whole that, by also including individual independence and mobility, could be defined as "invisible religion." One could assume that invisible religion is opposed to visible religion, the traditional object of study by sociology of religion, which is mainly concerned with measuring the levels of festive and sacramental practices.

Together with these main themes there are also other, less relevant, religious topics that have some claim to "sacred" status. The latter are, of course, equally available for the "autonomous" individual in the assortment of religious representations. They are subordinated to the major themes in the sense that they are less likely to be selected as cornerstones in the construction of subjective systems of "ultimate" significance. As pointed out earlier, many of the subordinate themes originate either in the traditional Christian cosmos or in the "secular" ideologies of the eighteenth and nineteenth centuries. (ibid.:113)

The theme of death is not present even among the subordinated ones. Thus, an element with an obvious religious character does not hold a central role and meaning in modern society. Instead, the "private sphere" acquires the central point and the ultimate meaning. This is then the "new social form of religion" (ibid.:163). Moreover, this "emergence of the new social form of religion is partly obscured by the more easily visible economic and political characteristics of modern industrial society. It is unlikely that the trend we have tried to describe is reversible" (ibid.:117). Finally, secularization would tend to have a unilinear progress—just the opposite of what Dobbelaere and others sustain—and would start with a symbolic differentiation from which would later derive a structural differentiation. Richard K. Fenn (1978), on the contrary, is convinced that secularization originates from this latter, structural differentiation.

The invisible religion hypothesis has generally caused more criticism than agreement among contemporary sociologists of religion. However, some sociological insights can emerge from it. Even the scholars of what Luckmann calls, perhaps polemically, the "new sociology of religion," must take those insights into account. According to Luckmann, the new sociology of religion is responsible for having "badly neglected its theoretically most significant task: to analyze the changing social—not necessarily institutional—basis of religion in modern society" (Luckmann 1967:18).

BERGER (1929–): FROM THE "SACRED CANOPY" TO THE TRANSCENDENCE OF THE COMIC

After working initially together with Luckmann (Berger and Luckmann 1966), Peter Berger has become highly original in his line of research, aiming at a basic coherence even though the objects of his studies appear to be different. Berger began his work on sociology of religion in a mood critical toward Protestant theologians and institutions. He was certainly under the influence of Durkheim and Weber, but he also was connected, like Luckmann, to Alfred Schutz.

In a volume entitled *The Sacred Canopy*, he envisions the social construction of religion as the projection of a sacred cosmos by human beings, in such a way that some sort of "sacred canopy" (Berger 1967) protects them in the course of their difficult and uncertain existence.

Inspired by Weber, Berger's methodology calls for a full use of the *Verstehen* operation, without however forgetting about the principle of value-free research.

His major themes touch upon secularization and pluralism. The former produces the latter because it tends to make religious institutions less credible, whereas pluralism gives rise to secularizing orientations. Later, Berger concentrates his attention on pluralism.

He is convinced that secularization is not irreversible. It is rather pluralism that creates new situations in contrast with the preexisting religious traditions. The necessary outcome is a resort to individualistic forms of religion.

Pluralism is not only an internal question of the various religious confessions. It also concerns competition with nonreligious rivals regarding the definition of reality and its social construction (Berger and Luckmann 1966). Such competitors are active both as revolutionary or nationalistic ideological movements and individualistic or sexually emancipating value systems. In the meantime, the answer of religious institutions points to an ever-greater rationalization and bureaucratization that imply a selection and a formation of personnel compatible with the functional needs of the modern world.

When speaking more specifically of secularization Berger refers to a process that conveys the rejection of religious dominance in various social and cultural sectors. Even education is then taken away from the direct influence of ecclesiastical authority. The dynamic of secularization affects not only the structure of society but also art, philosophy, literature, and in particular science. Science becomes more autonomous and secular in dictating its perspectives to social reality, but the phenomenon is obviously quite differentiated in the various groups and contexts.

As he stated in an editorial presentation and in an introduction (Berger 1969:9), Berger was aware that his book on the social reality of religion (*The Sacred Canopy* 1967) can be seen as a treatise on atheism. For this reason, in a subsequent volume he wrote almost polemically about a "rumour of angels" (Berger 1969) in order to show that the supernatural really emerges in many aspects of everyday life, including games and irony—in later years his interest returns to irony. Transcendence has not been reduced to a mere rumour. And modernity has not been able to supersede religion.

As a true Weberian, Berger knows that he must be objective (Berger 1973a:9). However, he confesses to be a Christian who has not yet found his option—he calls it appropriately heresy, a term that reappears in later works. For him "religion is of very great importance at any time and of particular importance in our own time" (ibid.:10). However, Berger goes on to say:

> Today the supernatural as a meaningful reality is absent or remote from the horizons of everyday life of large numbers, very probably of the majority, of people in modern societies, who seem to manage to get along without it quite well. This means that those to whom the supernatural is still, or again, a meaningful reality find themselves in the status of a minority, more precisely, a *cognitive minority* . . . a group of people whose view of the world differs significantly from the one generally taken for granted in their society. (ibid.:18)

On the basis of various reasons, the author maintains that "there are therefore some grounds for thinking that, at the very least, pockets of supernaturalist religions are likely to survive in the larger society" (ibid.:41). For this reason,

> It is a fairly reasonable prognosis that in a "surprise-free" world the global trend of secularization will continue. An impressive rediscovery of the supernatural, in the dimensions of a mass phenomenon, is not in the books. . . . This is not a dramatic picture, but it is more likely than the prophetic visions of either the end of religion or a coming age of resurrected gods. (ibid.:41–42)

A Rumor of Angels had been conceived from a liberal theological preoccupation in the sense of Schleiermacher—essentially it is a rebuttal to the secularizing theologians who reduced the supernatural to a simple rumor, which signals, however, some sort of presence, even though a minor one. This book makes a constant reference to the contemporary theological debate. In this framework an old perspective of Berger's reemerges. "The comic reflects the imprisonment of the human spirit in the world" (ibid.:90), but actually, "by laughing at the imprisonment of the human spirit, humor implies that this imprisonment is not final but will be overcome, and by this implication provides yet another signal of transcendence—in this instance in the form of an intimation of redemption" (ibid.). This interpretation of humor, which is theological and sociological at the same time, can be traced back to *The Precarious Vision* (Berger 1961) and makes a new appearance after thirty-five years in a systematic work on the comic as a metaphysical dimension that stands as a signal of transcendence (Berger 1997:205–15).

But why does Berger choose the term "rumor"? He provides the following explanation:

> A few years ago, a priest working in a slum section of a European city was asked why he was doing it, and replied, "So that the rumor of God may not

disappear completely." The word aptly expresses what the signals of transcendence have become in our situation—rumor—and not very reputable
rumors at that. This book has not been about angels. At best, it might be a
preface to angelology, if by that one meant a study of God's messengers as
His signals in reality. We are, whether we like it or not, in a situation in which
transcendence has been reduced to a rumor. . . . If the signals of transcendence have become rumors in our time, then we can set out to explore these
rumors—and perhaps to follow them up to their source. (Berger 1969:119,
120)

Undoubtedly, in these passages Berger is less Weberian than elsewhere: his
stand with regard to faith is evident. His orientation is quite theological, if
not pastoral. On the other hand, the objective is made quite explicit when
he remarks that in most of his book he has been reasoning to show that the
theological thought of our time has a possibility of rediscovering the
supernatural.

The intellectual development of Berger proceeds with the *Pyramids of
Sacrifice* (1974), a text not far from the tone of Ivan Illich, understanding
toward the needs of the Third World and against the sacrifices that are
imposed by capitalistic development. In this book Berger has in mind a
political ethic capable of producing profound social transformations.

Another key text is *The Heretical Imperative* (Berger 1979) in which the
influence of Schleiermacher is more explicit. The author considers three
hypotheses regarding religious tradition: deduction, that is, defense of
authority; reduction, that is, secularization of the existing situation; induction, that is, recovery of traditional experiences.

The central issue, however, is one concerning the choice of heresy
imposed by the contemporary situation: emblematically, it is no longer
necessary to look to Rome, but to Benares, therefore to the Indian traditions, in order to begin a confrontation among the world religions,
between Jerusalem and Benares. In a following book there is an attempt to
recover these aspects (Berger 1981).

Finally, in *A Far Glory: The Quest for Faith in an Age of Credulity* Berger's
thinking becomes even clearer. He remarks (Berger 1992:147–48), in fact,
that he can join the pilgrims getting together at dawn in order to go to the
river in Benares; he can stay together with them in one of the many
mosques that stretch from the Atlantic Ocean to the China Sea. But there is
of course, according to Berger, the next morning; then, remembering the
past experience of transcendent reality, it is impossible not to think of previous certainties and therefore to make comparisons and evaluations.

3

Civil Religion in Robert Bellah (1927–)

It can sometimes happen that a short essay is written that almost immediately becomes a classic, an indispensable reference, even more than a larger contribution on the same topic might be. This is the case with Robert N. Bellah, who is often quoted for an article he wrote on civil religion in America (Bellah 1967) and for another one concerning religious evolution (Bellah 1964). In both contributions the theory is so original that it is fascinating even before the necessary empirical verification. It is a fact that Bellah's challenges have succeeded in stimulating the field of contemporary sociology of religion. One might object to Bellah's ideas, but they cannot be ignored.

Bellah was director of the Center for Korean and Japanese Studies and then for a time chairman of the Department of Sociology at the University of California, Berkeley. His intellectual interests are far-reaching: the religion of the Tokugawa dynasty (1542–1868) (Bellah 1957) and also the habits of contemporary Americans depicted in a multidisciplinary book (Bellah et al. 1986).

A student of Talcott Parsons, Bellah has also been influenced by Durkheim and Weber. He also makes references to the work of Habermas, although he prefers the work of theologian Paul Tillich (1886–1965).

His collaboration with Parsons led to the publication of the essay *Religious Evolution* (Bellah 1964). Evolution here is seen as "a process of increasing differentiation and complexity of organization which endows the organism, social system, or whatever the unit in question may be, with greater capacity to adapt to its environment so that it is in some sense more autonomous relative to its environment than were its less complex ancestors" (ibid.:358). Equally balanced, although synthetic, is the definition of the concept of religion: "a set of symbolic forms and acts, which relate man to the ultimate conditions of his existence" (ibid.:359). Putting together the two concepts of evolution and religion, he establishes five phases of religious evolution:

1. primitive religion, for instance, that of Australian aborigines
2. archaic religion, that of native Americans
3. historical religions, ancient Judaism, Confucianism, Buddhism, Islam, primitive Christianity
4. premodern religion, represented by Protestantism
5. modern religion, in which religious individualism is predominant

Bellah considers the following dimensions: the symbolic religious system, religious action, religious organization, and their social implications.

The symbolic religious system of primitive religion belongs to a mythic and dreaming variety; religious action is based on participation, on identification, and on ritual. There is no separate religious organization; thus, the social implications of religion consist of the possibility of rituals reinforcing solidarity and socializing the young.

In archaic religion, the symbolic religious system shows a more direct interaction between mythological beings and men. Ritual is also an act in which the relationship between man and gods becomes evident; cult groups become more numerous; social structures appear to be organized within the frame of a cosmic order. With regard to historical religions, there is a great differentiation of symbolic systems; religious actions appear to be necessary for salvation; the religious organization is articulated in a number of communities; at the social level religion becomes an ideological bond that can influence reforms and revolutions.

In the case of premodern religion, symbolism makes reference to a direct relationship between man and God; religious action identifies itself with life and no longer with ascetic practices; religious organization is no longer hierarchic. Bellah remarks that "the direct religious response to political and moral problems does not disappear but the impact of religious orientation on society is also mediated by a variety of worldly institutions in which religious values have been expressed" (ibid.:370).

Finally, Bellah analyzes modern religion, which overcomes many dualisms of the past and rejects traditional symbolism. In this connection the philosophical-theological approach is more evident. In the first place Bellah states

> In many respects Schleiermacher is the key figure in early Nineteenth century theology who saw the deeper implications of the Kantian breakthrough. . . . By the middle of the Twentieth century, however, the deeper implications of Schleiermacher's attempt were being developed in various ways by such diverse figures as Tillich, Bultmann and Bohnhoeffer. Tillich's assertion of "ecstatic naturalism," Bultmann's program of "demythologization" and Bonhoeffer's search for a "religionless Christianity," though they cannot be simply equated with each other, are efforts to come to terms with the modern situation. (ibid.:371)

As far as religious action is concerned, Bellah writes that "how specifically religious bodies are to adjust their time-honored practices of worship and devotion to modern conditions is of growing concern in religious circles" (ibid.:373). On the contrary, at the level of the religious organization, trends of the type "my mind is my church" or "I myself am a sect" seem to prevail. From the social implication point of view:

> It remains to be seen whether the freedom modern society implies at the cultural and personality as well as at the social level can be stably institutionalized in large-scale societies. Yet the very situation that has been characterized as one of the collapse of meaning and the failure of moral standards can also, and I would argue more fruitfully, be viewed as one offering unprecedented opportunities for creative innovation in every sphere of human action. (ibid.:373–74)

A theoretical framework of this kind does not seem capable of effectively resisting specific criticism. However, the attempt is helpful, if for no other reason, for the debate connected with it.

Bellah's initial work on American civil religion goes back to a 1966 lecture published in *Daedalus* (Bellah 1967). At the outset he states that "this religion—or perhaps better, this religious dimension—has its own seriousness and integrity and requires the same care in understanding that any other religion does" (Bellah 1970:168). This quotation is taken from a later volume (*Beyond Belief*), which includes the 1966 lecture that was also published in *The Religious Situation* (1968). In Chapter 7 of *Beyond Belief* in a footnote he clarifies a few doubts:

> I think it should be clear from the text that I conceive of the central tradition of the American civil religion not as a form of national self-worship but as the subordination of the nation to ethical principles that transcend it and in terms of which it should be judged. I am convinced that every nation and every people come to some form of religious self-understanding whether the critics like it or not. (Bellah 1970:168)

The last observation seems to show a certain disappointment of Bellah with the many reservations some scholars harbor concerning his idea of civil religion. He states: "This public religious dimension is expressed in a set of beliefs, symbols, and rituals that I am calling the American civil religion. The inauguration of a president is an important ceremonial event in this religion. It reaffirms, among other things, the religious legitimization of the highest political authority" (ibid.:171). It is not by chance that the inaugural speeches of presidents from Washington to Kennedy as well as political rituals are carefully examined.

The term "civil religion" appears in Rousseau's (1712–78) *Social Contract*

(Chapter 7, Book 4) and concerns the existence of God, life after death, the reward for good and the punishment for evil, and interreligious tolerance. In the United States, "the words and acts of the founding fathers, especially the first few presidents, shaped the form and tone of the civil religion as it has been maintained ever since. . . . The God of the civil religion is not only rather "unitarian," he is also on the austere side, much more related to order, law, and right than to salvation and love" (Bellah 1970:175). Bellah remarks quite appropriately that civil religion is neither Christian nor anti-Christian, nor Christian in a sectarian way. On the other hand, it is not purely and simply "religion in general." Bellah claims that civil religion has been able to save itself from an empty formalism, emerging as a genuine vehicle of a national and religious self-awareness. Needless to say, Bellah adds his own contribution to this American conception of religion when he argues:

> It would necessitate the incorporation of vital international symbolism into our civil religion, or, perhaps a better way of putting it, it would result in American civil religion becoming simply one part of a new civil religion of the world. . . . A world civil religion could be accepted as a fulfillment and not as a denial of American civil religion. (ibid.:186)

The content of such religious forms has biblical roots: exodus, chosen people, promised land, New Jerusalem, sacrificial death, and resurrection. All these elements can be easily traced back in the historical development and formation of the United States of America.

Many of the hopes of Bellah are bound, however, to be disappointed. In the book *The Broken Covenant* (1975), he defines civil religion as an empty and broken container. Such pessimism is obviously justified by the contingent situation: on the one hand, the Vietnam War, and on the other, the delegitimation of the presidency resulting from the Watergate scandal.

A different outcome, and a more optimistic one, seems to be enjoyed by a subsequent work that is more systematic, multidisciplinary, and innovative, and deals with individualism and commitment in American society (Bellah, Madsen, Sullivan, Swidler, and Tipton 1986). The research on *The Habits of the Heart* is centered on the crisis of the 1960s, specifically understood as a religious crisis. Once it had rejected utilitarianism as a nongratifying solution, American culture showed a proclivity for a more individualistic approach through an emphasis, for instance, on subjective experience according to Zen Buddhism. For Bellah, however, this position does nothing but favor the return to utilitarian individualism.

The methodology of this research is qualitative. In fact, it uses qualitative interviews and life stories that help to describe a profile of the American "national character." The present and the future of contemporary society generate a malaise, which emerges from the transcribed text used in the volume as empirical verification of the hypothesis. Individualism appears as a significant aspect in the cultural heritage of the United States. This orientation has its own ideological connotation and assumes the character of a self-sufficient morality that is considered capable of acting also as a social and political guide. However, the lack of any basic value becomes evident. This is inevitable because the civil, biblical, and republican traditions have always avoided the most radical forms of individualism by emphasizing the social and communal dimensions of the person. But the crisis of civic belonging tends to blur such social propensity and to favor a way out of society in order to find a refuge in individualism. It seems that there is no longer a society in which to have faith, as organizational bonds, networks, norms, cooperation, and reciprocal help become weak. This trend, which was described in the year 1980, was confirmed in the subsequent decade. In the last analysis, modern religion presents itself as an extreme increment of individualism, that is to say, as a hyperprivatization ("my own religion"). A whole chapter of *Habits of the Heart* is dedicated to such a religion (Bellah et al. 1986:219–49):

> Radically individualistic religion, particularly when it takes the form of a belief in cosmic selfhood, may seem to be in a different world from conservative or fundamentalist religion. Yet these are the two poles that organize much of American religious life. To the first, God is simply the self-magnified; to the second, God confronts man from outside the universe. One seeks a self that is finally identical with the world; the other seeks an external God who will provide order in the world. Both value personal religious experience as the basis of their belief. Shifts from one pole to the other are not as rare as one might think.

Bellah also cites an example: "Sheila Larson is, in part, trying to find a center in herself after liberating herself from an oppressively conformist early family life. Her "Sheilaism" is rooted in the effort to transform external authority into internal meaning. The two experiences that define her faith took a similar form" (Bellah 1986:235). Finally, Bellah considers that religious individualism is, in many aspects, appropriate to our kind of society. Just as in the case of secular individualism, religious individualism is not going to disappear.

4

North American Trends

GUY E. SWANSON (1922–1995):
THE SOCIAL PSYCHOLOGY OF RELIGION

Guy Swanson, a social psychologist, did not exercise a great influence on American sociology of religion. His scientific marginality, however, does not justify neglecting his intellectual contribution to the study of religion (his name is not even mentioned in some of the most important handbooks of sociology of religion). The fact that the social psychology of religion is considered a collateral discipline was perhaps not helpful to him. In like manner, the philosopher and psychologist William James is still the object of a certain exclusion that denies him the role of protagonist that he deserves.

Guy E. Swanson taught at the University of Michigan and at the University of California, Berkeley. Adopting an interdisciplinary approach, he published a very stimulating essay in the *Journal for the Scientific Study of Religion* (Swanson 1971). In *Sociological Analysis* (renamed *Sociology of Religion*), *A Symposium of the Work of Guy E. Swanson* was published in 1984 (pp. 177–222) and, two years later, an essay by Swanson on immanence and transcendence (Swanson 1986).

Like Bellah, Swanson considered ultimate values as key concepts for the sociological interpretation of religious facts. He elaborated on this topic especially in his book on primitive religiosity, *The Birth of Gods* (Swanson 1960), following a trend of studies that had a long anthropological and also sociological tradition. On the basis of Durkheim's ideas, especially the concept of society as a producer of religious systems, Swanson assimilated structures to beliefs as if they were mirroring each other. In other words, a certain type of belief would correspond to an identical or similar kind of society. This led to a hierarchical classification of the gods, corresponding to an equally hierarchical power organization of groups in a given society. Thus, monotheism corresponded to the idea of a society ruled by an elite, that is, by a few dominant groups (sovereign groups). According to Swanson, a maximum of three sovereign groups constitutes a simple society. Four groups constitute the beginning of complexity.

These sovereign groups "exercise original and independent jurisdiction over some sphere of social life" (ibid.:42). This is true especially with regard to the family, the village, and the neighborhood. Swanson examined approximately fifty societies and he discovered that the sacralization of the individual is directly proportional to the weakness of the society. Unlike Durkheim, however, Swanson did not analyze the contribution and the meaning of ritual. The reference of supernatural beliefs appeared to him to be sufficient in order to understand religious phenomena from an individual and social point of view.

Swanson (1968) must also be remembered for an essay on secularization published in *The Religious Situation: 1968,* together with Bellah's essay on civil religion. Swanson's idea was that religious communities are no longer capable of producing significant and influential ultimate values, whereas roles and institutions in the secular society take on a sacred character at the same time.

ANDREW M. GREELEY (1928–):
A MULTIFACETED CATHOLIC SOCIOLOGIST

Distinct from most of his Catholic colleagues, Andrew M. Greeley has been an opinion leader who has also had a big influence in non-Catholic milieux. There are, however, other aspects of the Chicago priest that should be mentioned to prove his multifaceted personality. Indeed, he has been a serious scholar as well as someone who has been involved in social work and in essays in criticism.

In the first place, Greeley seems to confront reality as a global entity. Second, he is not a scholar who works only in the library. As a specialist in the Catholic world and in American Protestant denominations (Greeley 1972a), he is also active in the National Opinion Research Center. He is interested in pedagogical issues and has written novels (almost thirty) and poetry. He does not neglect the findings of other social sciences, in particular, anthropology, psychology, and history of religion. Greeley insists especially on the experiential dimension of religion, and laments the excesses of theorization in sociology of religion, preferring empirical research, which he conducts himself with refined methodological instruments.

Andrew Greeley contests the use and abuse of the concept of secularization, which he calls a myth (ibid.:127–55) and defends the thesis of a persistence of religion (Greeley 1972b). He maintains that neither the hypothesis of secularization nor the hypothesis of a serious crisis is empirically confirmed (Greeley 1972a:150). Greeley has clear-cut ideas for the future: religion will not lose its believers and its influence will not be diminished; the sacred is not about to be replaced by the secular; full-time parish clergy will not lose many members; there will not be any simplification of liturgy; religious institutions are about to become more sophisticated; denominations are not destined to disappear. At the same time Greeley thinks it not improbable that a new prophetic witness will come, local congregations will remain, but it will not be easy to shake the religious apathy of the masses.

Greeley conceives of religion as a circle that anybody can enter from any point: it is made of experience, image, narration, community, and ritual. Only later does it become doctrine, devotion, and a norm. Greeley speaks, in fact, of narrative symbols that are shared within the religious community and utilized to explain the meaning of life.

Greeley states that he has been influenced by Geertz (and thus Durkheim and Weber), James, and Otto. In particular, he says that his debt toward Geertz is "immense" (Greeley 1972a:iii).

Greeley has been associated with the University of Chicago and the University of Arizona. His vast bibliography includes almost four thousand titles, including many newspaper articles. He published his autobiography in 1986 under the title *Confessions of a Parish Priest*.

Among his preferred topics one can find the dynamics of the paranormal (Greeley 1975), ecstasy (Greeley 1974), stratification, alcoholism, and American Catholicism (Greeley 1977). He tries to verify the central role of symbols in organizing and orienting the meaning of life. He feels that religion is made of images that one can find in ritual and in narratives. These narratives allow the social subjects to tell and realize salvation stories in their own lives.

A sociological study of the parish where he worked (Greeley 1962) verifies Herberg's (1955) hypothesis concerning the triple religious affiliations of the Americans, inevitably divided among Protestants, Catholics, and Jews. Greeley also observed the prevalence of endogamic marriages, that is, marriage within one's religious community.

To reply to Lenski (1961), Greeley (1963) shows in *Religion and Career* that there are no substantive differences among Catholics and Protestants in scientific and economic fields. Moreover, Catholics do not look down either on scientific disciplines or on the basic values of American society, like autonomy, commitment, and material success. But Greeley continues to find evidence of distinctive Protestant, Catholic, and Jewish ethical systems that tend alternatively toward individualism or community (Greeley 1989).

RICHARD K. FENN (1934–):
A SOCIOLOGIST AGAINST THE GENERAL TREND

Richard K. Fenn had been an Episcopalian priest and then the supporter of a new sociology of religion and a *sui generis* theoretician of secularization. His scientific production goes beyond the traditional boundaries of the sociology of secularization by dealing with broader questions, like civil religion, and by expressing doubts on the nature of differentiation. Most of all, Fenn has had important discussions with North American sociologists, from Parsons to Bellah. All of this explains why Fenn appears in this section under "North American Trends" rather than in the "Secularization" section of this volume.

Unlike Talcott Parsons, in Fenn's opinion there cannot exist any consistency among culture, structure, and personality in a highly differentiated and secularized society. The Parsonian order cannot be maintained, because the same religious basis is threatened by secular theories, which undermine moral principles. Fenn (1970) observes that even the members of a church can give only extremely modest help to religious activities since other institutions require an active collaboration by the same subjects. Moreover, social individuals are attracted by a variety of models of ultimate significance. Thus, individuals are in conflict between differentiated or even opposed values. Fenn is very explicit on this point. He radically disagrees with Parsons, arguing that Parsons's congruence model does not serve any heuristic aim in such a complex and highly differentiated social system. Cultural diversity is too large to allow for a singular moral order. The notion of society as a moral order founded on a religious basis and characterized by congruence, according to Fenn, is no longer applicable to the facts that it is expected to interpret (ibid.). In the end "we may not be surprised to find that ostensibly secular activities have an ultimate significance to the actors involved and that traditionally religious institutions are of only proximate significance" (Fenn 1969:124).

In Fenn's opinion religion does not disappear; it loses, however, its strategic role within society. His secularization theory is articulated in five successive phases. Progress is not unilinear since regressions can occur from one phase back to a previous one. Moreover, secularization can create events as well as being dependent on them.

At the beginning there are neither religious ministries nor special operators. Thus, the first stage is characterized by the appearance of the clergy, which is active throughout the secularization process. In the second phase, there is a demand for a clear division between religious and secular elements. The result is a notion of secularization as "a process in which the parts of a society seek to define their relationship to each other and to the larger society" (Fenn 1978:29). The next stage deals with the problem of "civil religion." Fenn assumes a very critical stance when he considers Bellah's formulation. However, Fenn accepts the idea of "civil religion" if conceived as a "desecularization" device, that is, when conceived as a mediator of the conflict existing between the social parts. The fourth phase is characterized by a spreading of the discussion to define the limits of sacredness. Both the state and the clergy take part in it, together with other smaller organized groups. In the end, however, the sacred disperses itself and loses strength. In the meantime, there are some groups that demand legitimization for their notion of the sacred. This leads to a great increase of charismatic figures and elites. The last phase is the present situation, characterized by the hiatus between individual and society, the person and the community. While the collective values tend to secularization, the individual ones become sacralized.

The different forms of adaptations to secularized society can be determined by considering two parameters—the extent of the sacred and the integration between individual and collective values. Catholicism and Protestantism in their origins are the least suited forms for secularization because they have a rather wide notion of the sacred, the collective, and individual values, which are rather integrated among them. A minimum notion of the sacred and a strong integration characterize the Mormons. The other evangelical Protestants are not very integrated as far as values are concerned, but the extent of the sacred is noteworthy. Finally, magic and occultism are in last place since they show a good adaptation to secularization. Thus, secularization neither keeps religion away from society, nor prevents the agreement of some esoteric forms, like magic practices, with a secular context.

THE THEORIES OF HANS MOL (1922–) ON RELIGIOUS IDENTITY

Hans Mol was born in Holland. He has taught in New Zealand, Australia, the United States, and Canada, and is a pastor, a theology expert, and the former president of the Research Committee of Sociology of Religion in the International Sociological Association. He is a neofunctionalist and has discussed in a closely documented and accurate way the "inevitable" process of secularization (Mol 1989). He conceives a new scientific and social theory of religion (Mol 1976) and considers identity as a sort of religion (Mol 1978). He has written critically about Durkheim, Weber, Freud, Fromm, Bellah, and Berger.

Mol is convinced that men have an insuppressible need for a strong and reassuring identity. Religion would functionally satisfy this need. Notwithstanding the past and present changes, social, personal, and group identity are maintained because religions are able to handle the sociosymbolic renovation processes. Both convergence and conflictual situations are present. The final result is a sacralization of identity through four devices. The first one is objectification, that is, the tendency to put together the various elements of worldly existence within an orderly, lasting, and timeless reference frame. The second device is involvement, that is, an emotion centered on a specific identity, a system of meaning; the third element is the rite, as articulation and repetition of the system of meaning that aims at preventing its loss; finally, there is myth, that is, the sacralization of reality and personal experiences through statements concerning the role of human beings.

In Mol's opinion, tendencies toward change and those concerning preservation find a balance, a dialectical coexistence. Mol claims that religion reacts to a new element that changes a given situation just as an oyster adapts to the intrusion of a grain of sand by covering it with a mother-of-pearl secretion that accumulates on it in a concentric way (Mol 1976). Therefore, "conversion, charisma, and the rites of birth, initiation, marriage, and death are all essentially mechanisms for incorporating, rather than for annihilating, change" (ibid.:263). There is a desacralization process of what precedes and a sacralization process of the new. One identity substitutes for another. This further sacralization occurs through institutional modes. In fact, religion makes a system of meaning stable, while it strengthens the notion of reality and sacralizes identity. Religion's relevance lies both in the interpretation of life by stressing the struggle between sin and salvation and in the support of frail identities, those of the less privileged. An increase of "otherness" seems to parallel the growth of the socioeconomic and cultural complexity that leads to dominion over nature.

After analyzing the sects (ibid.:166–83), just as Weber and Troeltsch did, Mol writes about universal religions (ibid.:184–201). "The complexity of modern industrial societies has necessitated an increasingly greater independence of individuals and groups, which has created difficulties for the achievement of social integration and for the maintenance of comprehensive systems of meaning" (ibid.:200). Differently from the sects, universal religions tend to favor a mutual adaptation between men and society. Buddhism, Christianity, Confucianism, Hinduism and Islam tend to sacralize social identity without, however, creating particular difficulties for men. These universal religions survive in time because they can change, incorporate reluctant groups and reform, but also reinforce social unity (ibid.:184).

THE MULTIFORM SOCIOLOGY OF RODNEY STARK (1934–)

A prolific author, Rodney Stark has often written books in collaboration with other sociologists. He first worked with Charles E. Glock (Glock and

Stark 1965, 1966; Stark and Glock 1968), then with William S. Bainbridge (Stark and Bainbridge 1980, 1985, 1987, 1996), Laurence R. Iannaccone (Stark and Iannaccone 1994), and Roger Finke (Finke and Stark 1992). Together with these authors, Stark produced works that represent an essential reference even outside the realm of North American sociology of religion. Each contribution, in its own peculiar way, constitutes a conceptual and empirical work that becomes a first-rate methodological instrument, not without some noteworthy empirical backsliding. One could also say that the four phases of Stark's theoretical path correspond to each of the four coauthors—Glock, Bainbridge, Iannaccone, and Finke.

Glock in particular (Glock and Stark 1965), in writing about religious commitment, provides an important contribution with his proposition that commitment is made up of five dimensions: experiential, ritualistic, ideological, intellectual and consequential. The first dimension is concerned with what one experiences as sensations, feelings, and gratification in relation with the divine. The second stage includes all the celebration aspects, liturgies, prayers, official events, cults, and sacraments. The third stage includes the ideas, principles, values, contents, and aims in relation to beliefs. The fourth dimension regards the basic knowledge of sacred texts. Finally, the fifth dimension concerns the concrete outcomes of beliefs as expressed through behaviors, activities, and actions that occur in non-specifically religious contexts, like the family or the workplace. These dimensions could become indicators of religiosity, that is, useful measuring tools for empirical investigation.

Stark and Glock (1968) provide an example in their research on religious commitment. The aim of the research was to measure the religiosity levels on the basis of the following parameters:

1. generic certainty concerning the existence of God;
2. belief in a person-God;
3. belief in miracles on the basis of their biblical description;
4. belief in the afterlife;
5. belief in the existence of the devil;
6. belief in Christ as a divine person;
7. belief in the notion that a child is born without original sin.

The heuristic value of these propositions is exclusively founded on beliefs, while other important religious variables are not taken into consideration.

The objective of the two authors was to understand the nature of religious commitment (ibid.), and also to identify its origins and its sociopsychological consequences (however, the two projected volumes on these topics were never published). The whole work focused on four aspects: belief, practice, experience, and knowledge. Practice was in turn divided into ritual, that is, public, communitarian—which involves rites—and devotional, that is, private and personal, as in the case of individual prayer. Stark and Glock stressed the importance of the noninstitutional features of religion, thus contributing to widening the usual outlook of socioreligious investigations, which were often limited to the measurement of the ritual moments.

Stark and Bainbridge (1980; Bainbridge and Stark 1984) usually define religion as a compensation form for dissatisfaction deriving from frustrated aims. So religion is a substitute for a desired reward, and is a "proposal about gaining the reward" (Stark, cited in Young 1997:7). Then Stark and Bainbridge define a typology of church, denomination, sect, and cult that was already present in Swatos (1975). A church can be characterized by a strong self-legitimization that leaves out the legitimization of other religious forms, dismissing any dissent and alternatives. Society, on the other hand, with its institutions, appears to be competitive. The sect has both the self-legitimization trait and a tendency to fight against the other organized religious forms (the belief that only one's own religion is legitimate (Glock and Stark 1966). Sects deny society since it is considered hostile and thus should be confronted in various ways. This produces isolation, but at the same time it is a stimulus for social change. On the contrary, the denomination fits in well with society, recognizes the legitimacy of other religious creeds, and does not tend to exercise a strong control over society. Finally, the cult presents more particular aspects, accepts other religious solutions, but generally is not in line with society and differs markedly without exceeding it.

Stark's scientific work with Bainbridge is probably his most original contribution. They elaborated on exchange theory and on the idea of "compensation," to be viewed as a promise for a future reward that is not immediately verifiable, but that could be accepted as a compensatory form to be exchanged for the established objective (Stark and Bainbridge 1980).

Stark (Young 1997:3) recognizes his debt to Karl Popper (1902–94) for his rationalist criticism and his skepticism toward empirical knowledge, especially as presented in Popper's book *Conjectures and Refutations* (1969). Stark clarifies his conception: "I want it to be clear that the theory does not, and should not, imply anything about the truth or falsity of religious compensators. It merely postulates the process of rational choices by which humans value and exchange these compensators" (cited in Young 1997:7).

The universal form of religious commitment consists in the fact that *"regardless of power, persons and groups will tend to accept religious compensators for rewards that do not exist in this life"* (cited in ibid.:8; emphasis in the original). Stark is particularly interested in this perspective, which he indicates as his third axiom; however, he does not overlook the first two axioms, which function as a link in his theorizing on religion: "(1) *The power of an individual or group will be negatively associated with accepting religious com-*

pensators for rewards that are only scarce" (cited in ibid.:8; emphasis in the original). Expressed otherwise, this passage means that powerful and rich people will pursue immediate, material rewards, whereas poor people are more willing to accept religious compensators, thus hoping to store up considerable reward in the next life. This kind of religious commitment resembles the one concerning the sect. "(2) *The power of an individual or group will be positively associated with control of religious organizations and with gaining the rewards available from religious organizations"* (cited in ibid.:8; emphasis in the original). This axiom, on the contrary, is closer to a churchlike commitment. It is possible to infer from these three axioms that Stark is strongly oriented toward a specific theory of religion, and one can also deduce from them his orientation to empirical analysis. For this stance he shows an evident disposition, of Humean derivation, toward empirical knowledge. Since the mid-1970s William Bainbridge has also agreed with this position. Bainbridge is a scholar "mad enough to agree to collaborate on a full-length deductive theory of religion" (cited in ibid.:10).

The collaboration between Stark and Bainbridge continued to be rather productive. While Stark established the axioms, Bainbridge verified whether there were gaps in the logic sequence and suggested intermediate passages when needed. After having defined the theory, however, the two scholars encountered some difficulties in getting it published, as Stark (ibid.:11) recounted in an autobiographical form. Thus, they decided to make their theoretical approach known in small doses. They published twenty-two articles, which were collected in one volume, entitled *The Future of Religion* (Stark and Bainbridge 1985), and which won a prize from the Society for the Scientific Study of Religion. It is a work that goes against the general trend of secularization and shows the persistence of religion viewed as a substitute for prestige and privilege. The text provides a great deal of empirical documentation to support their theoretical framework.

After this success, the two authors started to work again on their theoretical book, published two years later under the title *A Theory of Religion* (Stark and Bainbridge 1987). In this book they present 7 axioms, 104 definitions, and 344 propositions, together with comments and discussion. Since it would be impossible to provide the full list of these elements, here follows the list of axioms, as well as one definition and one preposition:

> Axiom 1   Human perception and action take place through time, from the past into the future.
> Axiom 2   Humans seek what they perceive to be rewards and avoid what they perceive to be costs.
> Axiom 3   Rewards vary in kind, value, and generality.
> Axiom 4   Human action is directed by a complex but finite information-processing system that functions to identify problems and attempts solutions to them.

Axiom 5   Some desired rewards are limited in supply, including some that simply do not exist.

Axiom 6   Most rewards sought by humans are destroyed when they are used.

Axiom 7   Individual and social attributes which determine power are unequally distributed among persons and groups in any society. (ibid.:325)

Definition 23   Religious organizations are social enterprises whose primary purpose is to create, maintain, and exchange supernaturally-based general compensators. (ibid.:326)

Proposition 339   In the short run, secularization stimulates the development of sect movements. (ibid.:349).

Actually, the secularization process is capable of self-limitation, producing new religious movements, in particular, new sects that move away from traditional historical religions. At this point, it would be better to remind readers that the authors view the propositions as statements that work as a link between the axioms and the propositions on the one hand, and the empirical world on the other (ibid.:26). This expedient is useful for empirical surveys during fieldwork.

In the meantime, Stark also develops the notion of "religious economy" through which he wants to verify the existence of a market with its regular and potential customers (the believers), and a group of companies (religious organizations) that are ready to serve such a market and to act as a supplier in order to provide a line of religious products, thus creating a demand (Stark 1985). The consequence is that this market pluralism does not lead to the decline of religion and to secularization. Quite the contrary, the various religious confessions become stronger and competitive, thus favoring the participation of the believers, especially if they find an adequate answer to their personal expectations. Stark and Laurence R. Iannaccone (1994) applied this economic-based perspective to the European situation. Here they found that religious demand was present, but pluralistic church organization was rather inadequate.

The hypothesis of a growth of pluralism and revival of the religious organizations is supported in the volume *The Churching of America—1776–1990: Winners and Losers in Our Religious Economy* (Finke and Stark 1992). This holds true notwithstanding the various sects (especially Baptists) that are in a growing phase and the main denominations (first of all the Episcopalians, Presbyterians, and Congregationalists) that mark time or show some decline (this is also the case with Catholics, in the postconciliar phase of the last decades).

In line with this idea of a religious market, Stark also carries out research on religious conflict, on the stability and dynamics of religious economies, and on the development of primitive Christianity during Greek and Roman times. His primary goal, however, remains the construction of a "real" theory of religion that is not tied up with the theory of rational choice, not even in the manner of James S. Coleman (1926–95). This theory of rational choice is based on the freedom of the individual actor to choose, having his own resources, an ability to control them, some interests to protect, and rewards to maximize. This leads him to a rational calculation of costs and benefits, that is to say, the relative convenience of given actions when faced with special events requiring a rational choice, as regards, for instance, religious affiliation. There are, however, actors that are not individual but collective, that is, corporate actors, made up of "positions" more than of people and that have rights and responsibilities, interests and resources: business corporations, trade unions, and other associations including those of a religious character (Coleman 1990:part 4).

Finally it is worth mentioning Stark's return to his previous criminological studies and to the collaboration with Bainbridge (1996). This time they examine the relationship between religion and deviance, emphasizing the role of individual behavior and of social control on the part of the community. They talk about social and moral sources of integration having resort to four initial propositions. Regarding the social sources, at the individual level: *"Persons will conform to the norms to the extent that they are attached to others who accept the legitimacy of the norms.* Conversely, *people will deviate from the norms to the extent they lack attachments.* At the group level: *Deviance rates will be higher in groups having a lower mean level of attachments"* (ibid.:5; emphasis in the original). With regard to the moral sources at the individual level and in the same condition: *"Religious individuals will be less likely than those who are not religious to commit deviant acts.* At the group level: *Rates of deviant behavior will vary across ecological or collective units to the degree that they exhibit moral integration"* (ibid.:7). Religion itself is subjected to an analysis as deviance through the cult examination. However, it creates more communities of a Durkheimiam type. These communities promote integration and tend to limit deviant behaviors. For example, the consumption of alcohol and drugs is found to be related to religious affiliation (ibid.:81–99).

THE GLOBALIZING VISION OF ROLAND ROBERTSON (1938–)

Roland Robertson, a student of Bryan Wilson, draws his seminal ideas from Durkheim, Weber—whose theory on salvation he analyzed (Robertson 1978)—Simmel, and Parsons (Robertson 1982).

One of Robertson's major contributions is his approach to the phenomenon of globalization (Robertson 1992). Out of this debate we can see the main lines of his studies: the meanings of modernity, the creative role of religious movements, the perennial relevance of the classical authors, and the place of religion in sociology. (These themes are especially evident in the "Introduction" to the *Journal for the Scientific Study of Religion*—n. 3, 1992—by Frank J. Lechner. This issue of the journal is dedicated to a symposium devoted to Robertson held in Pittsburgh in 1991.)

In Garrett's terms, "Robertson is one of the few among a select group of contemporary theorists who have effectively applied symbolic interactionist categories at the macro-social level" (Garrett 1992:299). Over the years Robertson has offered important contributions, for instance with his book, *Sociology of Religion* (Robertson 1971).

With the transition of his interest from modernization to globalization, Robertson is moving along the path already indicated by both European and American sociology. Moreover, he does not believe in the privatization of religion. He believes that religion is capable of enhancing closeness among different cultures, creating in such a way the basis for a globalization based on the local units of an integrated social and cultural system at the world level. He shows indifference to the problem of secularization, which was however predominant when he published *The Sociological Interpretation of Religion* (Robertson 1970:34–47). Here he drew a distinction between a substantive definition, which he prefers, and a functional definition of religion. In his view, at any rate, religion is bound to persist for a long time, thanks especially to sectarian experiences. Later, he devotes his attention to the issue of ethnicity and multiculturalism, and he emphasizes the decisive role of religion in the process of globalization, similar to that which it has already had for modernization. In particular, Robertson stresses that he derives his interest in both the comparative and the interactive aspects that are typical elements of his sociological perspective from symbolic interactionism. In *Sociology of Religion* (Robertson 1971:15) he tries to outline a possible global framework that would include different contexts (from Africa to Latin America), different epochs (from the so-called primitives to the medieval and modern world), related social sciences (from history to anthropology), various beliefs (from magic to Protestantism). We are therefore confronted with a crucible of religious affiliations and analytical points of view. He has made an effort to cover a wide scope as far as religions and types of societies are concerned, along two dimensions: historical and geographical. Moreover, he emphasizes a sociological comparison of the various religions in different social and cultural contexts. Robertson has tried to escape from the tendency to deal principally with the Western industrial societies and he has paid a greater degree of attention than usual to anthropological materials.

In Robertson's view, religion is actually an integral part of the process of globalization. This process does not have an exclusively economic character, but is based on the relationship between individuals, mankind, national societies, and the systems of the various societies. The outcome is a reduction of individual and social identities. Within this framework, the churches and the states are also in conflict. In the meantime some religious organizations seem to be fostering a nationalistic fundamentalism in order to protect their own original roots and to reshape the world order. However, religious groups and movements are especially called upon to give the world a meaning that should be, at the same time, an interpretation of it.

In the last analysis, Robertson, on the one hand, rejects any hypothesis of secularization and then of desecularization (or return of the sacred); on the other hand, he insists that

> in an increasingly globalized world . . . issues concerning societal as well as civilizational and local, forms of identity become of increasing importance; largely because of increasing global interdependence and the concomitant process of relativization of traditional identities. It is almost inevitable that religion will play a very significant role in the construction and reconstruction of societal, and other, identities in such a circumstance and will do so in close conjunction or rivalry with political agencies. . . . In more general terms, our attention should be directed at the response of religious traditions and movements to the phenomenon of globality as such. (Robertson 1987:31–32)

MORALITY, RELIGION, AND CULTURE IN ROBERT WUTHNOW (1946–)

Robert Wuthnow has published many works of considerable originality and quality, among them *Christianity in the Twenty-first Century* (Wuthnow 1994a), *Communities of Discourse* (Wuthnow 1989a), and *Acts of Compassion* (Wuthnow 1991). Wuthnow's first book was *The Consciousness Reformation* (Wuthnow 1976), in which he outlines four meaning systems: theistic, individualistic, social-scientific, and mystical. The last two are characteristic of the most recent historical phase as empirically tested through specific research (the San Francisco Bay Area Survey). This research concerns one thousand young people, between sixteen and thirty, and examines the new California religious movements, especially those of Eastern derivation (transcendental meditation, yoga, Zen Buddhism, astrology, extrasensory perception). These movements represent some sort of "new consciousness," especially among young people, in contrast to the traditional churches (Wuthnow 1978). This could be interpreted also as a rejuvenation of American religion to the extent that religious organizations might be capable of providing adequate answers to new needs and to the new mystical forms. But as if anticipating the discussions on globalization, Wuthnow raises implicit questions: "The common-denomination

values of the American civil religion, it seems, may be particularly susceptible to such international influences, being marked by the nation's
efforts to differentiate itself from other nations of the world and to redefine
its mission to the world" (ibid.:200). In the last analysis, the United States
has been too closely interested in other areas of the world (intervening
twice in wars in both Europe and Asia) to the point of neglecting its own
national identity and of becoming easily influenced by external factors.
According to Wuthnow the time has come, perhaps, to think of a rejuvenation of American civil religion. Initially, he followed Bellah's hypothesis
concerning the existence of a religious bond capable of making the diversity of the American people compatible under shared values.

His later production is, on the contrary, more autonomous, more
detached from the common wisdom of the sociological school, even if he
always makes dutiful homage to his teachers Glock and Bellah. A first volume concerns cultural change and the role of ideologies (Wuthnow 1987).
In a later work, he (Wuthnow 1989a) studied the institutionalization of
ideologies during the Reformation, Enlightenment, and period of European socialism. His major interest, however, is American religion at the
end of World War II. This religion has not disappeared: it undergoes
changes, but it remains relatively active.

In a 1988 work, Wuthnow considered the character of the majority religion, the *mainstream* religion. His aim was to identify the relationship
between religious belief and American society (Wuthnow 1988). He took
notice of the difficulties faced by the denominations and, at the same time,
of the development of groups not attached to religious structures. He also
spoke about the split between liberals and conservatives, competing in
order to give "a soul to America" (Wuthnow 1989b). The reality of the
United States is, however, much more complicated and includes, for
instance, the vast sector of voluntary activity, in particular that connected
with religious communities (Wuthnow 1991). This sector enjoys the most
intense contribution from people belonging to institutional religious
organizations. Especially relevant are those support groups in which the
presence of God is more directly felt, as one can read in *Sharing the Journey*
(Wuthnow 1994c). In these contexts individualism is overcome, but these
are temporary situations, which are subject to change. Wuthnow argues
that the role of voluntary activity, including religiously oriented activity, is
strategic in the American social structure with regard to its constant attention to others.

He again commented on the public dimension of religion in another
book, *Producing the Sacred* (Wuthnow 1994b), which shows the ability of
religious organizations to be active in society and to send public messages
of a spiritual character. "Each of the five forms of religious organizations—
congregations, hierarchies, special interests, academies, and public ritu-

als . . . participate in the public arena, attempting to make the sacred manifest in public life, from a distinctive niche in the social environment" (ibid.:18). Wuthnow is firmly convinced that "the particular contributions of these organizational types, and the challenges facing them, deserve special attention, instead of merely speaking of religion as a uniform entity" (ibid.:18).

Robert Wuthnow is one of the youngest members of the growing group of American sociologists of religion. A century ago only a few articles of interest to sociologists of religion had been published in the United States, whereas today a noticeable growth, with several hundred essays each year, has to be taken into consideration. This growing interest in the sociology of religion is due to the work of the American scholars who have been mentioned here.

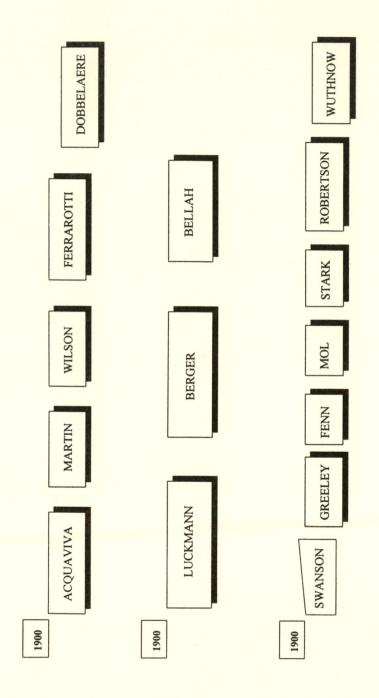

Synoptic Table 6:   From Acquaviva to Wuthnow

5

The European Trends

ÉMILE POULAT (1920–): BETWEEN HISTORY AND SOCIOLOGY

Émile Poulat, Directeur d'Études at the École des Hautes Etudes en Sciences Sociales and Directeur de Recherche at the Centre National de la Recherche Scientifique, is one of the few French sociologists of religion sufficiently known throughout the world. He can be considered one of the most important contributors to the *Archives de Sciences Sociales des Religions* (before 1973 called *Archives de Sociologie des Religions*) if for no other reason than his detailed reviews of books and for his collaboration in the publication of the journal as well as being a member of its reading committee.

His familiarity with other disciplinary sectors (through the jurist Le Bras and the psychologist Ignace Meyerson), and especially with historians, has also earned him great appreciation outside the sociological milieu. His way of conducting research in the field of sociology of religion is very original. A great specialist in Catholicism, he uses sociological instruments for detailed and persuasive analyses of phenomena, those belonging to both the present-day and the past. He moves with ease among different fields: Fourier's utopian socialism (Poulat 1957), the Jesuit Bremond's spiritualism (Poulat 1972), modernism (Poulat 1962, 1982), the worker priests (Poulat 1961, 1965), integralism (Poulat 1969), and from the problems of democracy to those of lay groups (Poulat 1987).

According to Poulat (1986:260), there is a "Ecclesiosphere" as we have an "Americansphere" and a "Sovietsphere." The Ecclesiosphere is for Poulat a "sphere of influence of the Roman Catholic Church that forces the other spheres but also other countries to come to terms with it." Moreover, Poulat maintains that the "sphere of the church goes well beyond the church itself as outlined in Canon Law; it can no longer be identified with the people of God, a doctrinal notion which is based on faith" (ibid.:267).

As is perhaps to be expected, Poulat centers his attention on France. But from this social laboratory he opens up to other contexts in order to reach conclusions that would be applicable to the wider Catholic world. He studies the origins of modern freedoms, of republican laypeople, and of the scientific culture, which are not favorable to religion (Poulat 1987). What he says about the two French worlds, the lay and the Catholic, is that there is a confrontation between them. This issue is very much alive in Italy, as well as in other countries. His conclusion is that none of the realities of

> conscience, church and state, has the means to remain self-enclosed. When one of the three elements is too invasive, oppressive, or threatening, it might happen that the other two make an alliance against it. Within human societies, between tyranny and anarchy, freedom points to a narrow path; it is a permanent invention, a fragile enterprise, but also a tremendous force. (ibid.:435)

A similar question concerns religion in Europe, which cannot only be a domain reserved to the churches. It is, in fact, also

> a question of the state, of the European states, although they conceive of themselves as being liberal and lay. They share the same conception of the state based on the rule of law and of freedom. This puts them up against a paradox: on the one hand, nothing can escape the law, not even freedom, on the other hand, they are all far from having an identical conception of law and of freedom. (Poulat 1993:408)

Poulat has also invented another word, "metheosociology," to define the sociology of religion. He justifies doing so:

> This neologism may be risky but . . . it expresses what he wants to say: a sociology of the climate of the times, that looks to the future and studies the sky (this is the least that a sociology of religion can do), sensitive to climatic zones, to their lasting stability about which voluntary action can do very little, but also to the seasonal ideas that live as long as a favorable wind lasts. (Poulat 1988:9)

Beyond rhetoric and metaphors, the author wishes to suggest a sociological approach to the religious phenomenon. This phenomenon should be stable and mobile at the same time, static and dynamic in its attention to the surrounding reality, capable of understanding the whole but also the detail, the persistent as well as the ephemeral: in sum, the well-defined historical institutions and the contingent small movements. To do this a rigorous method is necessary, a method open also to the unforeseeable and therefore to whatever is perennial and at the same time transitional. Poulat (1988) offers an extraordinary example of such a method through his work, which is made up of "small grains of reason or dust," in seven chapters, of a reason that is "applied," "universal," "received," "shared," "Catholic," "inhabited." From this metaphorical use of adjectives one can see the depth of Poulat's reflections that lead us to question the desire for peace and the need for war, spiritual power and the malaise of the intellectual, liberty and the sacred, sanctity and personal religion, the church and the economy, without ever having to resort to the notion of secularization.

Poulat is also a scholar who loves to do research in the archives, in which he finds key documents of the relationship between state and church (Poulat 1988:8–9), precious and enlightening letters, personal data (Poulat 1961), unpublished texts (Poulat 1957), or little known works (Poulat 1972).

His knowledge of the Catholic world, its clergy, and the religious intellectuals of the eighteenth and nineteenth centuries turns his publications into a gold mine of historical-sociological information and interpretations. Writing about the spiritual powers, Poulat defines the Holy See as a "power that is denied but recognized. Historians can tell us how, being practically excluded from political power at the time of Comte, the church has been able progressively to reenter the international scene, causing surprise on the part of many outside the church and scandal on the part of some inside the church" (Poulat 1988:53).

Regarding the present-day socioreligious situation (with respect to France) Poulat's perception appears to be well balanced between the attitudes of the laity and of religion as a private, personal experience. He wrote that it is "an institutionally lay society in all its great sectors: in politics, but also in economics, law, science, culture, education, sport, health, social insurance, etc. It does not exclude the religious but entrusts it to the free evaluation of each citizen, that is to say to free discussion and in this way it reintroduces it in the social circuit" (ibid.:97). In this way private values are being negotiated and evaluated in the social world almost as in some sort of stock market. But the signs of religious crisis are there (Poulat 1996).

THE SYMBOLISM OF THE SACRED IN THE WORK OF ISAMBERT (1924–)

François André Isambert is Directeur d'Etudes at the Ecole des Hautes Etudes en Sciences Sociales and former president of the Association Française de Sociologie Religieuse. He belongs to the current that follows the teachings of Le Bras. He carries out the mapping of French religiosity (Isambert and Terrenoire 1980) according to the original project of Le Bras.

At the time when Desroche (1962) was writing on Marxism and religion and Poulat (Poulat et al. 1961; Poulat 1965) was doing research on worker priests, Isambert was working on the relationship between Christianity and the working class (1961).

Later on, between the end of the 1970s and the beginning of the 1980s, aside from the valuable work on mapping, he also carried out studies on contraception and abortion (Isambert and Ladrière 1979). He then published two studies that mark a very productive phase of his working career. The first concerns institutional ritualism (Isambert 1979), while the second deals with popular ritualism (Isambert 1982). The aim of these studies is to provide a theory of the symbolic effectiveness that can be applied both to the religious and the social fields. In this way it is possible to avoid the traps of subjectivism that became prevalent after the end of the tendency to carry out research on religious practices.

At the same time, Isambert suggests a "sociological anthropology" aimed at analyzing a social phenomenon by appealing to intercultural analogies. In this way, the specificity linked to the particular place and time of the researcher can be overcome. As Isambert writes, this perspective should lead to the formulation of "a more general theory of symbolic action in social life" (Isambert 1979:25).

From the analysis of magic, with its immanent, manipulatory, and private character, Isambert deals with religion, which has on the contrary transcendental, propitiatory, and public traits. Isambert suggests that between magic and religion there is a polarity rather than a boundary (ibid.:44). In sum, "the sociological anthropology of religion would reinsert the conceptual tools of the sociology of magic within the analysis of the contemporary religious field" (ibid.:60).

In order to measure the symbolic effect, Isambert analyses three aspects of the symbol: the significant, that is, a meaning, which could become a mental content; the object (which could also be a gesture or a sound), which could be perceived within the material universe; the consent, that is, the social occurrence resulting from the link between the significant and the object. In this way, according to Isambert, "the symbolic effect comprehends three levels at the same time. In any case, the sociologist is particularly aware that the symbolic effect is a social effect" (ibid.:85).

Following Austin (1911–60) and his idea of the "performative utterance"—that is, the idea that an utterance performs what is being said by the simple fact that it has been uttered (Austin 1988)—Isambert suggests considering a rite as performative "when it realizes, according to a previously established modality, a relationship with the other—a person, an object or god—through the same symbolization of the relationship that has to be established." Isambert writes that "this procedure is not a mystery—I can always pray to God, even if He does not exist—insofar as behavior tends to correspond to the symbols—verbal or not—that designate them. In fact, without the symbols, behaviors are difficult to maintain" (Isambert 1979:99–100). Hence, it would be difficult for a person to pray without having the verb "to pray" and the symbolic gesture typical of the praying person.

Liturgy itself is a performative act par excellence. However, "today's liturgy," as Isambert writes, "is undergoing a crisis of institutional effectiveness; thus, often the effects of liturgy are sought elsewhere rather than in the performance itself and in its precise rules" (ibid.:113). Isambert then dedicates a whole long chapter to the analysis of the symbolic effectiveness of the Catholic sacrament of the "anointing of the sick."

The ambivalence of the sacred is the topic of an essay on the religiosity of popular festivals (Isambert 1982). After making a well-documented introduction on the developments of "religious" sociology in France, which is dominated by the figure of Gabriel Le Bras and by the discussions on "de-Christianization"—another term for secularization—Isambert outlines, deepens, and critically reexamines popular religion, the festivals, and the sacred. These three elements correspond, respectively, to the three parts of the book. The three concepts belong to a joint system, so that "popular religion and the festivals refer to the sacred as the fundamental meaning of which they are the expression through the acts" (ibid.:15).

Isambert underlines that talking about popular religiosity probably means being open to neither categorized nor qualified religious forms especially as regards their content.

> One would omit therefore the categories such as "pagan" and "Christian," the "naive" and the "rudimentary," but also categories like the "original" and the "authentic," in order to understand systems of belief with a unified criterion pertaining to them. The social position in which they would be placed could then no longer be helpful in explaining their deviations or in evaluating their foundation, but rather in understanding the "sigh of the creature," as collective enjoyment. (ibid.:122)

With these observations about the oppressed creature that has a Marxist resonance, Isambert concludes the section dealing with popular religion.

Important symbolic meanings and rituals are connected with the festival. First of all, it is a collective activity, made up of

> representations, material or mental images that are supportive of the activity. The same is true of the various material objects, decorations, and food and so forth, which are useful for the development of the festival. Secondly, the festival is, if not total, at least complex as it involves several levels of social life. In this respect, the notion of festivals goes beyond the notion of ritual and also of the ceremony, which is a sequence of rites. Finally, this activity is symbolic in the sense that it evokes a being, and an event, a collectivity. Symbolization is characteristic of the festivals. The symbolic character

implies another trait, which is nothing but an aspect: in order to make the symbols recognizable, it is important that it remain relatively fixed. (ibid.:160)

Isambert offers at this point a survey of various forms of festivals, from the family forms to the public ones, from those that are typically religious to those of a different nature. After a detailed examination of the notion of the sacred in Durkheim and in his disciples (ibid.:215–45) Isambert expounds the way in which popular religion, the festival, and the sacred appear to be interwoven.

> The idea of popular religion entails the globalizing idea of the sacred as being grounded in the unchanging essence of religion and would therefore connect it with the "original sacred" which seems to interest some modern theologians very deeply. If popular religion is said to be festive this would amount to a far-reaching conception of the festival that tends to make it a ritual modality which on the other hand is typically of the same "original sacred." (ibid.:286)

A last caveat concerns the sacred: it cannot be assimilated to any form close to the religious field. Its character cannot be confused, according to Isambert, with a resort to the supernatural as a substitute for science and technology, with the personification of nature, with the sacralization of certain values such as a political party, a special cause, or a people. In the end, a sociology "freed from its myths but open to the understanding of whatever the contemporary world can still hide in terms of myth and mystery," is outlined and advocated (ibid.:305).

JEAN SÉGUY (1925–): FROM THE STUDY OF THE CLASSICS TO THE INVESTIGATION OF RELIGIOUS MOVEMENTS

The work of Jean Séguy is known for two characteristics. First of all, he is an expert in the classic authors of sociology of religion, especially Durkheim, Weber (Séguy 1972, 1986, 1988a, Séguy in Guolo 1996:149), and Troeltsch (Séguy 1980, 1994a). Second, he is a pioneer in the studies on religious movements and minority groups (Séguy 1977, 1989), utopia (Séguy 1971), charisma (Séguy 1984b), religious orders (Séguy 1984a), and messianism and millenarianism (Séguy 1993). Séguy and his students have studied the relationship between religion and modernity (Séguy 1986), and he has paved the road for his pupils (among whom Hervieu-Léger). As chief editor of the *Archives de Sciences Sociales des Religions*, Séguy has maintained an interdisciplinary and interconfessional approach.

Since the 1960s Séguy has shown a proclivity toward far-reaching scientific outlooks (Desroche and Séguy 1970) in order not to create water-tight compartments among the various disciplines. After having criticized the unfriendliness of theologians toward the nontheological sciences of religion, he has recognized the new trend toward accepting the contributions of the human sciences of religion but he calls the theological sciences "abusive mothers" as compared to the lay sciences. According to him, theology, as a normative science, studies the sources, the doctrines, the practices, the institutions, of a given religion from the point of view of this same religion. Being normative and characterized by the claim of authority, theology is naturally in difficulty when it has to accept competition from what it calls, at least in a first phase, heresy or heterodoxy (Séguy in Desroche and Séguy 1970:38).

Through a concise excursus on the history of sociology and of sociology of religion, Séguy outlines the stages of a difficult road: "Sociology began, for instance in Comte, as a neo-theology. In Durkheim sociology assimilates society and the religious object through a total suppression of the 'supernatural.' With Max Weber, on the contrary, sociology sets aside the question of values. Ernst Troeltsch is at the same time a theologian and a sociologist of Christianity" (ibid.:45–46).

At the conclusion of his survey of the study of religions, Séguy seemed convinced that

> the non-religious and the non-theological studies of religions have constituted themselves in opposition to theology [and] the relationships between theology and the non-theological studies of religion have been always the same: opposition, composition, and integration. At the present time, the non-theological research on religious phenomena has become of interest to ecclesiastical as well as the non-ecclesiastical, to believers as well as to nonbelievers. (ibid.:51)

In order to overcome the obstacles (Séguy 1973) caused by the divergence of those groups closer to the religious institutions and those closer to the laity, Séguy described a nontheological ecumenology that could open the door "to a complex of hypotheses, of men and methods so far not considered like, for example, those of the Marxists." The final solution could be given by "collaboration from a particular point of view among the non-theological disciplines and eventually with the theological disciplines also on the basis of ways and approaches to be defined with great care" (Séguy in Desroche and Séguy 1970:257).

In 1977 Séguy published his work *Les assemblées anabaptistes-mennonites de France*. More than nine hundred pages in length,

> this work represents the most far-reaching research that has ever been done on the Mennonite Anabaptists in one country. Séguy's analysis is focussed on those historical-religious aspects that characterize the persistence of a given religious tradition. Séguy asks how it is possible that religious beliefs

and practices can transmit themselves over a long period of time. In his view this is possible because of the ability to transform themselves that such beliefs and practices show according to the social conditions and despite their tendency to fight against them. . . . At any rate, the social actors of this process find their identity only through a constant return to their past, which is relived in new terms. (Prandi in Séguy 1994a:10–11)

As far as definitions are concerned, Séguy follows Weber's idea of a "metaphorical religion" or "analogical religion" that "does not have recourse to supernatural powers, but which has most of the other characteristics of religion in a global sense." Moreover, "this metaphoric religion produces meaning; it is an object and instrument of inner experience; but it does not pretend to open a way to a world, beings, or powers that escape the realm of the senses. It puts one in contact with a transcendence that, since it does not come from everyday life, does not require an other-worldly sanction" (1988a:178). This does not prevent access to moral obligations or even to ecstasy, as in the case of art. "Substitute religions" of a Weberian origin are therefore acknowledged.

Actually, it is for Troeltsch that Séguy reserves his major attention. Séguy here fills a gap not only with regard to the figure and the work of Ernst Troeltsch, whom he studies in order to offer a balanced image, keeping in mind the various aspects of this scholar and the way these different aspects play dialectically with each other. There is also an issue that is identified with the object of the study and at the same time goes beyond it. It is not by chance that this issue represents the central point and the preferred theme to which Séguy has devoted most of the volume. "It concerns the introduction, by examining the history of Christianity, of 'models' and 'types'—church, sect, mystic—on whose basis Troeltsch sees the development of the Middle Ages, of the Reformation, and its subsequent fragmentation" (Séguy 1980, 1994a).

Séguy's interest in Troeltsch is not without reason. It is an interest that must be underscored, as Troeltsch has contributed to a widening or confirmation of some of Weber's perspectives or conceptions. "His dependency on Dilthey and Weber does not mean that he was not capable of transforming their contributions according to his own goals. This is especially true as regards Dilthey, but it also true as far as Weber is concerned." Séguy maintains that "the sociology of Troeltsch is an historical sociology of Christianity and is expressed in the 994-pages of the *Soziallehren*" (Séguy 1980, 1994a:88).

Séguy's reconstruction of the thinking and work of Troeltsch is exemplary. It considers, in fact, the German scholar in his complete formation and development, before and after the publication of *Social Teaching of the Christian Churches* (Troeltsch [1912] 1976). Séguy analyzes the early years of primary socialization of Troeltsch and in the end discusses works that are usually neglected, for instance, posthumous productions such as the lectures that Troeltsch would have given in England had he not died in 1923. Séguy describes with great sensitivity and full knowledge all the details of Troeltsch's social life as well as the cultural influences connected with his scientific work.

Séguy's conclusion (1980, 1994a:347) on Troeltsch is quite definite and does not leave any room for doubt. He maintains that the development of Troeltsch remains extraordinary. Weber, whose concepts were largely utilized by Troeltsch, was quite aware of the high quality of this work. In Séguy's view, Troeltsch's shortcomings can be found in some secondary aspects, especially in his allegiance to the philosophy of Dilthey and his constant references to transcendence.

THE ANALYSIS OF JEAN RÉMY (1938–) ON THE RELATIONSHIP BETWEEN CITY LIFE AND RELIGION

Jean Rémy's academic courses and his publications are a point of reference both in Belgium and also in other countries: the University of Louvainla-Neuve is an important center for the study of religion.

[Rémy] has analyzed the structures and the roles of the Catholic church as well as the meanings of the practice of popular religion passing from the confrontation of the religious with the political and the economic and through its compromises with modernity. Jean Rémy has never stopped renovating the thinking in this field which, for a long time, has been enclosed in a reductive sociography. Rémy has studied the classics of sociology, in particular Max Weber, but his reading has always been enlivened by his sociological imagination. (Voyé 1996:5)

Rémy is also a specialist in urban sociology. For this reason he is able to couple the aspects of religiosity with those of urbanization. This was especially true at the very beginning of his research activity under the influence of Le Bras and of Fernand Boulard (Boulard and Rémy 1968).

For Rémy the basic structure is an economic one. Felice Dassetto summarizes his curriculum: collaborator of François Houtart at the Center of Sociology of Religion in the Diocese of Malines-Bruxelles, Rémy has conducted a vast research in the industrial area of Charleroi.

Already in this research one can detect the typical characteristic of his thinking, that is, a profound theoretical and analytical autonomy combined with a fervent imagination. The result is a constant opening of new observational spaces and of new interpretive models. . . . From the observation of urban reality and from an institutional request for an essay on pastoral practice, Rémy elaborates a series of reflections whose aim consists in showing the ways in which the church's pastoral practice was adapted to modernity in the urban environment. . . . Rémy tries to describe the problem of pluralism

at the various levels of social formation and of its effects on the religious system. (Dassetto in Houtart and Rémy 1969, 1974:12–13)

For this reason Rémy draws a distinction between a society that is not very
differentiated (rather simple, culturally monolithic, with a homogeneous
legitimation of norms and values) and a society that is differentiated or on
the way to becoming differentiated (with eventually a still Christian legitimization, but with severe disagreements among the same Christians about
the norms and the values that should regulate social life). In this second type
of society, religious pluralism emerges, with citizens in a constant tension
due to their overlapping memberships. "They might pass from one field to
another and desire that their religious leader represent this point of view in
confrontation with different orientations" (Houtart and Rémy 1969:80).

In doing research Rémy suggests keeping the descriptive separate from
the analytical concepts. However, such separation does not imply the
renunciation of any concept. In effect, one should distinguish "observation
at the descriptive level from the global level of explanation. The confusion
between these two aspects often ends up in a false debate between macro
and micro sociology" (Rémy 1981:44). More explicitly he stresses:

> Some sociologists, unable to distinguish the descriptive and the analytical
> level, see religion as a fundamental phenomenon of social life. Religion is
> therefore interpreted as some sort of functional need. This leads unfortu-
> nately to a false debate. Some see religions as a positive characteristic, the
> deficiency of which amounts to a social distortion.

Atheists, therefore, would have to be considered as being deprived of an
essential element, the religious one. "However, if in such actors a totaliz-
ing commitment is discovered, it is called a pseudo-religion." Marxism,
for instance, has been considered as some sort of religion because it
implies a total commitment on the part of its militants. "Some sort of
downgraded substitute is seen here to take the place of religion" (ibid.:37).

Rémy aims at preserving the essence of religion by avoiding illegitimate
and ill-grounded confusions. A definition of religion that is too far-
reaching would extend in his view the applicability of the concept beyond
the limits of an acknowledgeable sociological reality, moving toward
fields that would be too differentiated to be considered comparable and
homologous.

THE INQUIRIES OF BURGALASSI (1921–)
ON RELIGIOUS BEHAVIOR

Silvano Burgalassi, a sociologist at the University of Pisa, is a pioneer in
Italian sociology of religion. However, mention should first be made of

Lorenzo Milani (1923–67), whose *Esperienze pastorali* (Milani 1974) was first published in 1957. Milani's text is a rigorous and detailed study of the parish of San Damiano (in Tuscany) and it deals, in particular, with catechism and sacraments, recreation, education, political orientation, emigration, housing, and work problems. The book contains numerous and diverse data gathered through the help of a number of collaborators among whom, for instance, were "widows and spinsters" and relies somewhat on "local gossip" (ibid.:474).

In 1967 Silvano Burgalassi wrote *Italiani in chiesa* (*Italians in Church*) with findings that

> are very simple and do not have the presumption of perfection and completeness as required by scientific research. If the first chapter gives an idea of the religious and social Italian reality, the second chapter analyzes the psychological and sociological components of religious behavior; the other chapters are concerned with some aspects of religious vitality or with general interpretations. (Burgalassi 1967:5)

The author criticizes the notion of the eclipse of the sacred (Acquaviva 1971), writing of "a more and more frequent use of phrases such as world crisis, crisis of the sacred, flattening or crisis of values, crisis of civilization." In his view "such statements and insights, often no more than simple hypotheses, should be empirically tested with extended research" (Burgalassi 1967:67).

Terminological precision is also considered important to avoid misunderstanding. For instance, Burgalassi defines the sacred as "a type of relationship between human beings and things through the divinity that functions as mediator, or also a relationship with the divine lived through the mediation of a thing (totem, etc.)" (ibid.:70). Religiosity is "any manifestation, exterior or inner, of the relation between divinity and man." Religious practice, finally, is "the external obedience that a person or a social group observes with regard to obligations (precepts) or suggestions (devotions) given by a church" (ibid.).

Burgalassi studies empirically the delayed administration of baptisms and attendance at communion and participation in devotions.

Burgalassi's book *Il comportamento religioso degli italiani* (*The Religious Behavior of Italians* 1968) is more articulated at the empirical level. In this book Burgalassi examines Italian religiosity (3,418 parishes in 1,072 municipalities) by subdividing the three main geographical zones: the north, where there is a clear connection between religious practice, income, and education; the center, where the connection between practice and income is prevalent; and the south, where practice increases slightly in the urban zones in subjects with a higher education.

Regarding religiosity in Tuscany, a higher rate "is always associated with strong religious traditions and especially with a sustained formation activity" (ibid.:176). The Tuscan data suggest a vast plan for the restructuring of the dioceses of the region (ibid.:77–310).

The most important work by Burgalassi (1970a), on so-called hidden Christianity, is the first attempt to study religiosity at the national level. It precedes by almost twenty-five years the research that is statistically more representative and that has been conducted at the Catholic University of Milan (Cesareo, Cipriani, Garelli, Lanzetti, and Rovati 1995).

The pilot study of Burgalassi discovers five "subcultures" (the use of this term has provoked some debate). The first subculture is the atheist one, which is a "belief limited to human social values" and includes Marxists, anarchists, and atheists only. The second category is rather large, perhaps too large, as it tries to make very different variables homologous. It concerns the "religiously indifferent" affiliated with Catholicism and unwilling to break their ties with religion, who although not very observant are nonetheless sensitive to religious values, fluctuating between particularism and universalism. The third classification is the "official Catholic Church model," which believes in the teachings of the church and is characterized by an energetic religious practice and by a strong sense of belonging to Catholicism. The fourth subculture is the "magic sacred," rather traditional, family oriented, particularistic, embedded in popular religiosity, ritualistic, with a proclivity toward superstition and magic. The last subculture—"diffused state"—is given by the prophetic innovation characterized by "an extreme opening toward the future and often by a violent rupture," with religious institutions.

The research was carried out in twenty-seven parishes, three in each of the nine regions studied (Piemonte, Veneto, Emilia, Tuscany, the Marches, Lazio, Apulia, Calabria, and Campania) with the administration of 2,160 questionnaires. The indifferent subculture accounted for 55 percent of the interviewees; the magic-sacred 20 percent; the official church model 15 percent; whereas atheism and prophetism 5 percent each.

In the same year Burgalassi (1970b) published the results of a study on the crisis of priestly vocations in Italy.

THE RELIGIOUS GESTURE AS A CULTURAL INSTITUTION: LILIANE VOYÉ (1938–)

A student of Jean Rémy, Liliane Voyé represents the French-Belgian school of the sociology of religion, which includes, among others, Leclercq and Houtart. Her works began with a traditional approach following Le Bras, but with some original viewpoints (Voyé 1973). Later she offered a more elaborate research work (Voyé, Bawin-Legros, Kerkhofs, and Dobbelaere 1992).

Her essay on the *Sociology of the Religious Gesture* (Voyé 1973) belongs to sociology applied to religious practice, but it took new and more open directions and led to an unusual perspective in the sociology of religion: the theory of cultural institutions.

In his foreword (ibid.:1), Rémy recalls the antecedents of Le Bras and Boulard, but also of a competitor of Boulard in the realization of a map of religious practice in Belgium: Eugène Collard (1952). Rémy goes on to say that such antecedents place

> the work of Voyé at the center of the traditional preoccupation of the sociology of Catholicism in France and in Belgium. This volume is of great interest, in the first place because it presents an inventory and a synthesis of various research carried out in Belgium. Moreover, for the Sunday practices considered as religious gestures, which is specific and recurrent, it proposes an interpretation that binds the social to the cultural. By underlining the fact that religious gestures are connected to an unaware collectivity that has a capacity for growth, this research is a contribution to the sociology of Catholicism in industrial and urban society.

Put differently, the result of the survey shows that the persistence of festive religious practice is not only the result of a socializing activity, i.e., to instruct the new generations with regard to festive obligations, but rather a local culture within which families maintain a relevant role. Attending mass becomes a sort of institution, a cultural institution, which transforms a repeated gesture into a peculiar action of cultural belonging that is lasting and unchanging.

Voyé shows that religious practices are subject to the influence of different places, to the current of emigration, and to limitations of a linguistic nature. Actually, the gesture of participating in the mass seems to order the very rhythm of everyday life, of conditioning and of managing it. This function, typical of certain sociocultural institutions, is maintained thanks to its ability to perpetuate itself. The differences between Flemish and Walloons or between Catholics and Socialists are further parameters that enter into play at the level of religious practice and that condition the statistical rates. Basing her analysis on an approach to everyday life that makes a cultural model operational, Voyé aims at interpreting the effects at the behavioral level, especially regarding the stabilization of the religious gesture due to historical cultural stratification over a long period. These stratifications produce equally lasting effects.

The self-reproduction of the gesture has the advantage of showing new synthetic solutions when confronted with the global evolution of the social framework. While this framework changes the substance of the religious, the festive gesture does not seem to change.

Quite unexpectedly, more than the diversification between rural and urban contexts and the various types of agricultural activity, fieldwork organization is the factor that explains the territorial levels of religious practice. The complex organization of this research, using maps and historical data, factorial analysis and cultural variables, provides findings that must be taken into account and that are certainly necessary for subsequent comparative studies.

With reference to farming, a synthetic indicator is given by the fact that "diverse involvement in the agricultural work is tied up in an almost univocal way to the Sunday practice, corresponding to direct work organization in regions of an elevated practice while indirect farming work corresponds to areas characterized by a weaker practice" (Voyé 1973:182). Moreover, "a connection between the religious gesture and the local culture by showing that each disorganization of this culture has effects on the practice causing its diminution" (ibid.:202) is empirically proven. However, it should be taken into account that this empirically tested conclusion might be valid only for Sunday practice, whereas there is no evidence in the same sense for other dimensions of religiosity.

EMOTIONS, MEMORY, AND RELIGION BEING CONSIDERED BY DANIÈLE HERVIEU-LÉGER (1947–)

Danièle Hervieu-Léger teaches at the Ecole des Hautes Etudes en Sciences Sociales, and at the Centre d'Etudes Interdisciplinaire des Faits Religieux, and succeeded Jean Séguy as chief editor of the *Archives de Sciences Sociales des Religions*. Hervieu-Léger has made some innovative contributions to sociology of religion and has published work with Françoise Champion (Champion and Hervieu-Léger 1990; Hervieu-Léger, with Champion, 1986, 1989).

She analyzed Catholic students during the protests of 1968. Ten years later, together with Bertrand Hervieu, she published another study on the anti-institutional utopian and community movements (Léger and Hervieu 1983). The center of attention of this research consists of the "community experiences of young students who were born in the intellectual middle-class and had left for the underpopulated regions of southern France. . . . The main interest of the research was to test the possibility of economic conversion and realization of those utopian plans" (Hervieu-Léger 1993, 1996:120).

She must be credited with a revision of the concept of secularization, which is to be understood not only as a crisis of religious institutions that are unable to have an impact on contemporary societies. In fact, these societies themselves are at present capable of producing some alternative ways of socializing through diversified forms of experience, such as the new religious movements (ibid.).

The contradictory symptoms of a sacred in crisis and at the same time of new religious enthusiasm calls the relationship between religion and modernity to the attention of Danièle Hervieu-Léger. The problem is to understand, between decline and renewal, what religious dynamic is at present developing, after "the disappearance of the practicing believers" (Hervieu-Léger 1986, 1989:27) and following the "de-Catholicization" (ibid.:41) and the "end of parish culture and 'civilization'" (ibid.:57). The conclusion is that the accent on the affective relationship with God, as a source of personal fulfillment and of enrichment of relationships with others, tends to move the practicing Catholic toward a "transcendent humanism that seems to jeopardize an ethical affective conception of salvation with a dominant worldly characterization" (Hervieu-Léger, with Champion, 1989:61). She then examines the situation of the clergy, of popular religion, and of the new religious movements, especially with regard to the relationship between modernity and secularization. In particular, she emphasizes the role of the new religious movements. In her view these movements "show how secularization does not imply the disappearance of religion when confronted with rationality. It rather points to a process of permanent reorganization of the activities of religion in a society that is structurally unable to satisfy the expectations which it must raise in order to exist as such" (Hervieu-Léger 1986, 1989:198).

After having considered separately the future perspectives of Protestantism and of Catholicism, Hervieu-Léger argues that a new Christianity consisting of "emotional communities" is on the rise. This is a religion composed of voluntary groups in which one becomes a member on the basis of an explicit choice. This strongly personalized choice creates a very intense bond between the community and each of its members (Hervieu-Léger, with Champion, 1989:298). These militant members distance themselves from the most observant believers. In the last analysis, Hervieu-Léger maintains that "the expansion of religion based on emotional communities corresponds to the quest for a new type of compromise, in terms of self-realization between Christianity and a modernity that has broken up its contacts with the Christian eschatology" (Hervieu-Léger 1986, 1989:306-7). In the end religion becomes some sort of "authorized collective memory" based on the recognition of its values.

The theme of the religion of emotions is taken up by Hervieu-Léger in a new key of renovation. The "emotional communities" play a critical role vis-à-vis the institutions; they allow adequate room for the experiences of the believers, and they reject dogmatic formulations. Hervieu-Léger discovers, therefore, an emotional dimension that helps to overcome the impasse of secularization—a secularization that is far from having been completed.

After recalling the proposal of Séguy (1988a:177–78) concerning a "metaphorical" or "analogical" religion, Hervieu-Léger defines religion as a way of believing with a constant reference to the authority of a tradition and to the continuity of a family of believers, or "believing descendency." By the term "believing" Hervieu- Léger means

> a totality of individual and collective persuasions, which do not depend on empirical verification and, in general, on recognized methods of scientific control. On the contrary, these persuasions find their justification in the fact that they give coherence and meaning to the subjective experience of those who believe. If we speak of believing rather than faith, this is due to the fact that we include, besides the usual persuasions, all those practices, languages, gestures, spontaneous automatism through which beliefs manifest themselves. (Hervieu-Léger 1993)

Believing, according to Hervieu-Léger, means having faith in action, that is to say, the "lived faith" (Hervieu-Léger 1996:113–14).

On these premises a definition of religion is finally reached: "Religion is an ideological, practical, and symbolic instrument through which the individual and the collective consciousness of belonging to a specific believer's descendency is formed, maintained, developed, and controlled" (Hervieu-Léger 1993, 1996:129).

In particular, Hervieu-Léger notes the detachment from tradition is a typical element of contemporary society, which is no longer a society based on memory, whereas the "individualistic immediatism" has the upper hand. One thinks of getting better physically, but not of saving one's soul.

Hervieu-Léger feels that as far as the religious memory is concerned the normativity of collective memory is reinforced by the fact that the group defines itself, "both objectively and subjectively, as the descendency of believers" (ibid.:193). Faith in the continuity of descendants of believers

> shows itself in the act of remembering the past in such a way as to give meaning to the present and to anticipate the future. The practice of anamnesis develops itself in the form of a ritual. What characterizes the religious rite as compared with all the other forms of social ritual, is the fact that the regular repetition of gesture and of words aims at inserting itself into the temporal sequence of memory, resembles the course of the life of any individual, where some foundation-events occur. These events have allowed the descendency to constitute itself and they document its ability to perpetuate itself beyond any jeopardizing experience. (ibid.:194)

However, in modern society memory tends to be fragmented and to lose its specificity (ibid.:200); religious memory is in crisis. Because of secularization the crisis concerns both "the imagination of continuity" and "the family" (ibid.:206–7). The outcome is the religious emptiness of modern societies and the disappearance of any memory that is not immediate and functional (ibid.:218). In the last analysis, one could talk of a process that goes from anamnesis to amnesia. But new reinventions of descendency are emerging (ibid.:219–33): utopia; "elective fraternities," that is to say, religious groups that have chosen in absolute freedom a shared living experience that produces a common progeny; new "ethnoreligions" are developing, with a special bond between ethnicity and religion. This bond assumes the character of an "abandonment of religion because religion has lost any autonomous social reality" (ibid.:252). In other words, we are here confronted with a "post-traditional religion" that goes "beyond secularization" (ibid.:261–70).

6

Religion as Function in the Work of
Niklas Luhmann (1927–1998)

Having studied and followed Talcott Parsons, German sociologist Niklas Luhmann was a coherent systemic functionalist who wrote about religion. Luhmann recalled that, for his late wife (and also for himself), religion's meaning went beyond whatever a theory could say (Luhmann [1977] 1991:20).

The basic objection to Luhmann, who taught at the University of Bielefeld, concerned the comprehensive character of his theory. Neither alternatives to nor ways to verify a possible dysfunctional effect of religion on society were left open. Empirical research seemed to show that the relationship between individual, religion, and society was much more articulate than the one taking place in a society that was by definition functionally complex.

Luhmann's essay ([1977] 1991) on the function of religion was not born out of a unified project, nor was it part of an intellectual plan especially dedicated to the study of religious phenomena. The five chapters of Luhmann's volume dealt with different questions: the social function of religion, religious dogma and social evolution, contingency transformations in the social systems of religion, secularization, and organization. Each of these topics could constitute the subject of a special volume. The second chapter, the longest, is a discussion directed to theologians and is accompanied by numerous footnotes. Quite a few insights do not belong to a purely sociological domain and amount to a call for specific activities in the religious field (in the first place in the theological one). One must add that Luhmann's contribution was part of his theory of functional differentiation, which he applied to many other fields, from politics to law. It is somewhat difficult to understand his reasoning completely, especially because of his concise conceptual definitions.

His main point is that religion, as a social system, regulates the relationships of people with the world in a comprehensive and ultimate meaning. Naturally, society is the essential condition for being in the world in a

225

meaningful way. "With the concept of system the difference between internal and external, between environment and system is introduced in the analysis. This difference can be illustrated as a difference in complexity so that the environment is always more complex than the system itself" (ibid.:83). In practice a society is a social (external) system that aims to regulate the environment (internal). The system serves to reduce the complexity of the environment. For this reason the former is always less complex than the latter.

At the same time it should be kept in mind that the environment is external with respect to the system, which is "that whole mechanism of elaboration that answers to the enormous and infinite variability of the environment." It is necessary, at this point, to take into account the fact that society as a system means for Luhmann that it is essential to imagine it as an entirety of subsystems, each keeping under control a portion of the external environment. There are, of course, various subsystems, or partial systems (politics, law, religion, and so forth). Finally, it should be remembered that individuals with their various forms of living, desiring, behaving, and believing constitute a vast, unpredictable series of social models and actions: hence, the complexity of the social environment (Acquaviva and Pace 1996:45). The function of each system consists in reducing the differentiation through subsystems or partial systems that provide rules and procedures for better communication.

Systemic differentiation presupposes, therefore, the presence of two systemic orders: the global and the partial. The two orders are characterized by some particular traits:

> For the global system the single function is only one among many; a system cannot specialize itself by favoring one of its functions against the other, but it can do it with respect to a function of the global system, considering the global system as a particular environment, which it takes advantage of and to which it finally provides the satisfaction of the specific function. If applied to the case of religion: . . . *religion* remains a function of the global social system and therefore preserves its reference to the environment of the system. The religious *system* remains, despite its functional specification, a social system in which a multiplicity of other functions must at the same time be satisfied. (Luhmann 1991:54)

If this functional systemic logic is applied to religion, one finds that religion fulfills for the social system the function of transforming the indeterminate world, in the sense that it was not possible to limit it toward the external (environment) and towards the internal (system), in a determinable world in which system and environment can have a relationship which excluded both from arbitrary change (ibid.:36). But what is the world? Luhmann thinks that "the properly systemic action recalls the environment, and the environmental event opens the possibility of the system acceding to itself. It is therefore possible to say: through the use of meaning the world is constituted as total horizon. Within this horizon the system refers to its own environment and refers its own environment to itself" (ibid.:32). However, "the world itself is not a system" (ibid.:26). The world is therefore identifiable as a biunivocal nexus, as a two-way relationship between the system and its environment. But again: what is the environment of a system? Luhmann stated that it is

> everything that is delimited by the system. . . . Thus, the concept of environment is defined in relationship to the system and each system possesses a particular environment. . . . The environments of different systems cannot therefore be identical; they can only overlap for a long stretch. The totality of whatever does not belong to a system cannot in itself constitute a system. Even when reunited, the environments of the system do not constitute a larger system. (ibid.:26)

Although it includes "all the rest," "the environment becomes relevant for each system only as a contingent selection. In order to draw selectively from its environment, the system must utilize a network that is defined inside the environment and that only as such gains informative value. In this way the environment becomes 'legible'" (ibid.:28).

Regarding the system-environment-world triad, it is the first two elements that play a strategic role in the theory of Luhmann. Most of the integrative functions are based on the concepts of system and environment. The almost unique perspective is that of the system. Individuals are minimal entities that express themselves in actions, which are constantly regulated by procedural norms. These norms minimize the contribution of the subject and maximize systemic functionality.

There is a socially objective nature in the religion *of societies,* but an objective nature also in the religion *of the psychic systems.* In both cases two procedures exist, and these two procedures lead to the construction of meaning. In this field religion appears to be more effective than other functional equivalents.

> The distinction is also evident, *together with the correlation,* between religion (of a social context) and the religiosity of an individual character. In fact, there are personal as well as social sources of religiosity. Being united for the other environment of the system, they depend on one another without being, however, reducible to one another. (ibid.:39)

Religion, therefore, does not disappear, but certainly it does not have a central function. The same is true for science, economics, and politics. Religion produces its own communications that do not have, however, a meaning for the whole social complex. This, also, is a sign of secularization because the religious subsystem is only one among the many possible subsystems. It gives a meaning, it determines a sense, but with a limited valid-ity. Despite this fact, Luhmann maintained that the function of religion is no longer integrative but *interpretative*. That is to say, for the individual it represents a resource of meanings that allows one to imagine as united what is in reality divided, as absolute what is relative. Therefore, it offers individuals interpretative keys that other subsystems have rejected (Pace, in Acquaviva and Pace 1996:46). In the end, the partial system of religion remains like an oasis in a desert in which there is a scarcity of meaning providers, because there are many abdications in favor of the systemic reg-ulations. Luhmann, however, was adamant in stating that "functional analysis cannot be satisfied merely by introducing such interpretative need as an existential status, which leaves things as they are" (Luhmann 1991:25).

The autopoietic and the autoreferential functionality of religion as a subsystem was still able to build by itself presence and symbolic commu-nication forms. But its main task remained the one concerning the reduc-tion of complexity. Religion surrendered to other subsystems some of its peculiar characteristics; however, it succeeded in surviving thanks to its adaptation to modernity.

Luhmann thought that religion is called upon to develop the function of "representing the non-representable" (ibid.:36). "In other words, religion has the functional task of representing, that is, specifying, determining or rendering at least determinable, what is not presentable and determinable: the world, the whole" (S. Belardinelli cited in Luhmann 1991:3). The prob-lem consists in transforming complexity from indeterminate to determi-nate: "Religion has to do, in the last analysis, with the contingency of the world" (S. Belardinelli cited in ibid.:5). Religion in fact postulated the idea of God as a contingency formula that was helpful in order to make the tran-sition from indeterminable to determinate and therefore it reduced com-plexity. In this way religion proceeded through a "meta-differentiation" (*Ausdifferenzierung*), that is to say, it went out of itself and it created itself (here it is the autopoiesis) with regard to the answer of a single God (the uniqueness of the divine was also a reduction of complexity, as compared with the polytheism of gods or of values). If this is one point favorable to religion, one should not neglect at the same time its inadequacy in keeping up with the pace of functional differentiation in society.

The secularization of society is tied up with the difficulties of the partial religious system. In Luhmann's view,

> secularization is only one of the many consequences of a society such as ours that has become a differentiated system in functional form, that is to say a system in which each functional environment acquires greater stability and greater autonomy, but it also becomes more dependent from the fact and from the way in which other functions are satisfied. The religious system

cannot have the same integrative ability that it used to have in the past. (S. Belardinelli cited in ibid.:12)

In the light of such a premise, Luhmann surveyed theological dogmas as if they were the expression of autoreferentiality (ibid.:81–176), and conceived of the organization of the religious system as a regulator of affiliation (ibid.:261–302).

At the very outset, Luhmann made his point of view explicit: "The starting point concerns socio-cultural evolution not in its normal functional modality but rather in its collateral effects. This evolution increases the complexity of the social system, giving predominance to those ordering structures that face the selection requests through a functional specification" (ibid.:22). This statement introduces the realization that religion was sanctioned or penalized because as a subsystem it did not succeed in facing the need for differentiation; at the same time, however, it found instruments to persist in developing its functional task of reducing the indeterminable to the determined.

In order to clarify the question concerning the "metadifferentiation" of the religion system, Luhmann wrote:

It is not only a sociological phenomenon but, as a condition of possibility for superior forms, it is at the same time a theme of faith. In terms of our tradition it is often developed in the concept of a *church*. It is not possible to believe in meta-differentiation, but undoubtedly, by adding concrete contents and excluding an excessively abstract exchangeability, it is possible to believe in the church. The transition from the sociological theory to religious dogmatic doctrine is consciously thought about and implemented. It should arrive at a reduction of complexity as a process of inserting and broadening of conceptual elements with reference to an abstract systemic model. (ibid.:135)

In this respect, it might be helpful to remember that believing in the church is one of the "articles" of faith as witnessed by the Credo, which in the Catholic world is a profession of faith par excellence.

Luhmann (ibid.:292–94) outlined a social system as seen from the perspective of a religious system. The intrasocial environment and the religious system entered into it. The organized official church was placed at the center; the roles of the members, subdivided into intensive and nonintensive ones, were indicated within the intersecting part of two concentric circles; in the nonintersecting part were placed the nonmembers, again divided between intensive and nonintensive ones. It is a typical system-environment scheme that adequately

illustrates within which limits the central position of the ecclesiastical ministerial organization puts itself in terms of interdependence in need of control: the ecclesiastical apparatus must refer its decisional processes to the relationship that members of a highly different grade of intensity establish or could establish, between their lived experience and their religious and non-religious actions; equally for those who are not members and, as the status of a member cannot be achieved or rejected on the basis of a decision, also for the relationships among member and non-members. (ibid.:292–94)

In other words, complexity was such as to discourage any attempt to take into account all the interdependencies. The right choice became impracticable. For instance, in the case of an economic operation, the organized official church entered into the internal social environment and became in this respect part of the economic system, often of the political and the legal system. Within itself, the organized official church must put specifically religious decisions into relationship with nonreligious ones and place them both in relationship to the internal social environment and to the environment that is internal to the religious system and, finally, in relationship to the members and the nonmembers, to the extent that their attitude towards religion is positive. Each decision implies a relationship that could have rather differentiated characteristics. The options were many and the basic religious dimension got lost in the magma of possible situations, which were neither easily controllable nor justifiable.

7

The New Religious Movements

BEYOND THE PREJUDICES AGAINST THE NEW RELIGIOUS MOVEMENTS: EILEEN BARKER (1938–)

Eileen Bartan Barker teaches at the London School of Economics. She founded the Information Network Focus on Religious Movements (INFORM) and has been president of the Society for the Scientific Study of Religion and of the Sociology of Religion Study Group of the British Sociological Association.

Barker's best-known book is *The Making of a Moonie: Brainwashing or Choice?* (1984) in which she reconstructs the affiliation dynamics of the followers of Reverend Sung Myung Moon, leader of the Unification Church.

Eileen Barker is very well known for her study *New Religious Movements* (Barker 1989). An indefatigable researcher and traveler, she has already carried out a number of fieldwork studies and has organized many international conferences.

Eileen Barker has gained the confidence of the various churches of the United Kingdom—the Anglican, Catholic, Baptist, Methodist, and so forth—in order to study in depth the phenomenology of the new religious experiences.

As far as the religious movements are concerned, Barker adopts a neutral, social science approach; she respects the different behaviors and rituals, and is far from promoting any kind of antimovement campaign. Her ability to interact with the various groups is noteworthy. She shows adaptability to different situations.

At first glance her book *New Religious Movements* (also NRM) appears to be a practical introductory guide. However, more than that, it is a serious and well-documented study, provided with firsthand materials, in which the characteristics of the single groups are described in an impartial and scientifically rigorous manner. Barker herself writes that many scholars have invested quite a bit of time in studying the new religious movements in the field, living at times in very uncomfortable conditions and finding themselves involved in a myriad of strange activities, even though, as scholars, there are limits to their participant observation. Members of the new religious movements have been interviewed in depth. With the exception of Jim Jones's People's Temple and the Charles Manson family, Barker has been able to talk to members of almost all the movements cited in her book. Moreover, she has been listening to former members and to hundreds of parents and friends of members, supporters, enemies, and whoever could shed some light on the various ways in which a movement operates and on its impact on the external world. As a researcher, together with her group Barker has constructed and analyzed questionnaires. She has laboriously tried to master the huge amount of existing material and has studied "control groups" in order to evaluate the material collected on the movement by confronting it with the data of other "populations" (Barker 1989).

After clarifying possible misunderstandings of the term "new religious movements," Barker defines them as groups that can provide ultimate answers to fundamental questions—such as the meaning of life or the role of human beings in nature (ibid.).

Barker's book contributes in a fluent and understandable style to disproving prejudices, and provides useful information for a better knowledge of the various groups and movements. Her data furnish information on the different conversions, the persuasion techniques being used, the totalitarian authoritarianism, the tension within the family. The book is the result of years of fieldwork, which is the only research method that allows an in-depth and competent understanding of the problems together with the possibility of finding an adequate solution—in fact, in the second part of the text, the author faces the question of "forced de-conditioning" as opposed to the "intermediate" solution, to be discussed together with the converted one.

JAMES BECKFORD (1942–):
RELIGIOUS MOVEMENTS AND CHANGE

James Beckford's first work (Beckford 1975) was research on the Jehovah's Witnesses that has become a classic study on religious movements. After that Beckford worked at a survey on new religious movements and on the reaction they cause—especially in the "anticult" groups. This research partly appears in *Cultural Controversies* (Beckford 1985), which analyzes the new religious movements as well as the activities of those who oppose them. Beckford provides a classification of the different degrees of affiliations, from the most distant (apostasy) to the closest (devotion). Within these two opposite stances there are various modalities of membership. Equally meaningful is the relationship between the members and the nonmembers of a movement. After his long experience as a researcher on new religious movements, Beckford feels able to formulate definitions and to advance hypotheses to be verified. He writes that the concept of religious movements implies an organized attempt to introduce changes within a religion. This normally entails tensions and conflicts between the religious movements and their competitors or opponents (Beckford 1986). The movement's essence is always in antithesis to the nature of the institution and appears to be in conflict with it.

> But the term "movement" also suggests that broad shifts in people's religious ideas and sensibilities may occur independently of organized religious movements—at least, initially. Examples from the recent era include the growing sympathy of Christians of many persuasions for the cultivation of charismatic Gifts of the Spirit; the resurgence of Islam, often in a puritanical spirit, in many parts of the Islamic world; and the veritable craze for spiritist activities in Brazil. (ibid.:x)

The fact is that the "religious movements have always existed, despite the fact that there is a tendency in most academic studies of religion to deny their importance in favor of emphasizing the continuity, if not dominion, of large and stable complexes of teachings, sentiments and rituals in the major world religious traditions" (ibid.:xi).

Beckford concludes: "Rapid social change in the twentieth century is associated with the rise of a large number of new religious movements. They are both a response to change and a means of contributing to it" (ibid.:xv).

More than once Beckford happened to have expressed a strong preoccupation for the future of his discipline. For this reason he has been looking for points of reference and support from related sectors, thus favoring the development of a full social science for the sociology of religion. His objective is to prevent the isolation of the sociologists of religion.

In *Religion and Advanced Industrial Society* (1989), Beckford presents his project. He argues that the contemporary attempts to grasp the sociological meaning of religion should take into account theories regarding the peculiar characteristics of advanced industrial societies and of the new world order. Then Beckford presents a critical-historical review of the classics and of their later results. He emphasizes the decline in scientific tension especially during the last part of the twentieth century. Beckford in fact affirms that only in the recent past has there been a tendency to renounce the consideration of the issues of an industrial society. As a result this has led to new insights concerning the sociological impact of religion (ibid.).

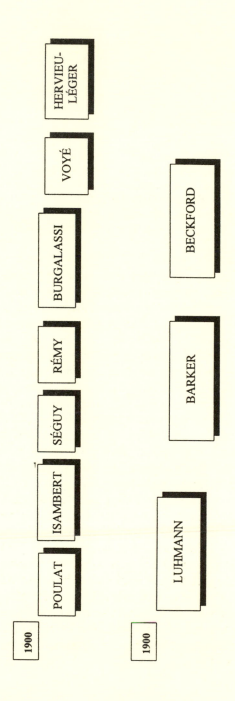

Synoptic Table 7:   From Poulat to Beckford

Afterword

Since an author writes the preface to a book when the book is finished, it would be more appropriate to speak of an afterword. The afterword offers the opportunity to say something outside the context of the book, but not totally estranged from the text.

First of all, I have to express my gratitude to a number of scholars: William H. Swatos, executive officer of the Association for the Sociology of Religion, who kindly guided me through the maze of North American sociology; Salvatore Abbruzzese, Sabino Acquaviva, Silvano Burgalassi, Luca Diotallevi, Franco Ferrarotti, Piergiorgio Grassi, François Houtart, Stefano Martelli, David Martin, Davide Meghnagi, Emile Poulat, Elio Roggero, Jean Séguy, and Tullio Tentori for having read and commented on some chapters; Karel Dobbelaere, Danièle Hervieu-Léger, Rodney Stark, and Liliane Voyé for the precious information on their scientific work; Laura Ferrarotti for translating this book from Italian into English, and Katrina McLeod and William D'Antonio for their editorial work and important suggestions; special thanks go to Maria Saveria, Pietro Cipriani, and Giuseppe Palumbo, to whose memory I dedicate this book for having nourished my sensitivity in dealing with issues of religion both with participation but also with a critical distance.

This volume could not have been written until a few years ago, at least in this form. Only a protracted study of the European and of the North American context has allowed me to understand the different importance of authors and trends as far as socioreligious thinking is concerned.

This book aims at overcoming the gap between European and North American scholars through a careful retrieval of their common theoretical and research interests. In other words, I have been trying to go beyond the shortcomings in many English and American textbooks, which tend to be parochial to the point of not even mentioning European classical authors of the sociology of religion. On the other hand, in Europe there is a shortage of handbooks in this field.

This book is hopefully a step forward and beyond past scholarly experiences. However, I must admit it does not render justice to other sociologies of religion that are especially thriving and alive in Central and South America as well as in Africa, Asia, and Australia. It is to be hoped that in the near future it will be possible to cover such areas.

This treatise is aimed at the reader, scholar, or student. I have chosen to offer specific "sketches" in order to give articulated, theoretical, and biographical information about the various authors. From this point of view it seems certain that, when personalized, the interplay of reciprocal suggestions and influences becomes more visible.

Out of some seventy scholars who have been analyzed, only four are women. However, it must be said that they are all contemporary women. This means a positive change especially for the future role and contributions of women.

The graphic synopsis and the synoptic outline for authors, principal works, influence, key-concepts, and themes are helpful in order to place issues and scholars within a line of historical and thematic continuity. It must be kept in mind that we are always dealing with summaries and descriptive syntheses that in general avoid the further problematization of the various topics.

The positive reception of the various authors is in some way presupposed in the very presentation of their works. Whenever possible, mention is made of different interpretations for which I am fully responsible. But in general the relative importance of the authors becomes understandable in terms of the space allocated to each scholar, of the presentation, of the qualitative adjectives used, of the number of books that have been quoted and/or described. Special attention has been used to try to convey the real thinking of the authors quoted in this handbook. For this reason preference has been given to direct quotations whenever a reference is made to a key passage in their thinking.

SYNOPTIC OUTLINE
(AUTHORS, INFLUENCES,
KEY CONCEPTS, TOPICS)

For each author, the synoptic outline is as follows:

(a) the title in English of a main work (year of publication of the original edition);

(b) the scholars who have influenced ($\Rightarrow$) the author;

(c) the key concepts and the basic topics;

(d) ($\Rightarrow$) the scholars who have been influenced by the author; ($\Leftrightarrow$) the scholars who have influenced the author and who have been influenced by him/her.

THE ORIGINS

The Historical-Philosophical Background

SPINOZA: the historical-critical method and the freedom of thought

VICO
New Science (1744)
Empirical Rationalist
History as a new science
The three ages: gods, heroes, men
Divine Providence in history
Educational impact of religion

HUME
Natural History of Religion (1757)
Empiricist
Natural religion
Sentiment as the basis of religion
Ethics and religion
$\Rightarrow$ Comte   Berger

SCHLEIERMACHER: Religion as the feeling of absolute dependency

FEUERBACH
The Essence of Christianity (1841)
Hegel ⇒
Self-alienation of man in the divinity
Centrality of man
Opposition to Hegelian idealism
⇒ Marx   Buber   Barth   Bohnhoeffer

MARX
Theses on Feuerbach (1888)
Religion as the "opium of the people"
Religion as the "sigh of the oppressed creature"
Religious alienation
Religion as a form of knowledge
Religion as "perverted world consciousness"
The ideological character of religion
The criticism of religion
⇒ Maduro

The Universal Religion

COMTE
Course of Positive Philosophy (1830–42)
Positivist
Saint-Simon
The law of the three stages: theological, metaphysical, positivistic
The religion of Humanity

Religion and Democracy

TOCQUEVILLE
Democracy in America (1835-40)
Religious spirit and liberal spirit
The influence of religion on politics
The future of religion

Religion and "Élan Vital" (vital impetus)

BERGSON
The Two Sources of Morality and Religion (1932)
The philosophy of life (élan vital)
Spencer   Comte   Tocqueville   James ⇒
Religion as social feeling
Science and ethics

The Contribution of Anthropology

TYLOR: Animism

ROBERTSON SMITH
Lectures on the Religion of the Semites (1889)
MacLennan ⇒
Sacrifice as unity
Rites before doctrines
The dynamics between myth and rite
⇒ Frazer   Durkheim   Freud

FRAZER
The Golden Bough (1890)
Mannhardt ⇒
Rites and customs
Imitative magic and contageous magic
The mystical bough of mistletoe at Nemi and Ariccia
Totemism
⇒ Durkheim   Freud   Eliade

MALINOWSKI
A Scientific Theory of Culture and Other Essays (1944)
Functionalist
Robertson   Smith   Durkheim   Frazer ⇒
The theory of needs
The biological bases of human behavior
The principle of integration
Magic and religion

RADCLIFFE-BROWN
Structure and Function in Primitive Society (1952)
Functional structuralist
Durkheim ⇒
Instrumental rites and symbolic rites
Social function of religion
The effects of religion

MAUSS
The Gift (1925)
Structural-functionalist
Durkheim   Radcliffe-Brown ⇒
The gift and the exchange

Total social facts
Myths and symbols
The sacrifice and the *mana*
Magic and religion
Prayer as an oral rite
⇒ Lévy-Bruhl   Hubert   Lévy-Strauss

THE CLASSICS

The Religious Forms

DURKHEIM
The Elementary Forms of Religious Life (1912)
Fustel   de Coulanges   Tylor   Spencer   Comte   Robertson   Smith
   Müller   Frazer ⇒

The totemic system
Primitive religion
Individual and society
Beliefs and rites
Sacred and profane
Magic and the church
⇒ Mauss   Hubert   Hertz   Lévy-Bruhl   Van Gennep   Lévi-Strauss
Parsons   Berger   Luckmann

The Universal Religions

WEBER
The Protestant Ethic and the Spirit of Capitalism (1904–5)
Channing   Alfred Weber   Mommsen   Naumann   Troeltsch
   Simmel ⇒
"Marx of the bourgeoisie"
Opposed to the materialistic conception of history
The ideal-type
Predestination and salvation
Vocation
Time is money
Economic success
Ascesis
The accumulation of capital
The sects
The economic ethics of religions

Religiosity and Religion

SIMMEL
Religion (1906–12)
Durkheim ⇒
The concept of religiosity
Sociability
Religious life as social relation
The concept of religion

The Psychic Dimension of Religion

FREUD
Totem and Taboo (1913)
Spencer   Wundt   Tylor   Frazer   Robertson Smith ⇒
The technique of free association
Obsessions and religiosity
The Oedipal complex
The taboo of the totem
Animism
The prohibition of incest
Religious representations
Moses and the Hebrew question

Religion in the Psycho-Social Perspective

JAMES
The Varieties of Religious Experience (1902)
Pragmatist
Peirce   Starbuck   Paul Sabatier ⇒
The James-Lange theory of emotions
The variety of religious forms
Institutional religion
Personal religion
Religion and neuropathologies

THE CONTEMPORARIES

The Universal Religion

LÉVY-BRUHL
The Supernatural and Nature in the Primitive Mentality (1931)
Pre-logical thought of the primitives

The unity between the visible and the invisible
The mystical virtues of blood

EVANS-PRITCHARD: Religion in relation to other social phenomena

VAN DER LEEUW
The Phenomenology of Religion (1933)
Husserl   Dilthey   Weber ⇒
The close relationship between object and subject
Verstehen and *Erlebnis*
The ideal-type and structure
Religion as salvation

The Macrosociological Approach

PARSONS
Structural-functionalist
Durkheim   Weber ⇒
Criticism of Sorokin
The differentiation
The denominational pluralism

SOROKIN
The Social and Cultural Dynamics (1957)
The ideational model
The sensist model
The idealistic model
Asceticism and activism

The Historical-Cultural Dynamic

TROELTSCH
The Social Doctrines of the Churches and of the Christian Groups (1912)
Dilthey ⇒
The church
The sect
Mysticism
⇔ Weber

OTTO
The Sacred (1917)
Schleiermacher   James ⇒
The rational and the irrational
The "numinous"
The *"mysterium tremendum"*

The "utterly other"
The sacred as a priori category

VAN GENNEP: myth and rite

TAWNEY
Religion and the Rise of Capitalism (1926)
Troeltsch   Weber ⇒
Puritanism and capitalism
Criticism of Weber and Troeltsch

NIEBUHR
The Social Sources of Denominationalism (1929)
Weber   Troeltsch   Tawney ⇒
Church, sect and denomination
Nationalism, capitalism and "sectionalism"

ELIADE
Treatise of the History of Religions (1948)
The return to the origins
Cultural relativism
Symbolism of the "center" and the "binding"
Sacred and profane

DE MARTINO
The Magic World (1948)
The crisis of the presence
The dehistoricization of the negative

Religion According to the Frankfurt School

HORKHEIMER: the "non-denial" of religion
ADORNO: the problem of the "otherness"
FROMM: psychoanalysis and religion as a system object of devotion
JUNG: unconscious, religion, and symbolism of the mass

The New European Suggestions

WACH
Sociology of Religion (1944)
Schleiermacher   Dilthey   Troeltsch   Otto   Heiler ⇒
The science of religion
The *Verstehen* as a methodological approach
Religion as experience
The founded religion (created by a leader)

Ecclesiola in ecclesia
Protest groups within the Church

MENSCHING: The "comprehending" phenomenology of religion

LE BRAS
Studies of Sociology of Religion (1955)
The religious practice
Religious sociology and sociology of religions
The "seasonal conformist," the "practitioners," and the "pious and
    zealous people"
The religious geography
⇒ Poulat   Isambert   Desroche   Séguy

LECLERCQ
Introduction to Religious Sociology (1948)
Founder of the C.I.R.S. (Conférence Internationale de Sociologie
    Religieuse)
The theology of sociology

DESROCHE
Religious Sociology (1968)
Troeltsch   Le Bras ⇒
Socio-theology and non-theological sociology
Marxism and religions

HOUTART
Sociological Aspects of American Catholicism (1957)
Religion and institutional power
Religion and revolution
Functional religion and dysfunctional religion

The Socioanthropological Perspectives

HERBERG
Protestant, Catholic, Jew (1955)
Religion and the "American way of life"
Forerunner of the "civil religion"

YINGER
Religion, Society and the Individual (1957)
Functional definition of religion
Church/sect classification
Field theory of religion

LENSKI
The Religious Factor (1961)
Multidimensional analysis of religion
Associative and community ties
Religion and "race"
The disengagement of Catholics in economic and scientific activities

GEERTZ
Islam (1968)
Durkheim Weber Malinowski Parsons Eliade Schutz Bellah ⇒
Religion as a cultural system
Charismatic Islam (Morocco) and centralized Islam (Indonesia)
The religious symbols
Symbols *of* reality and symbols *for* reality
Criticism of Durkheim, Malinowski and Lévy-Bruhl

SPIRO
Burmese Supernaturalism (1978)
The psycho-anthropological approach
Needs and desires
Personality, structures and beliefs
Functional and causal explanations of religion
Centrality of the family

TURNER: ritual process (structure, antistructure, liminality)

DOUGLAS
Natural Symbols (1970)
Durkheim Evans-Pritchard Lévi-Strauss ⇒
Neo-structuralist
The religiosity of the Lele
The *frame/group* scheme

THE RECENT DEVELOPMENTS

Secularization

ACQUAVIVA
The Eclipse of the Sacred in the Industrial Civilization (1961)
The decline of the religious practice
End of the magic use of the sacred
The biopsychological hypothesis of religion
Secularization and desacralization

MARTIN
A General Theory of Secularization (1961)
Durkheim   Parsons   Wilson ⇒
Opposition to the concept of secularization
Rationalism, Marxism and existentialism: ideologies of secularization
Monopoly, duopoly, pluralism and mixed model
The ambiguities of secularization

WILSON
Sects and Society (1961)
Criticism of Troeltsch
Typologies of the sects
From conversion to utopia
The loss of influence of religion

FERRAROTTI
A Theology for Non-Believers (1983)
Groundlessness of the eclipse of the sacred
Religion-of-the-church and personal religiosity
The desecralizing religion
The need for the meta-human
Religion as the administrative structure of the sacred

DOBBELAERE
Secularization: A Multidimensional Concept (1981)
Secularization, religious change, religious participation
Non-unilinearity but reversibility of secularization
Criticism of "civil religion"
Religion as a system of meaning

Religious Pluralism

LUCKMANN
The Invisible Religion (1963)
Durkheim   Weber   Mead   Schutz ⇒
The conception of the world as a social form of religion
Ecclesiastically oriented religiosity and individual religiosity
The "private sphere" as a sacred cosmos
Autonomy, self-expression, self-realization, sexuality, familism
Overcoming of the theme of death
Irreversibility of the "invisible religion"

BERGER
The Sacred Canopy (1967)
Schleiermacher   Durkheim   Weber   Schutz ⇒
Secularization and pluralism

Bureaucratization of religious institutions
Irony as a sign of the transcendence
Religion as a "cognitive minority"
Religion as "rumor"
Comparison among world religions

Civil religion

BELLAH
Habits of the Heart (1985)
Durkheim   Weber   Parsons   Habermas   Tillich ⇒
Religious evolution as differentiation
Primary religion, ancient religion, historical religion, premodern religion,
   modern religion
Symbolic-religious system, religious action, religious organization, social
   implications
Civil religion as public fact and as religious and national self-
   understanding
Individualism and social commitment
"Sheilaism": between external authority and inner meaning
⇒ Wuthnow

The North American trends

SWANSON
The Birth of the Gods (1960)
Durkheim ⇒
The ultimate values
Primitive religiosity
Social structure and religious beliefs
The sovereign groups

GREELEY
Unsecular Man (1972)
Durkheim   Weber   James   Otto   Geertz ⇒
The myth of secularization
Narrative symbols
Protestants, Catholics, and Jewish endogamy

FENN
Toward a Theory of Secularization (1978)
Parsons ⇒
Incongruence among culture, structure, and personality
The five phases of secularization
The scope of the sacred and integration between individual
   and collective values

Mol
Identity and the Sacred (1976)
The sacralization of identity
Objectification, involvement, rite, myth
The balance between stable tradition and change
The universal religions as adaptation between man and society

Glock: religious commitment (experiential, ritualistic, ideological, intellectual, consequential)

Stark
A Theory of Religion (1987; coauthored with W. S. Bainbridge)
Popper $\Rightarrow$
Parameters of religiosity: certainty of the existence of God, belief in God, in miracles, in afterlife, in the existence of the devil, in Christ and in his sinless birth
Belief, practice, experience, and knowledge
Rewards and compensators
The church, denomination, sect, and cult
Persistence of religion
7 axioms, 104 definitions, 344 propositions
Religious economics

Robertson
Globalization: Social Theory to Global Culture (1992)
Durkheim   Weber   Simmel   Parsons $\Rightarrow$
Modernization
Globalization
Indifference toward the theses of secularization
Comparison and interaction
Religion and globalization

Wuthnow
Producing the Sacred (1994)
Glock   Bellah $\Rightarrow$
Systems of meaning: theistic, individualistic, social-scientific, mystic
The "new conscience"
The mainstream religion
Voluntary work
Small support groups
Public religion
Forms of religious organization: congregations, hierarchical, special interests, academic institutions, public rituals

The European Trends

POULAT
The Church is a World (1986)
Le Bras ⇒
The "Ecclesiosphere"
Lay culture and Catholic culture
"Metheosociology"
The spiritual power

ISAMBERT
The Sense of the Sacred (1982)
Le Bras ⇒
Symbolic effectiveness
Sociological anthropology
Significance, object, and consent
Performative rite
Popular religion, feast, and sacred

SÉGUY
Christianity and Society. The Sociology of Ernst Troeltsch (1980)
Le Bras ⇒
Theology and nontheological sciences of religion
Nontheological ecumenology
Metaphorical or analogical religion
The research on the Mennonites-Anabaptists
⇒ Hervieu-Léger

RÉMY
Church and Society in Evolution (1969; in collaboration with F. Houtart)
Religion and urbanization
Church and modernity
Little differentiated society and differentiated society (or about to
    become differentiated)
Affiliations pluralism
Descriptive level and interpretative-analytical level
⇒ Voyé

BURGALASSI
The Hidden Christianities (1973)
Atheist subculture, indifferent subculture, formal model, sacral sub-
    culture, prophetic subculture

Voyé
The Sociology of the Religious Gesture (1973)
Rémy ⇒
The theory of cultural institution
Self-repetition of the religious gesture
The work organization of farming and the religious practice

Hervieu-Léger
Religion and Memory (1993)
Séguy ⇒
The emotional communities
The progeny of believers
The break away from tradition
From anamnesis to amnesia
The post-traditional religion

Religion as Function

Luhmann
The Function of Religion (1977)
Parsons ⇒
The theory of functional differentiation
Society as a system
Environment, system, and world
Global system and partial system (or subsystem)
From the indeterminable to the determined
Secularization as differentiation
Self-referentiality of the religious system
Meta-differentiation: the church
The complexity of the organization as affiliation regulator

The New Religious Movements

Barker
The Making of a Moonie (1984)
NRM (New Religious Movements)
Neutrality of the analysis
Ultimate answers to crucial questions

Beckford
The Trumpet of Prophecy (1975)
Investigations on the Jehovah's Witnesses
The concept of movement
The isolation of the sociology of religion

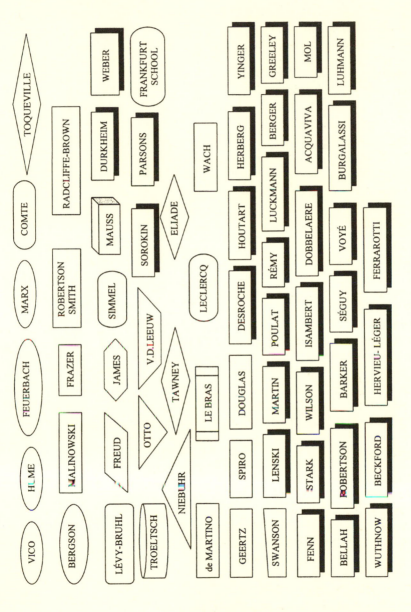

General Synoptic Table

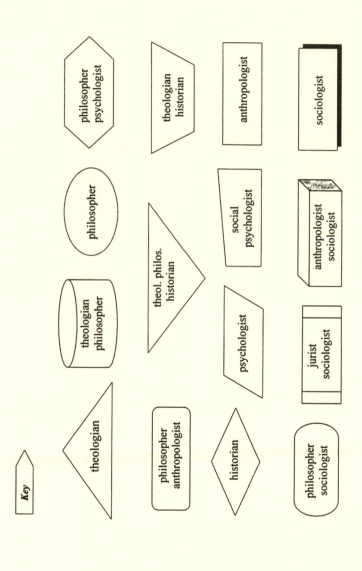

Key to the Synoptic Tables

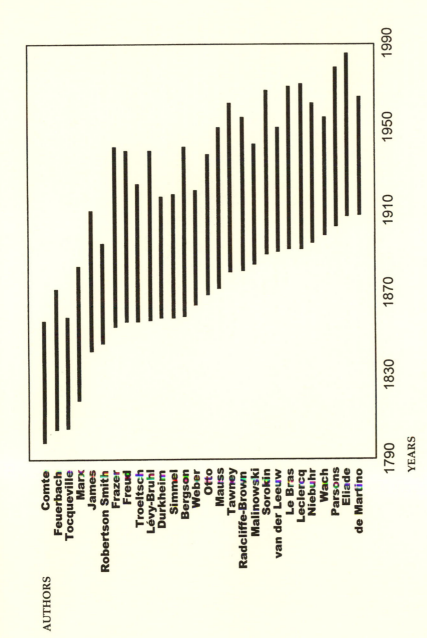

AUTHORS

Comte
Feuerbach
Tocqueville
Marx
James
Robertson Smith
Frazer
Freud
Troeltsch
Lévy-Bruhl
Durkheim
Simmel
Bergson
Weber
Otto
Mauss
Tawney
Radcliffe-Brown
Malinowski
Sorokin
van der Leeuw
Le Bras
Leclercq
Niebuhr
Wach
Parsons
Eliade
de Martino

YEARS

1790   1830   1870   1910   1950   1990

The Classics

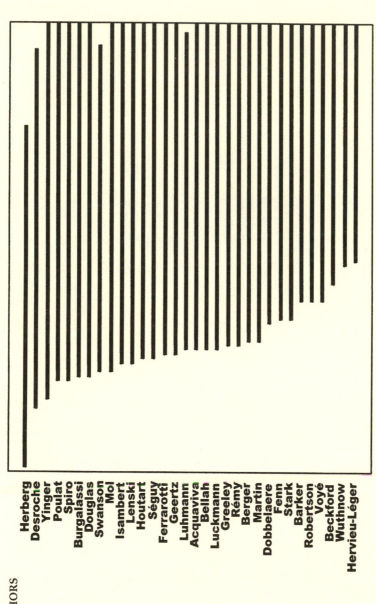

YEARS

AUTHORS

The Contemporaries

Bibliography

Abraham, J. H. 1973. *Origins and Growth of Sociology*. Harmondsworth: Penguin.

Acquaviva, S. S. 1971. *L'eclissi del sacro nella civiltà industriale*. Milan: Comunità. [Reprint: Mondadori, Milan, 1992.]

———. 1979. *The Eclipse of the Holy in Industrial Society*. London: Blackwell.

———. 1979. *Il seme religioso della rivolta*. Milan: Rusconi.

———. 1990. *Eros, morte ed esperienza religiosa*. Rome and Bari: Laterza.

Acquaviva, S. S., and E. Pace. 1996. *Sociologia delle religioni. Problemi e prospettive*. Rome: Borla.

Acquaviva, S. S., and R. Stella. 1989. *Fine di un'ideologia: La secolarizzazione*. Rome: Borla.

Adorno, T. W. 1975. "The Stars Down the Earth: the Los Angeles Times' Astrology Columns." In *Soziologische Schriften*. Vol. 2. Frankfurt: Suhrkamp.

———. [1966] 1990. *Negative Dialectics*. Vol. 1. Translated by E. B. Ashton. New York: Continuum. [Original edition in German.]

———. [1951] 1993. *Minima Moralia: Reflections from a Damaged Life*. London: Verso. [Original edition in German.]

Aron, R. 1970. *Main Currents in Sociological Thought*. New York: Doubleday. 2 vols.

———. [1955] 1977. *The Opium of the Intellectuals*. Reprint. Westport, CT: Greenwood.

———. 1998. *Main Currents in Sociological Thought*. Vol. 1. New Brunswick, NJ: Transaction.

Austin, J. L. 1988. In M. Sbisa and J. O. Urmsson, eds., *How to Do Things with Words*. Cambridge, MA: Harvard University Press.

Bainbridge, W. S., and W. Stark. 1984. "Formal Explanation of Religion: A Progress Report." *Sociological Analysis* 45:145–58.

Banton, M., ed. 1966. *Anthropological Approaches to the Study of Religion*. London: Tavistock.

Barker, E. V. 1984. *The Making of a Moonie: Brainwashing or Choice?* Oxford: Blackwell.

———. 1989. *New Religious Movements: A Practical Introduction*. London: HMSO.

Becker, H. 1932. *Systematic Sociology on the Basis of the Beziehungslehre and Gebildelehre of Leopold von Wiese*. New York: Wiley.

Beckford, J. A. 1975. *The Trumpet of Prophecy: A Sociological Analysis of Jehovah's Witnesses*. Oxford: Blackwell.

———. 1985. *Cult Controversies: The Societal Response to New Religious Movements*. London: Tavistock.

———, ed. 1986. *New Religious Movements and Rapid Social Change*. London: Sage.

———. 1989. *Religion and Advanced Industrial Society*. London: Unwin Hyman.

Bellah, R. N. 1957. *Tokugawa Religion: The Cultural Roots of Modern Japan*. Glencoe, IL: Free Press.

———. 1964. "Religious Evolution." *American Sociological Review* 29(3):358–74.

———. 1967. "Civil Religion in America." *Daedalus* 96:1–21.

———. 1968–69. *The Religious Situation*. Boston: Beacon. 2 vols.

———. 1970. *Beyond Belief: Essays on Religion in a Post-Traditional World*. New York: Harper & Row.

———. 1975. *The Broken Covenant: American Civil Religion in Time of Trial*. New York: Seabury.

Bellah, R. N., R. Madsen, W. M. Sullivan, A. Swidler, and S. M. Tipton. 1986. *Habits of the Heart*. Berkeley: University of California Press.

Benedict, R. 1934. *Patterns of Culture*. Boston: Houghton Mifflin.

Berger, P. L. 1961. *The Precarious Vision*. Garden City, NY: Doubleday.

———. 1967. *The Sacred Canopy. Elements of a Sociological Theory of Religion*. Garden City, NY: Doubleday.

———. 1969. *A Rumor of Angels: Modern Society and the Rediscovery of the Supernatural*. Garden City, NY: Doubleday.

———. [1967] 1973. *The Social Reality of Religion*. Harmondsworth: Penguin. [Originally published as: *The Sacred Canopy: Elements of a Sociological Theory of Religion*. Garden City, NY: Doubleday, 1967.]

———. 1974. *Pyramids of Sacrifice: Political Ethics and Social Change*. New York: Basic Books.

———. 1979. *The Heretical Imperative: Contemporary Possibilities of Religious Affiliation*. Garden City, NY: Doubleday.

———. 1981. *The Other Side of God: A Polarity in World Religions*. Garden City, NY: Doubleday.

———. 1992. *A Far Glory: The Quest for Faith in an Age of Credulity*. New York: Free Press.

———. 1997. *Redeeming Laughter: The Comic Dimension of Human Experience*. Hawthorne, NY: Aldine de Gruyter, and Berlin: Walter de Gruyter.

Berger, P. L., and T. Luckmann. 1966. *The Social Construction of Reality*. Garden City, NY: Doubleday.

Bergson, H. [1934] 1946. *La Pensée et le mouvant*. Paris: Alcan.

———. [1974] 1986. *The Two Sources of Morality and Religion*. Translated by R. A. Audra and C. Brereton. South Bend, IN: University of Notre Dame Press.

Blumer, H. 1954. "What Is Wrong with Social Theory?" *American Sociological Review* 19:3–10.

Boccassino, R. 1974. *Etnologia religiosa*. Naples: Edizioni del Delfino.

Bonanate, U. 1975. *Antropologia e religione*. Turin: Loescher.

Boulard, F., and J. Rémy. 1968. *Pratique religieuse urbaine et regions culturelles*. Paris: Éditions Ouvrières.

Buber, M. 1952. *Das Problem des Menschen*. Heidelberg: L. Schneider.

Bucaro, G. 1988. *Filosofia della religione: Forme e figure*. 2nd ed. Rome: Città Nuova.

Burgalassi, S. 1967. *Italiani in chiesa: Analisi sociologica del comportamento religioso.* Brescia: Morcelliana.

————. 1968. *Il comportamento religioso degli italiani: Tre saggi di analisi socio-religiose.* Florence: Vallecchi.

————. 1970a. *Le cristianità nascoste: Dove va la cristianità italiana?* Bologna: Dehoniane.

————. 1970b. *Preti in crisi? Tendenze sociologiche del clero italiano.* Fossano: Esperienze.

Candeloro, G. 1966. "Prefazione" [Preface], in A. de Tocqueville, *La democrazia in America.* G. Candeloro, ed. Milan: Rizzoli.

Casanova, J. 1994. *Public Religions in the Modern World.* Chicago: University of Chicago Press.

Cassirer, E. 1962. *An Essay on Man: An Introduction to a Philosophy of Human Culture.* New Haven, CT: Yale University Press.

Cavalli, L. 1968. *Max Weber: Religione e società.* Bologna: Il Mulino.

Cazeneuve, J. 1968. *Sociologie de Marcel Mauss.* Paris: Presses Universitaires de France.

Cesareo, V., R. Cipriani, F. Garelli, C. Lanzetti, and G. Rovati, G. 1995. *La religiosità in Italia.* Milan: Mondadori.

Champion, F. and D. Hervieu-Léger, eds. 1990. *De l'émotion en religion.* Paris: Centurion.

Cipriani, R., ed. 1986. *La teoria critica della religione.* Rome: Borla.

————. 1988a. *Claude Lévi-Strauss: Una introduzione.* Rome: Armando.

————. 1988b. *La religione diffusa: Teoria e prassi.* Rome: Borla.

Cocchiara, G. 1965. "Prefazione" [Preface], in J. G. Frazer, *Il ramo d'oro Studio sulla magia e la religione [The Golden Bough].* Turin: Boringhieri.

Codrington, R. H. 1891. *The Melanesians: Studies in Their Anthropology and Folklore.* Oxford: Clarendon.

Coleman J. S. 1990. *Foundations of Social Theory.* Cambridge MA: Harvard University Press.

Collard E. 1952. "Commentaire de la carte de la pratique dominicale en Belgique." *Lumen Vitae* 4:644–52.

Comte A. [1830–42] 1967. *Corso di filosofia positiva.* F. Ferrarotti, ed. Turin: UTET. 2 vols. [Original edition: *Cours de philosophie positive.* Paris: Ed. Rouen; reprint: Paris: Societé Positiviste, 1892; text uses Italian edition: 1967.]

————. 1851–54. *Système de politique positive, ou traité de sociologie instituant la religion de l'humanité.* Paris: L. Mathias.

————. 1852. *Catéchisme positiviste ou sommaire exposition de la religion universelle, en onze entretiens systématiques entre une femme et un prêtre de l'humanité.* Paris: Chez l'auteur et chez Carilian- Goeury et V. Dalmont.

Corradi C. 1993. "Conclusioni: L'attore religioso del moderno." In R. Cipriani, ed., *Sentieri della Religiosità: Un'indagine a Roma,* 263–66. Brescia: Morcelliana.

de Martino, E. 1941. *Naturalismo e storicismo nell'etnologia.* Bari and Rome: Laterza.

————. 1958. *Morte e pianto rituale nel mondo antico: Dal lamento pagano al pianto di Maria.* Turin: Boringhieri.

————. 1960. *Sud e magia.* Milan: Feltrinelli.

————. 1961. *La terra del rimorso: Contributo a una storia religiosa del sud.* Milan: Il Saggiatore.

————. 1962. *Furore, simbolo, valore.* Milan: Il Saggiatore.

————. [1948] 1973. *Il mondo magico: Prolegomeni a una storia del magismo.* Turin: Boringhieri.

————. 1975. *Mondo popolare e magia in Lucania.* Rome and Matera: Basilicata.

————, ed. 1976. *Magia e civiltà.* Milan: Garzanti.

————. 1977. *La fine del mondo.* Turin: Einaudi.

Demarchi, F., ed. 1988. *Wilhelm Schmidt: Un etnologo sempre attuale.* Bologna: Dehoniane.

Desroche, H. 1955. *Les Shakers américains: D'un néochristianisme à un pré-socialisme.* Paris: Éditions du Minuit.

————. 1962. *Marxisme et religions.* Paris: Presses Universitaires de France.

————. 1965. *Socialismes et sociologie religieuse.* Paris: Cujas.

————. 1968. *Sociologies religieuses.* Paris: Presses Universitaires de France.

————. 1969. *Dieux d'hommes: Dictionnaire des messianismes et millénarismes de l'Ère Chrétienne.* Paris and the Hague: Mouton.

————. 1972. *L'homme et ses religions: Sciences humaines et expériences religieuses.* Paris: Éditions du Cerf.

————. 1974. *Les religions de contrebande: Essai sur les phénomènes religieux en époques critiques.* Paris: Mame.

Desroche, H., and J. Séguy, eds. 1970. *Introduction aux sciences humaines des religions.* Paris: Cujas.

di Nola, A. M. 1974. *Antropologia religiosa: Introduzione al problema e campioni di ricerca.* Florence: Vallecchi.

Dobbelaere, K. 1981. "Secularization: A Multi-Dimensional Concept" *Current Sociology* 29:2.

Douglas, M. 1966. *Purity and Danger.* London: Routledge and Kegan Paul.

————. 1970. *Natural Symbols: Explorations in Cosmology.* Harmondsworth: Penguin.

————. 1975. *Implicit Meanings: Essays in Anthropology.* London: Routledge and Kegan Paul.

————. 1982. *In the Active Voice.* London: Routledge and Kegan Paul.

Dumais, A. 1997. *Historicité et foi chrétienne: Une lecture du théologien Ernst Treoltsch.* Québec City: Les Presses de l'Université Laval.

Durkheim, E. [1898] 1996. "De la définition des phénomènes religieux," *L'Année Sociologique* 2:1–28.

————. 1996. *Per una definizione dei fenomeni religiosi.* Rome: Armando.

————. [1912] 1995. *The Elementary Forms of the Religious Life: The Totemic System in Australia.* Translated by K. E. Fields. New York: Free Press. [Original edition in French.]

Eliade, M. [1948] 1976. *Trattato di storia delle religioni.* Torino: Boringhieri. [Original edition in French: *Traité d'histoire des religions.* Paris: Payot.]

————. [1952] 1991. *Images and Symbols: Studies in Religious Symbolism.* Translated by P. Mairet. Princeton, NJ: Princeton University Press. [Original edition in French.]

————. [1949] 1991. *Myth of the Eternal Return: Or Cosmos and History*. Translated by W. R. Trask. Princeton, NJ: Princeton University Press. [Original edition in French.]

————. [1958] 1996. *Patterns in Comparative Religion*. Translated by R. Sheed. Reprint. Lincoln: University of Nebraska Press.

————. 1998. *Myth and Reality*. Reprint. Prospect Heights, IL: Waveland.

Evans-Pritchard, E. E. 1956. *Nuer Religion*. Oxford: Oxford University Press.

————. 1965. *Theories of Primitive Religion*. Oxford: Oxford University Press.

————. 1971. *Teorie sulla religione primitiva*. Introduction by V. Lanternari. Florence: Sansoni.

Fenn, R. K. 1969. "The Secularization of Values: Analytical Framework for the Study of Secularization." *Journal for the Scientific Study of Religion* 1:112–24.

————. 1970. "The Process of Secularization: A Post-Parsonian View." *Journal for the Scientific Study of Religion* 2:117–36.

————. 1978. *Toward a Theory of Secularization*. Storrs, CT: Society for the Scientific Study of Religion.

Ferguson, A. [1767] 1980. *An Essay on the History of Civil Society*. Reprint. New Brunswick, NJ: Transaction. [Original published in Edinburgh.]

Ferrarotti, F. 1965. *Cultorologia del sacro e del profano*. G. Harrison, ed. Milan: Feltrinelli.

————. 1970. *Toward the Social Production of the Sacred*. San Diego, CA: Essay.

————. 1983. "Il paradosso del sacro." Rome-Bari: Laterza.

————. 1984. "The Paradox of the Sacred." *International Journal of Sociology* 14(2):3–108.

————. [1983] 1987. *A Theology for Non-Believers: Post-Christian and Post-Marxist Reflections*. Millwood, NY: Associated Faculty Press.

————. 1993. *Faith without Dogma: The Place of Religion in Postmodern Societies*. New Brunswick, NJ: Transaction.

————. 1990. *Una fede senza dogmi*. Rome-Bari: Laterza.

Feuerbach, L. A. 1839. *Über Philosophie und Christentum* (On Philosophy and Christianity).

————. [1830] 1980. *Thoughts on Death and Immortality*. Translated by J. A. Massey. Berkeley: University of California Press. [Original published in German anonymously.]

————. [1841] 1989. *The Essence of Christianity*. Translated by G. Eliot [M. A. Evans]. Reprint. Amherst, NY: Prometheus Books. [Original edition in German.]

Filoramo, G. 1984, "Prefazione" [Preface], in G. Videngren, *Fenomenologia della religione*. Bologna: Dehoniane.

————. 1985. *Religione e ragione tra ottocento e novecento*. Rome and Bari: Laterza.

Finke, R., and R. Stark 1992. *The Churching of America—1776–1990: Winners and Losers in Our Religious Economy*. New Brunswick, NJ: Rutgers University Press.

Firth, R. 1975. *Symbols: Public and Private*. London: George Allen & Unwin.

Fleischmann, E. 1964. "De Weber À Nietzsche." *Archives Européennes de Sociologie* 5:190–238.

Frazer, J. G. 1887. *Totemism*. Edinburgh: A. & C. Black.

————. 1910. *Totemism and Exogamy*. London: Macmillan. 4 vols.

————. [1907–15] 1994. *The Golden Bough: A Study in Magic and Religion*. Oxford: Oxford University Press. [Reprint: 1 vol. abridged ed. London: Macmillan, 1922.]

Freud, S. 1953a. *The Interpretation of Dreams. The Standard Edition of the Complete Psychological Works of Sigmund Freud*, vols. 4, 5. J. Strachey, ed. London: Hogarth. [*Die Traumdeutung*, Leipzig-Wien, 1900 (1899).]

————. 1953b. *Totem and Taboo. The Standard Edition of the Complete Psychological Works of Sigmund Freud*, vol. 13, pp. 1–161. J. Strachey, ed. London: Hogarth. [*Totem und Taboo*, Helle, Leipzig-Wien; Italian edition: *Totem e Tabù*, in *Opere*, vol. 7, pp. 1–64 (1912–14), C. Musatti, ed.; S. Daniele, trans. Boringhieri, Torino.]

————. 1959. *Obsessive Actions and Religious Practices. The Standard Edition of the Complete Psychological Works of Sigmund Freud*, vol. 9, 115–27. J. Strachey, ed. London: Hogarth. ["Zwandsbandlungen und Religionsübungen," *Zeitschrift für Religionspsychologie*, 1(1, 1907), 4–12.]

————. 1961a. *A Seventeenth Century Demonological Neurosis. The Standard Edition of the Complete Psychological Works of Sigmund Freud*, vol. 19. J. Strachey, ed. London: Hogarth. ["Eine Teufelsneuroses im siebzehnten Jahrhundert," *Imago*, 4(1, 1923), 1–34.]

————. 1961b. *The Future of an Illusion. The Standard Edition of the Complete Psychological Works of Sigmund Freud*, vol. 21, pp. 5–56. J. Strachey, ed. London: Hogarth. [*Die Zukunft einer Illusion*, Internationaler Psychoanalytischer Verlag, Leipzig-Wien-Zürich, 1927.]

————. 1961c. *A Religious Experience. The Standard Edition of the Complete Psychological Works of Sigmund Freud*, vol. 21, pp. 167–73. J. Strachey, ed. London: Hogarth. ["Ein Religiöse Erlebnis," *Imago*, 14(1, 1928 [1927], 7–10.]

————. 1964. *Moses and Monotheism. The Standard Edition of the Complete Psychological Works of Sigmund Freud*, vol. 23. J. Strachey, ed. London: Hogarth. [*Der Mann Moses und die Monotheistische Religion: Drei Abhandlungen*, Allert de Lange, Amsterdam, 1939 (1938).]

Fromm, E. [1950] 1958. *Psychoanalysis and Religion*. New Haven, CT: Yale University Press.

Fustel de Coulanges, N. D. [1864] 1980. *The Ancient City*. Reprint. Baltimore: Johns Hopkins University Press. [Original edition in French.]

Garrett, W. R. 1992. "Thinking Religion in the Global Circumstance: A Critique of Roland Robertson's Globalization Theory." *Journal for the Scientific Study of Religion* 3:297–303.

Geertz, C. 1960. *The Religion of Java*. Glencoe, IL: Free Press.

————. 1966. "Religion as a Cultural System." In M. Banton, ed., *Anthropological Approaches to the Study of Religion*, 1–46. London: Tavistock.

————. 1968. *Islam Observed: Religious Development in Morocco and Indonesia*. New Haven, CT: Yale University Press.

Gisel, P. 1992. *Histoire et théologie chez Ernst Troeltsch*. Geneva: Labor et Fides.

Glock, C. Y., and R. Stark. 1965. *Religion and Society in Tension*. Chicago: Rand McNally.

————. 1966. *Christian Beliefs and Anti-Semitism*. New York: Harper and Row.

Gollwitzer, H. 1970. *The Christian Faith and the Marxist Criticism of Religion.* Edinburgh: Saint Andrew.

Grassi, A. M. 1984. *Modelli di filosofia della religione,* Urbino: Quattroventi.

Greeley, A. M. 1962. "Some Aspects of Interaction Between Religious Groups in an Upper Middle Class Roman Catholic Parish." *Social Compass* 9:39–61.

————. 1963. *Religion and Career: A Study of College Graduates.* New York: Sheed and Ward.

————. 1972a. *The Denominational Society: A Sociological Approach to Religion in America.* Glenview, IL: Scott, Foresman.

————. 1972b. *Unsecular Man: The Persistence of Religion.* New York: Schocken.

————. 1974. *Ecstasy: A Way of Knowing.* Englewood Cliffs, NJ: Prentice-Hall.

————. 1975. *The Sociology of the Paranormal: A Reconnaissance.* Beverly Hills, CA: Sage.

————. 1977. *The American Catholic: A Social Portrait.* New York: Basic Books.

————. 1989. "Protestant and Catholic: Is the Analogical Imagination Extinct?" *American Sociological Review* 54(4):485–502.

Gunn, A. 1922. *Modern French Philosophy: A Study of the Development since Comte.* London: Fisher Unwin.

Guolo, R., ed. 1996. *Il paradosso della tradizione: Religioni e modernità.* Milan: Guerini e Associati.

Herberg, W. 1955. *Protestant-Catholic-Jew: An Essay in American Religious Sociology.* Garden City, NY: Doubleday.

Hervieu-Léger, D. 1973. *De la mission à la protestation: L'évolution des étudiants chrétiens 1965–1970.* Paris: Éditions du Cerf.

————. 1993. *La religion pour mémoire.* Paris: Éditions du Cerf.

————. 1996. *Religione e memoria.* Bologna: Il Mulino.

————., with D. Champion. 1986. *Vers un nouveau christianisme? Introduction à la sociologie du christianisme occidental.* Paris: Éditions du Cerf.

————, with D. Champion. 1989. *Verso un nuovo cristianesimo? Introduzione alla sociologia del cristianesimo occidentale.* Brescia: Queripiana.

Horkheimer, M. 1931. "Die gegenwärtige Lage der Sozialphilosophie und die Aufgaben eines Instituts für Sozialforschung." *Frankfurter Universitätsreden* 37:3–6.

————. 1969. "Himmel, Ewigkeit und Schönheit." *Der Spiegel* 33:108–9.

————. 1970. *Die Sehnsucht nach dem ganz Anderen: Ein Interview mit Kommentar von Helmut Gumnior.* Hamburg: Furche-Verlag H. Renneback KG.

Horkheimer, M., and T. W. Adorno. [1947] 1997. *Dialectic of Enlightenment.* Reprint, Oxford-London: Blackwell. [Original edition in German published in Netherlands.]

Houtart, F. 1957. *Aspects sociologiques du catholicisme américain.* Paris: Les Éditions Ouvrières.

Houtart, F., and J. Rémy. 1969. *Église et societé en mutation.* Paris: Mame.

————. 1974. *Chiesa e società in evoluzione.* Bologna: Dehoniane.

Houtart, F., and A. Rousseau. 1973. *L'église force anti-révolutionnaire?* Brussels: Éditions Vie Ouvrière and Paris: Les Éditions Ouvrières.

Hubert, H., and M. Mauss. 1909. *Mélanges d'histoire des religions.* Paris: Alcan.

Hume, D. 1754–63. *History of England: From the Invasion of Julius Caesar to the Revolution of 1688*. Reprint. Indianapolis, IN: Liberty Fund. 6 vols.

———. [1757] 1969. *Storia naturale della religione*. Florence: La Nuovo Italia.

———. (anon.). [1739–40] 1986. *A Treatise of Human Nature*. Reprint of 3 vols. in one vol. New York: Viking Penguin.

———. [1758] 1988. *An Enquiry Concerning Human Understanding*. Reprint. Amherst, NY: Prometheus.

———. [1757] 1996. *Four Dissertations: The Natural History of Religion, Of the Passions, Of Tragedy, Of the Standard of Taste*. Reprint. Herndon, VA: Books International.

———. [1777] 1996. *Essays on Suicide and the Immortality of the Soul*. Reprint. Herndon, VA: Books International.

———. [1875] 1996. *Philosophical Works*. T. H. Green and T. H. Gross, eds. Bristol: Thoemmes. 4 vols.

———. [1779] 1998. *Dialogue Concerning Natural Religion*. Reprint, 2nd ed. Indianapolis, IN: Hackett.

Husserl, E. [1950] 1977. *Cartesian Meditations*, vol. 1. Translated by D. Cairns. The Hague: Kluwer/Martinus Nijhoff. [Original edition in German.]

Isambert, F.-A. 1961. *Christianisme et classe ouvrière*. Paris: Casterman.

———. 1979. *Rite et efficacité symbolique: Essai d'anthropologie symbolique*. Paris: Éditions du Cerf.

———. 1982. *Le sens du sacré: Fête et religion populaire*. Paris: Éditions du Minuit.

———, with P. Ladrière. 1979. *Contraception et avortement*. Paris: CNRS. Isambert, F.-A., and J. Terrenoire. 1980. *Atlas de la pratique religieuse des catholiques en France*. Paris: CNRS.

James, W. [1890] 1912. *Principles of Psychology*. Mineola, NY: Dover.

———. 1904. *Pragmatism: A New Name for Some Old Ways of Thinking*. New York: Longmans.

———. [1902] 1961. *Varieties of Religious Experience: A Study in Human Understanding*. New York: Collier Macmillan.

Jung, C. G. [1942] 1954. *Das Wandlungssymbol in der Messe*. Olten: Walter Verlag.

———. 1958. *Psychology and Religion*. New Haven, CT: Yale University Press.

Kerényi, K. 1969. "Introduzione." In S. Freud, *Totem e Tabù*. Translated by S. Daniele, 7–22. Turin: Boringhieri.

Lambert, Y. 1991. "La 'Tour de Babel' des définitions de la religion." *Social Compass* 38(1):73–85.

Le Bras, G. 1955–56. *Études de sociologie religieuse*. Paris: Presses Universitaires de France. 2 vols.

Leclercq, J. 1948. *Introduction à la sociologie*. Louvain: IRES.

———. 1955. "Sociologie religieuse et théologie." In *Actes du IVe Congrès De Sociologie Religieuse*. Paris: Éditions Ouvrières.

Léger, D. and B. Hervieu 1983. *Des communautés pour des temps difficiles: Néo-ruraux ou nouveaux moines*. Paris: Centurion.

Lenski, G. 1961. *The Religious Factor: A Sociological Study of Religion's Impact on Politics, Economics and Family Life*. Garden City, NY: Doubleday.

Lepenies, W. 1988. *Between Literature and Science: The Rise of Sociology*. Cambridge: Cambridge University Press.

Lévy-Bruhl, L. [1931] 1935. *Primitives and the Supernatural.* New York: E. P. Dutton. [Original edition in French.]

———. 1938. *L'éxperience mystique et les symboles chez les primitifs.* Paris: Alcan.

———. 1973. *Sovrannaturale e natura nella mentalità primitiva.* Rome: Newton Compton. [Original edition in French.]

Luckmann, T. [1963] 1967. *The Invisible Religion: The Transformation of Symbols in Industrial Society.* New York: Macmillan. [Original edition in German.]

Luhmann, N. [1977] 1991. *Funzione della religione.* Introduction and translated by S. Belardinelli, ed. [Original edition in German: *Funktion der Religion.* Frankfurt: Suhrkamp.]

Maduro, O. 1979. *Religión y lucha de clases.* Caracas: Editorial Ateneo de Caracas.

Malinowski, B. 1915. "The Natives of Mailu: Preliminary Results of the Robert Mond Research Work in British New Guinea." *Proceedings of the Royal Society of Southern Australia, Adelaide* 39:494–706.

———. 1922. *Argonauts of the Western Pacific.* London: Routledge.

———. 1944. *A Scientific Theory of Culture and Other Essays.* Chapel Hill: University of North Carolina Press.

———. 1948. *Magic, Science and Religion and Other Essays.* Glencoe, IL: Free Press.

Mannhardt, W. 1875–77. *Antike Wald- und Feldkulte.* Berlin. 2 vols.

Martelli, S. 1987. *Marcel Mauss: Una introduzione.* Rome: Armando.

Martin, S. 1967. *A Sociology of English Religion.* London: Heinemann.

———. 1969. *The Religious and the Secular: Studies in Secularization.* London: Routledge & Kegan Paul.

———. 1978a. *A General Theory of Secularization.* Oxford: Blackwell.

———. 1978b. *The Dilemmas of Contemporary Religion.* Oxford: Blackwell.

———. 1990. *Tongues of Fire: The Explosion of Protestantism in Latin America.* Oxford: Blackwell.

———. 1997. *Does Christianity Cause War?* Oxford: Oxford University Press.

Marx, K. [1888] 1935. "Theses on Feuerbach." In F. Engels, *Ludwig Feuerbach and on the Outcome of Classical German Philosophy.* C. P. Dutt, ed. New York: International.

———. [1844] 1959. "Towards the Critique of Hegel's Philosophy of Right." In *Marx and Engels: Basic Writings on Politics and Philosophy.* L. S. Feuer, ed. Garden City, NY: Doubleday.

———. 1973. "Tesi su Feuerbach." In K. Marx and F. Engels, *Scritti sulla Religione.* M. Fedele, ed. Rome: Savelli. Mauss, M. 1899. "Essai sur la nature et la fonction du sacrifice." *L'Année Sociologique* 2.29–138.

———. 1902–3. "Esquisse d'une théorie générale de la magie." *L'Année Sociologique* 7:1–146.

———. 1947. *Manuel d'ethnographie.* Paris: Payot.

———. 1968. "La prière." In *Oeuvres*, vol. 1 (*Les fonctions sociales du sacré*), 357–478. Paris: Editions du Minuit.

———. 1975. *Teoria generale della magia.* Rome: Newton Compton.

———. [1925] 1990. *The Gift: The Form and Reason for Exchange in Archaic Societies.* Translated by W. D. Halls. New York: Norton. [Original edition in French.]

Mensching, G. 1951. *Sociologie religieuse.* Edited and translated by P. Jundt. Paris: Payot.

Milani, L. 1974. *Esperienze pastorali*. Florence: Libreria Editrice Fiorentina.

Millar, J. [1771] 1996. *The Origin of the Distinction of Ranks*. Reprint of 2nd ed., 1806. Herndon, Virginia: Books International.

Mitzman, A. 1985. *The Iron Cage: An Historical Interpretation of Max Weber*. New Brunswick, NJ: Transaction.

Mol, H. 1976. *Identity and the Sacred: A Sketch for a New Social- Scientific Theory of Religion*. Oxford: Blackwell.

———, ed. 1978. *Identity and Religion: International Cross-Cultural Approaches*. Beverly Hills, CA: Sage.

———. 1989. "The Secularization of Canada." *Research in the Social Scientific Study of Religion* 1:197–215.

Müller, M. 1889. *Natural Religion*. London.

Nesti, A. 1985. *Il religioso implicito*. Rome: Ianua.

Niebuhr, H. R. [1929] 1972. *The Social Sources of Denominationalism*. New York: World.

Niebuhr, R. 1932. *Moral Man and Immoral Society*. New York: Scribners.

Nietzsche, F. W. [1886] 1989. *Beyond Good and Evil*. Translated by W. Kaufmann. New York: Random House. [Original edition in German.]

Olivetti, M. M. 1992. *Analogia del soggetto*. Rome and Bari: Laterza.

Otto, R. [1917] 1958. *The Idea of the Holy: An Inquiry into the Non-Rational Factor in the Idea of the Divine and its Relation to the Rational*. Oxford: Oxford University Press. [Original edition in German.]

Pace, E. 1996. In Acquaviva, S. S., and E. Pace, eds., *Sociologia delle religioni. Problemi e prespettive*, Rome: La Nuova Italia Scientifica.

Parinetto, L. 1976. *Né dio, né capitale: Marx, marxismo, religione*. Milan: Contemporanea Edizioni.

Parsons, T. 1962. "In Memoriam: Richard Henry Tawney (1880–1962)." *American Sociological Review* 27(6):880–90.

———. 1963. "Christianity and Modern Industrial Society." In E. Tiryakian, ed., *Sociological Theory, Values, and Sociocultural Change: Essays in Honor of Pitirim A. Sorokin*. Glencoe, IL: Free Press.

———. 1968."Emile Durkheim." In D. L. Sills, ed., *International Encyclopedia of the Social Sciences*, vol. 4, 311–19. New York: Macmillan.

———. 1972. "Religious Perspectives in Sociology and Social Psychology." In W. A. Lessa and E. Z. Vogt, eds., *Reader in Comparative Religion*, 88–93. New York: Harper & Row.

———. 1978. "Durkheim on Religion Revisited." In *Action Theory and the Human Condition*, 213–32. New York: Free Press.

Pettazzoni, R. 1965. *L'essere supremo nelle religioni primitive*. Turin: Einaudi.

Pinard de la Boullaye, H. 1922. *L'étude comparée des religions: Essai critique*. Paris: Beauchesne. [3 vols.: vol. 1 contains the study proper; vol. 2 deals with the methods; vol. 3 contains alphabetic tables.]

Popper, K. R. 1969. *Conjectures and Refutations*. London: Routledge & Kegan Paul.

Poulat, É. 1957. *Les cahiers manuscrits de Fourier*. Paris: Éditions du Minuit.

———. 1961. *Le "Journal d'un prêtre d'après-demain" (1902–1903) de l'abbé Calippe*. Paris: Casterman.

———. 1962. *Histoire, dogme et critique dans la crise moderniste*. Paris: Casterman.

———. 1965. *Naissance des prêtres ouvriers*. Paris: Casterman.

————. 1969. *Intégrisme et catholicisme intégral.* Paris: Casterman.

————. 1972. *Une oeuvre clandestine d'Henri Bremond: "Sylvain Leblanc. Un clerc qui n'a pas trahi: Alfred Loisy d'après ses mémoires (1931)."* Rome: Edizioni di Storia e Letteratura.

————. 1982. *Modernistica: Horizons, physionomies, débats.* Paris: Nouvelles Éditions Latines.

————. 1986. *L'Église, c'est un monde: L'Ecclésiosphère.* Paris: Éditions du Cerf.

————. 1987. *Liberté, laïcité: La guerre des deux Frances et le principe de la modernité.* Paris: Éditions du Cerf.

————. 1988. *Poussières de raison. Esquisses de météosociologie dans un monde au risque de l'homme.* Paris: Éditions du Cerf.

————. 1993. "L'Europe religieuse des États." In G. Vincent and J.-P. Willaime, eds., *Religions et transformations de l'Europe.* Strasbourg: Presses Universitaires de Strasbourg.

————. 1996. *L'era post-cristiana. Un uomo uscito da Dio.* Turin: SEI.

Poulat, É., et al. 1961. *Priests and Workers: An Anglo-French Discussion.* London: SCM.

Prandi, C. 1989. *Lucien Lévy-Bruhl: Una introduzione.* Rome: Armando.

Prontera, A. 1991. "Henri Bergson." In *Novecento filosofico e scientifico: Protagonisti.* A. Negri, ed. Vol. 1, 767–77. Settimo Milanese: Marzorati.

Radcliffe-Brown, A. R. 1922. *The Andaman Islanders.* Cambridge: Cambridge University Press.

————. 1952. *Structure and Function in Primitive Society: Essays and Addresses.* Glencoe, IL: Free Press.

Rémy, J. 1981. "Micro ou Macro Sociologie du Religieux." *Actes 16ème conférence internationale de sociologie des religions,* 23–45. Lausanne: CISR.

Robertson, R. 1970. *The Sociological Interpretation of Religion.* Oxford: Blackwell.

————, ed. 1971. *Sociology of Religion: Selected Readings.* Harmondsworth: Penguin.

————. 1978. *Meaning and Change: Explorations in the Cultural Sociology of Modern Society.* Oxford: Blackwell.

————. 1982. "Parsons on the Evolutionary Significance of American Religion." *Sociological Analysis* 4:307–26.

————. 1987. "From Secularization to Globalization." *Journal of Oriental Studies* 1:28–32.

————. 1992. *Globalization: Social Theory and Global Culture.* London: Sage.

Saint Simon, C. H. de. 1975. *Opere.* M. T. Pichetto, ed. Turin: UTET.

Schleiermacher, F. D. E. [1799] 1988. *On Religion: Speeches to Its Cultured Despisers.* Cambridge, England: Cambridge University Press. [Original edition in German.]

————. 1821. *The Christian Faith.* Schmidt, W. 1934. *Manuale di storia comparata delle religioni.* Brescia: Morcelliana.

Schutz, A. 1962. *Collected Papers.* The Hague: Martinus Nijhoff.

Séguy, J. 1970. "Introduction au sciences humaines des religions." In *Panorama des Sciences des religions,* pp. 37–52. Paris: Cujas.

————. 1971. "Une sociologie des sociétés imaginées: Monachisme et utopie." *Annales, E.S.C,* 2:328–54.

————. 1972. "Max Weber et la sociologie historique des religions." *Archives de Sociologie des Religions,* 1:71–103.

————. 1973. *Le Conflits du Dialogue*. Paris: Éditions du Cerf.

————. 1977. *Les assemblées anabaptistes-mennonites de France*. Paris and the Hague: Mouton.

————. 1980. *Christianisme et société: Introduction à la sociologie de Ernst Troeltsch*. Paris: Éditions du Cerf.

————. 1984a. "Pour une sociologie de l'ordre religieux." *Archives de sciences sociales des religions* 57(1):55–68.

————. 1984b. "Charisme, Prophétie, Religion Populaire." *Archives de sciences sociales des religions* 57(2):153–68.

————. 1986. "Rationalisation, modernité et avenir de la religion chez Max Weber." *Archives de sciences sociales des religions* 51(1):127–38.

————. 1988. "L'approche wébérienne des phénomènes religieux." In R. Cipriani and M. I. Macioti, eds., *Omaggio a Ferrarotti*, 163–85. Rome: SIARES.

————. 1989. "Un cas d'institutionnalisation du croire: Les assemblées anabaptistes-mennonites de France." *Recherches de Science Religieuse*, 2:165–96.

————. 1993. "Messianismes et millénarisme. Ou de l'attente comme catégorie de l'agir social." In F. Chazel, ed., *Action collective et mouvements sociaux*. Paris: Presses Universitaires de France.

————. 1994a. *Cristianesimo e società. La socioogia di Ernst Troeltsch*. Introduction by C. Prandi. Brescia: Morcelliana.

————. 1994b. "In memoriam: Henri Desroche (1914–1994)." *Archives de sciences sociales des religions*, 87:5–12.

————. 1996. In *Il paradosso della tradizione: Religioni e modernità*, Guolo, R., ed. Milan: Guerini e Associati. Simmel, G. 1908. *Soziologie: Untersuchungen über die Formen der Vergesellschaftung*. Leipzig: Duncker & Humblot.

————. [1900] 1990. *The Philosophy of Money*. London: Routledge. [Original edition in German.]

————. [1906, 1912] 1997. *Essays on Religion*. H. J. Helle, ed. New Haven, CT: Yale University Press. [Original edition in German.]

Sironneau, J. P. 1982. *Sécularisation et religions politiques*. Paris and the Hague: Mouton.

Skorupski, J. 1983. *Symbol and Theory: A Philosophical Study of Theories of Religion in Social Anthropology*. Cambridge: Cambridge University Press.

Smith, W. Robertson. [1889] 1956. *The Religion of the Semites*. New York: Meridian.

Sorokin, P. 1957. *Social and Cultural Dynamics*. Boston: Porter Sargent.

Spencer, H. 1882–85. *Principles of Sociology*. London: Williams and Norgate. 2 vols.

Spinoza, B. (anon.). [1670] 1991. *Tractatus Theologico-Politicus*. 2nd ed. Translated by S. Shirley. Leiden: Brill. [Original edition in Latin, published in Amsterdam.]

Spiro, M. E. [1978] 1996. *Burmese Supernaturalism*. New Brunswick, NJ: Transaction.

Starbuck, E. D. 1899. *The Psychology of Religion: An Empirical Study of the Growth of Religious Consciousness*. New York: Charles Scribner's Sons.

Stark, R. 1985. "From Church-Sect to Religious Economies." In P. E. Hammond, ed., *The Sacred in a Post-Secular Age*, 139–49. Berkeley: University of California Press.

Stark, R., and W. S. Bainbridge. 1980. "Towards a Theory of Religion: Religious Commitment." *Journal for the Scientific Study of Religion* 2:114–28.

————. 1985. *The Future of Religion: Secularization, Revival and Cult Formation*. Berkeley: University of California Press.

———. 1987. *A Theory of Religion*. Bern and New York: Peter Lang.

———. 1996. *Religion, Deviance, and Social Control*. New York: Routledge.

Stark, R., and C. Y. Glock. 1968. *American Piety: The Nature of Religious Commitment*. Berkeley: University of California Press.

Stark, R., and L. R. Iannaccone. 1994. "A Supply-Side Reinterpretation of the 'Secularization' of Europe." *Journal for the Scientific Study of Religion* 3:230–52.

Swanson, G. E. 1960. *The Birth of the Gods: The Origin of Primitive Beliefs*. Ann Arbor: University of Michigan Press.

———. 1968. "Modern Secularity." In D. Cutler, ed., *The Religious Situation: 1968*. Boston: Beacon.

———. 1971. "Life with God." *Journal for the Scientific Study of Religion* XX:169–99.

———. 1986. "Immanence and Transcendence." *Sociological Analysis* 47(3): 189–213.

Swatos, W. 1975. "Monopolism, Pluralism, Acceptance, and Rejection: An Integrated Model for Church-Sect Theory." *Review of Religious Research* 3:174–85.

Tawney, R. H. 1975. *Opere*. F. Ferrarotti, ed. Torino: UTET.

———. [1926, 1936] 1977. *Religion and the Rise of Capitalism*. London: Murray. *The Religious Situation*. 1968. Annual.

Tocqueville, A. de. 1856. *L'Ancien Régime e la Révolution*. Paris.

———. 1996. *La democrazia in America*. G. Candeloro, ed. Milan: Rizzoli.

Towler, R. 1974. *Homo Religiosus: Sociological Problems in the Study of Religion*. London: Constable.

Troeltsch, E. [1912] 1976. *The Social Teaching of the Christian Churches*. Chicago: University of Chicago Press. [Original edition in German.]

Tschannen, O. 1992. *Les théories de la sécularisation*. Geneva: Droz.

Turner, B. S. 1991. *Religion and Social Theory*. London: Sage.

Turner, V. W. 1967. *The Forest of Symbols. Aspects of Ndembu Ritual*. Ithaca, NY: Cornell University Press.

———. 1969. *The Ritual Process: Structure and Anti-Structure*. Chicago: Aldine.

Turner, V. W., and E. Turner. 1978. *Image and Pilgrimage in Christian Culture: Anthropological Perspectives*. New York: Columbia University Press.

Tylor, E. B. [1871] 1958. *Primitive Culture*. Vol. 1: *The Origins of Culture*; vol. 2: *Religion in Primitive Culture*. New York: Harper & Row.

van der Leeuw, G. [1933] 1986. *Religion in Essence and Manifestation: A Study in Phenomenology*. Princeton, NJ: Princeton University Press. 2 vols. [Original edition in German.]

van Gennep, A. [1909] 1961. *The Rites of Passage*. Translated by M. B. Vizedon and G. L. Caffee. Chicago: University of Chicago Press. [Original edition in French.]

Vico, G. [1844] 1984. *The New Science of Giambattista Vico*. Translated by T. G. Bergin and M. H. Fisch. Ithaca, NY: Cornell University Press. [Based on 3rd ed. of original work, published in 1744.]

Voyé, L. 1973. *Sociologie du geste religieux: De l'analyse de la pratique dominicale en belgique à une interprétation théorique*. Brussels: Les Éditions Vie Ouvrière.

———, ed. 1996. *Figures des dieux: Rites et mouvements religieux: Hommage à Jean Rémy*. Brussels: De Boeck Université.

Voyé, L., Bawin-LeGros, B., Kerkhofs, J., and Dobbelaere, K. 1992. *Belges, heureux et satisfaits: les valeurs des Belges dans les années 90*. Brussels: De Boeck Université.

Voyé, L., Dobbelaere, K., Rémy, J., and Billiet, J., eds. 1985. *La Belgique et ses Dieux: Églises, mouvements religieux et laïques*. Louvain-la-Neuve: Cabay.

———, eds. 1992. *Belges, heureux et satisfaits: Les valeurs des belges dans les années 90*. Brussels: De Boeck Université.

Wach, J. 1944. *Sociology of Religion*. Chicago: University of Chicago Press.

Weber, M. 1906. "Kirchen." *Frankfurter Zeitung*, 13 April; "Sekten." *Frankfurter Zeitung*, 15 April; "'Kirchen' und 'Sekten' in Nordamerika," *Christliche Welt*, 20.

———. 1920–21; 1922–23. *Gesammelte Aufsätze zur Religionssoziologie*. Tübingen: Mohr.

———. 1922. *Wirtschaft und Gesellschaft*. Tübingen: Mohr.

———. 1962a. "Science as a Vocation." In *From Max Weber: Essays in Sociology*, 129–56. Translated by H. H. Gerth. H. H. Gerth and C. W. Mills, eds. New York: Oxford University Press. [1st Galaxy edition, 1958.]

———. 1962b. "The Protestant Sects and the Spirit of Capitalism." In *From Max Weber: Essays in Sociology*, 302–22. Translated by H. H. Gerth. H. H. Gerth and C. W. Mills, eds. New York: Oxford University Press. [1st Galaxy edition, 1958.]

———. 1962c. "Religious Rejections of the World." In *From Max Weber: Essays in Sociology*, 323–59. Translated by H. H. Gerth. H. H. Gerth and C. W. Mills, eds. New York: Oxford University Press. [1st Galaxy edition, 1958.]

———. [1921–22] 1976a. *Sociologia delle Religioni*. C. Sebastiani, ed. Torino: Utet. 2 vols.

———. [1904–5] 1976b. *The Protestant Ethic and the Spirit of Capitalism*. London: Allen and Unwin.

———. 1978. *Economy and Society. An Outline of Interpretive Sociology*. G. Roth and C. Wittich, eds. Berkeley: University of California Press. 2 vols.

———. [1917–19] 1990. *Ancient Judaism*. D. Martindale, ed. Translated by H. H. Gerth. New York: Free Press. [Original edition in German.]

———. [1915] 1990. *The Religion of China: Confucianism and Taoism*. C. K. Yang, ed. New York: Free Press. [Original edition in German.]

———. [1920–23] 1990. *The Sociology of Religion*. Translated by E. Fischoff. Boston: Beacon. [Original edition in German, 3 vols.]

———. [1916–17] 1992. *Religion of India: The Sociology of Hinduism and Buddhism*. New Delhi: Munshiram Manoharial Publishers Pvt. [Original edition in German.]

———. [1904–6] 1998. *The Protestant Ethic and the Spirit of Capitalism*. Translated by T. Parsons. 2nd rev. ed. Los Angeles: Roxbury. [Original edition in German.]

Whimster, S. 1995. "Max Weber on the Erotic and Some Comparisons with the Work of Foucault." *International Sociology* 10(4):447–62.

Whimster, S., and S. Lash, eds. 1987. *Max Weber, Rationality and Modernity*. London: Unwin Hyman.

Widengren, G. 1969. *Religionsphänomenologie*. Berlin: Walter de Gruyter.

Wilson, B. 1961. *Sects and Society*. Berkeley: University of California Press.

———. 1976. *Contemporary Transformations of Religion*. New York: Oxford University Press.

————. 1982. *Religion in Sociological Perspective.* New York: Oxford University Press.

Wilson, B., and K. Dobbelaere. 1994. *A Time to Chant: The Soka Gakkai Buddhists in Britain.* Oxford: Clarendon, Oxford University Press.

Wuthnow, R. 1976. *The Consciousness Reformation.* Berkeley: University of California Press.

————. 1978. *Experimentation in American Religion: The New Mysticisms and Their Implications for the Churches.* Berkeley: University of California Press.

————. 1987. *Meaning and Moral Order: Explorations in Cultural Analysis.* Berkeley: University of California Press.

————. 1988. *The Restructuring of American Religion: Society and Faith since World War II.* Princeton, NJ: Princeton University Press.

————. 1989a. *Communities of Discourse: Ideology and Social Structure in the Reformation, the Enlightenment and European Socialism.* Cambridge, MA: Harvard University Press.

————. 1989b. *The Struggle for America's Soul: Evangelicals, Liberals, and Secularism.* Grand Rapids, MI: Eerdmans.

————. 1991. *Acts of Compassion.* Princeton, NJ: Princeton University Press.

————. 1994a. *Christianity in the 21st Century.* Oxford: Oxford University Press.

————. 1994b. *Producing the Sacred: An Essay on Public Religion.* Urbana and Chicago: University of Illinois Press.

————. 1994c. *Sharing the Journey: Support Groups and America's New Quest for Community.* New York: Free Press.

Yinger, J. M. 1957. *Religion, Society and the Individual.* New York: Macmillan.

————. 1965. *Toward a Field Theory of Religion.* New York: McGraw-Hill.

————. 1970. *The Scientific Study of Religion.* New York: McGraw-Hill.

Young, L. A., ed. 1997. *Rational Choice Theory and Religion.* New York: Routledge.

Zadra, D., ed. 1969. *Sociologia della Religione: Testi e Documenti.* Milan: Hoepli.

Author Index

General Index